The Homeric]

Peter McDonald was born in Belfast in 1962, and educated at Methodist College, Belfast and University College, Oxford. He has published four books of literary criticism, and six volumes of poetry, most recently *Herne the Hunter* (2016). His *Collected Poems* appeared in 2012. He has lectured in English at the Universities of Cambridge and Bristol, and since 1999 has been Christopher Tower Student and Tutor in Poetry in the English Language at Christ Church, University of Oxford, where he is also Professor of British and Irish Poetry. He has edited the *Collected Poems* of Louis MacNeice (Faber, 2007), and is currently editing a multi-volume edition of the *Complete Poems* of W. B. Yeats for Longman.

Details of **Homer**'s life, including his dates, are a matter of scholarly speculation. He is thought to have been born on the Greek island of Chios sometime between 700 and 900 BC, and is credited with authoring the first recorded European literature in the *Iliad* and the *Odyssey*. Whether Homer was in reality an individual or rather a loose school of writers spanning generations is a matter for conjecture; his works, nevertheless, are of unparalleled importance in the Western literary canon.

FyfieldBooks aim to make available some of the great classics of British and European literature in clear, affordable formats, and to restore often neglected writers to their place in literary tradition.

FyfieldBooks take their name from the Fyfield elm in Matthew Arnold's 'Scholar Gypsy' and 'Thyrsis'. The tree stood not far from the village where the series was originally devised in 1971.

Roam on! The light we sought is shining still.
Dost thou ask proof? Our tree yet crowns the hill,
Our Scholar travels yet the loved hill-side

from 'Thyrsis'

The Homeric Hymns

Translated by

PETER McDONALD

Fyfield*Books*

CARCANET

First published in Great Britain in 2016 by
Carcanet Press Limited
Alliance House
Cross Street
Manchester M2 7AQ

www.carcanet.co.uk

FSC
www.fsc.org
MIX
Paper from
responsible sources
FSC® C014540

A CIP catalogue record for this book is available from the British Library

ISBN 978 1 784101 76 3

The publisher acknowledges financial assistance from Arts Council England

Supported by
ARTS COUNCIL
ENGLAND

Typeset by XL Publishing Services, Exmouth
Printed and bound in England by SRP Ltd, Exeter

TO MY TEACHERS

R.H. JORDAN
T.W. MULRYNE

SEMPER IN MEMORIA

Contents

Appendices

Notes

Acknowledgements

My work on these translations began before I had any idea that they would turn into a book. Over the course of a year in 2008–9 I translated the Hymn to Demeter (Hymn 2), intending it as part of my collection *Torchlight* (2011), in which in due course it appeared. That Hymn, and subsequently my version of Hymn 5 (to Aphrodite), were both published in *PN Review*: I am grateful to the editor for this, since readers' reactions gave me the confidence to carry on and undertake the whole of the Homeric Hymns. I was very fortunate, as I went about my work, to have the encouragement and attention of the poets Michael Longley and Seamus Heaney: this confirmed me in my course, and kept me going at those moments when stamina seemed in danger of flagging. I was lucky, too, to have been working amongst classicists in Oxford: I am grateful to Stephen Harrison, Dirk Obbink, Peter Parsons, Christopher Pelling, and Oliver Thomas for their helpful responses to my many queries. At home, help of a different kind was just as vital; and I am indebted again, as ever, to Karen, Louisa, and Sammy.

Woodstock, Oxfordshire
July, 2015

Introduction

If asked to name the poems written by Homer, most of us would come up with the *Iliad* and the *Odyssey* without too much trouble. How many people would add the Homeric Hymns to that list? These are not, we might tell ourselves, *by* Homer in quite the same sense that the epics are by him: they are merely 'Homeric', and we do not talk about the 'Homeric *Iliad*' or 'Homeric *Odyssey*'. And yet, of course, those epics are more 'Homeric' than they are Homer's, for they almost certainly came into their received forms over a number of generations, at the hands of different schools of composition and performance who became known as 'Homer'. The Hymns, which mostly derive from such schools a century or two after the bulk of the epics had been consolidated, are by the same 'Homer'.

This is how things appeared, at any rate, to those who saw Homer's works through the process of printed publication in the renaissance and after. The first printed edition of Homer in 1489 was of the *Opera*, the complete works. It was edited in Florence by the scholar Demetrius Chalcondyles (1423–1511), and included the Hymns as a part of the poet's whole output; that these were indeed the works of a particular named poet was made all the clearer by the inclusion of three Lives of Homer, beginning with the (pseudo-) Herodotean Life in which Homer's Epigrams are contained. From then on, Homer had both a biographical identity and a recognized *oeuvre*: the *Iliad* and *Odyssey*, the Epigrams, the *Batrachomyomachia* (a late mock-epic piece on a war between the Frogs and the Mice), and the Hymns.

It was as Homer's Hymns, then, rather than the Homeric Hymns, that the poems in the present volume for centuries made their way in the world. For George Chapman, the pioneering (and still perhaps the greatest) translator of Homer into English verse, these were 'The Hymnes of Homer' and, far from being pale, late imitations of the genuine article, formed part of *The Crowne of All Homers Workes* when he published his versions in 1624. As late as P.B. Shelley's time, these were still Homer's Hymns, and it was not until 1838 that 'Homeric' crept in, when an English article spoke of 'the Hymn to Apollo ... The Hymn to Hermes ... The Hymn to Aphrodite and that to Demeter' as 'the principal of the Homeric hymns', adding that 'these, with the 'Battle of the Frogs and Mice', make up the sum of the Homeric poems, genuine and spurious.'[1] In this context, from the mid-nineteenth century onwards, 'Homeric' could mean, instead of verse characteristic of Homer, Homer of the second order, or something merely Homer-like.

The ancient world itself was perhaps less strict in the rigour of its methods of literary attribution. While someone as close to the originals as the historian Thucydides in fifth century BC Athens could refer to readily (and quote from) 'Homer in the Hymns' (see Notes to Hymn 3, page 209), there is a distinct scarcity of surviving evidence about either the nature or the general circulation of that collection. It might, of course, have been something very like the Hymns as we have them (certainly, it contained the Hymn to Apollo), but there are no firm grounds for assuming this; also, we should remind ourselves that allusions to, imitations of, and citations or discussions of the Hymns in antiquity, though they do exist, are many times scarcer than those relating to the *Iliad* and the *Odyssey*. The learned Hellenistic poets of the second century BC, notably Callimachus, imitated and elaborated ingeniously upon Hymns that were either the ones we know as Homeric, or something very like them. Oddly, though, the many scholars who commented in detail on classics like the ancient epics, dramas and lyric poetry seem neither to have lavished their attention on the Hymns nor (more remarkably) to have found

---

1   *The Penny Cyclopaedia* Vol. 12 (1838), 1.

much need to refer to or quote from them in the course of their editorial and lexicographical labours. Given the obscurity of some of the Greek literature that we know from just these kinds of source, that is all the more curious a thing. Where had the Hymns gone?

Obviously, they had not gone altogether: we possess them now thanks to medieval scribes, who produced the thirty-one surviving manuscripts from the fourteenth and sixteenth centuries. They were, in their turn, the beneficiaries of a tradition in which the Homeric Hymns had been transmitted from the ancient world: somebody, somewhere, at some time, had cared enough to preserve them. To judge from these manuscripts, they were transmitted as part of a larger collection, sometimes containing narrative by Homer and others, but more generally containing other Hymns by writers like Callimachus and the supposed 'Orpheus'.[2] Working back from this, it would seem likely that late ancient compilers (possibly in Alexandria) had been gathering together a compendium of Hymns, in which they included as a distinct group the Hymns of Homer.

The term Hymn is, for modern audiences, initially rather a misleading one. We think of a hymn as something sung in the course of religious services, but for the Greeks this was not at all the primary meaning of the word. The word *hymnos* is used for a verse composition in praise of a god, or seeking that god's sponsorship; it is a performance piece, intended to impress human as well as divine audiences. But another word is also used to describe these compositions, one which helps us come closer to some kind of early context for them: this is *prooimion*, best translated perhaps as a 'prelude'. The concept takes us back to the rhapsodic tradition, in which a performing poet would sing to his own accompaniment some epic or heroic narrative,

2 N.J. Richardson notes that the Italian humanist scholar Giovanni Aurispa Piciunerio wrote in 1424 that he possessed a manuscript of the Homeric Hymns, and that 'It is possible, but not certain, that this was the archetype from which many of our manuscripts of the hymns were drawn' (Introduction to *The Homeric Hymns* (London: Penguin, 2003), xxiv.

preceding this with a short piece in honour of a god. The god in question might sponsor the performance, in the sense that an event would be taking place in her or his honour; or the god might be particularly associated with the city or town in which the performance was taking place. There is a possible glimpse of this context preserved in epic verse itself, when in the eighth book of the *Odyssey* the bard Demodocus gives performances in front of Odysseus, and begins 'from the god' (*Odyssey* 8: 499). That is all Homer says, and it is plainly quite enough for an audience to understand him: an initial address to a divinity was conventional, therefore, before the performance of a verse narrative. The Homeric Hymns seem likely to be versions of such opening addresses, the shorter ones more obviously so than the five longer pieces which the collection contains.

The discrepancy in length between those pieces and the others appears odd at first sight. Can the longer poems really have been performed as *prooimia*? The Hymn to Hermes (Hymn 4), for instance, would require ninety minutes or so, even read briskly; read to musical accompaniment it would probably be a good deal longer. The only way this would be a practical proposition as a prelude would be if the main performance went on for a whole day, or possibly over more than a day. This is perfectly plausible if the Homeric epics (and other slightly later narratives in the so-called 'epic cycle', now almost completely lost) were being performed as major events at religious or sporting festivals. It is just as plausible to imagine the shorter *prooimia*, such as many of the short Homeric Hymns, serving as the manageably brief introductions to less extended runs of narrative verse (the equivalent of two books of Homer, say). For none of this, however, is there anything in the way of proof; and it is possible that the longer Hymns were originally self-standing. The oddity of the collection containing a series of long pieces, followed by a lot of much shorter poems, all under the same generic classification as *hymnoi* (or *prooimia*) does seem to imply that, however different they are, these works have some original function in common.

The collection moves from its long poems (the fragmentary

Hymn to Dionysus (Hymn 1) is thought to have been around
the five-hundred-line mark) to short pieces, some of them
markedly compressed and utilitarian. There are poems which
do not fit the divided scheme: narrative accounts of Dionysus
(Hymn 7) or Pan (Hymn 19) are of 'middle' length, and feel self-
contained. Towards the end of the sequence, a series of poems
of about nineteen lines each in length give the appearance of
being more artful compositions (these may well be amongst the
latest in date, and could be independent literary productions
which, if not themselves Hellenistic, might have appealed to
sophisticated taste in the Hellenistic period). From whatever
older tradition the medieval copyists drew their source-text of
the Hymns, the collection which they inherited seems to have
served more than one purpose: it preserved some substantial
pieces about major Greek gods, which added to (as they drew
upon) material in both Homer and Hesiod, and they included
a selection of useable *prooimia*, collected perhaps at some point
after their original function as performed preludes had fallen
into neglect, thus rendering them literary curiosities. Although
this whole collection was doubtless attributed to 'Homer'
– which, as an indication of the tradition within which the
poems situate themselves, is perfectly fair – there are no very
strong indications that the Alexandrian or Byzantine scholars
of Greek letters took them very seriously. In this, they were
probably following the general pattern of attention paid by
the ancient readership: it is indicative of relative obscurity that
so few papyrus fragments of the Hymns have turned up, in
comparison with the multitudinous fragments of Homeric
epic, or classical Greek authors.

So the renaissance Homer, for whom the Hymns were
firmly part of his *Opera*, is not quite the Homer of antiquity.
And, it should be added, the Hymns remained relatively easy
to pass over for many Homeric enthusiasts from the sixteenth
century onwards. In the course of his gigantic project of
translation, Chapman came to them last of all, with the *Iliad*
and the *Odyssey* safely behind him; and his versions were never
accorded a great deal of attention, even by his admirers (when

Keats first looks into Chapman's Homer, it is probably not the
Hymns that he is reading). In the early eighteenth century,
William Congreve declared his admiration for the Hymns,
and in particular Hymn 5 (to Aphrodite), which he translated
with brilliance. It was at Congreve's hands that this Hymn
was first made into a fully successful piece of contemporary
English poetry, as in the delicate, precise account of the lines on
Tithonus' slow decline, and Aphrodite's (here Aurora's) tender
and deliberate abandonment of her failed experiment:[3]

> *Tithonus*, while of pleasing youth possess'd,
> Is by *Aurora* with delight caress'd;
> Dear to her arms, he in her court resides,
> Beyond the verge of earth, and ocean's utmost tides.
>   But, when she saw grey hairs begin to spread,
> Deform his beard, and disadorn his head,
> The goddess cold in her embraces grew,
> His arms declin'd, and from his bed withdrew;
> Yet still a kind of nursing care she show'd,
> And food ambrosial, and rich cloaths bestow'd:
> But when of age he felt the sad extream,
> And ev'ry nerve was shrunk, and limb was lame,
> Lock'd in a room her useless spouse she left,
> Of youth, of vigour, and of voice bereft.

The poetic quality of the Greek was, for Congreve, the thing
that really mattered, and so obviously merited translation into
English poetry. 'A poem which is good in it self,' he wrote,
'cannot really lose any thing of its Value, tho' it should appear,
upon a strict enquiry, not to be the work of so eminent an
Author, as him, to whom it was first imputed ... The Beauties
of this ensuing Poem, in the Original, want not even the name

---

3   William Congreve, 'Homer's Hymn to Venus. Translated into English
    Verse', *The Poetical Works of Mr. William Congreve* (Dublin, 1736),
    324–325.

of Homer to recommend 'em'.[4] The effort here was to wrest the Homeric Hymns from the clutches of minute scholarly attention, in which they were subjects for philological analysis and dispute, effectively a series of puzzles of attribution and dating, and to make them into current poetry by recognizing their inherent artistic worth. Alexander Pope, who dedicated his enormously consequential *Iliad* to Congreve, made that poem again (for the first time since Chapman) a touchstone of contemporary English verse; and Congreve might have done the same for the Hymns: but the Hymn to Venus was as far as his project got. This was a major loss, which was not made good for another century, and then only in part.

In 1818, Shelley began to translate some of the Homeric Hymns: beginning with Hymn 33, he worked backwards in the collection to Hymn 30, then tackled Hymn 28; he also began work on Hymn 5 (producing a draft of about 65 lines). If a full translation was in Shelley's mind, it was put on hold there; and no more translation work on the Hymns was attempted by him until the summer of 1820, when he rendered the whole of Hymn 4 into *ottava rima* stanzas, as 'Homer's Hymn to Mercury'. The 1818 poems are all rendered as rhyming couplets, but their accomplishment is more elegant than it is arresting; the 'Hymn to Mercury', on the other hand, is a major achievement, and certainly the best translation of any of the Hymns, whether in Shelley's time or since. Initially, Shelley's interest in these poems was probably aroused by the enthusiasm of his friends T.L. Peacock (who himself incorporated a translation of Hymn 7 into his *Rhododaphne* (1817)), and T.J. Hogg, who called the Hymns 'miraculous effusions of genius' when recommending them to Shelley.[5] The poetry's appeal was amply registered in

---

4 Ibid, 312.
5 Another factor might have played a part in making Shelley (and his friends) think about the Hymns: 1818 also saw the republication of Chapman's version of *The Hymns of Homer*, edited by S.W. Singer, with a lengthy Preface that quotes with approval and fully the opinions on Homer of Shelley's father-in-law, William Godwin.

Shelley's 1818 translations, but it became something different (and greater) in 1820; while the judgement of one modern critic that 'the feature most likely to attract [Shelley] in the Hymns was their resemblance to his own work' is going too far, the deep creative connection between these Greek poems and Shelley's developing art was a real one.[6]

The 'Hymn to Mercury', in its stanzaic translation, presents itself as a modern poem – at first glance on the page, it could be mistaken for a further instalment of (say) Lord Byron's *Beppo* (1818) or *Don Juan* (1819 and after): the work, however, is an alchemical transformation of the Byronic form into something quite new. Liberated from the need to strike a suitable classical register in his formal deportment, Shelley can simultaneously give the Greek poetry its full mischievous dash and use the rhyming dynamics of the stanza form to generate his own kinds of eloquence:[7]

39
And Phoebus stooped under the craggy roof
    Arched over the dark cavern – Maia's child
Perceived that he came angry, far aloof,
    About the cows of which he had been beguiled,
And over him the fine and fragrant woof
    Of his ambrosial swaddling-clothes he piled –
As among fire-brands lies a burning spark
Covered, beneath the ashes cold and dark.

40
There like an infant who had sucked his fill
    And now was newly washed and put to bed,
Awake, but courting sleep with weary will,

6 Timothy Webb, *The Violet in the Crucible: Shelley and Translation* (Oxford: Clarendon Press, 1976), 67.
7 P.B. Shelley, 'Hymn to Mercury' (1820, 1st publ. 1824), *The Poems of Shelley Volume 3 1819–1820* eds. Jack Donovan et al. (Harlow: Longman, 2011), 524.

And gathered in a lump hands, feet, and head,
He lay, and his beloved tortoise still
He grasped and held under his shoulder-blade.

One of the gains made by Shelley here is a result of his need to fill up the stanzas' room: rhyme encourages extra associative energies in poetic style, and here the infant Mercury has 'sucked his fill' partly to help the rhymes on their way (for he has done no such thing in the Greek); but without this, Shelley's attention could hardly have produced 'gathered in a lump hands, feet, and head', in which the Greek line 'in a small space he drew together his head, his hands, and his feet' is utterly transformed, even while it is being translated, into a moment of direct observation. 'In a lump', like the 'beloved' Shelley adds to the tortoise without any warrant from the text, suddenly makes Mercury a real baby.[8] In a larger sense, the 'Hymn to Mercury' becomes also a real poem of Shelley's at the same time as being a superb translation of the Hymn; and within weeks, both the stanza form and the mercurial power and liberty of the verse had sparked his rapid composition of 'The Witch of Atlas', an 'original' poem which could never have happened without the translation that preceded and provoked it.

Many English poems issued from the Homeric Hymns in the later nineteenth century, and into the twentieth, although none of them (including even work by Tennyson and Swinburne) fully matches Shelley, Congreve, and Chapman. Hymn 2 (to Demeter) tended to speak a little too readily to half-formed mystical aspirations in Victorian poetry, and too temptingly to mythologically over-excited purveyors of twentieth-century

8 Shelley's infant son William had died at the age of three and a half, just over a year before the translation was undertaken, and at almost the same time as it was being written, the little girl who was probably his illegitimate daughter, Elena Adelaide Shelley, died in Naples, aged one and a half. Does love sharpened by grief help to energise Shelley's treatment of the infant Mercury? There is no documentary evidence whatsoever to prove that it does; but perhaps the acuteness of the poetic attention is its own kind of evidence here.

and contemporary verse. Greek poetry of the classical and the
early periods in general is not 'mystical' in any modern sense,
and poets attempting to make it so end up looking faintly
ridiculous in their ancient fancy-dress. Nor, it would be useful
to add, should Greek poetry be presumed to be relevant to
the pressing and worthy concerns which a modern poet may
share with her or his contemporary readership. There is a line,
one maddeningly difficult to draw, between the kind of poetic
translation that results in originality, and that which fails to be
anything more than merely poetic. In general, when a poet's
translation resembles too closely (and that can also mean too
pleasingly, too satisfyingly or easily) that poet's original verse,
something is going wrong. The Homeric Hymns present the
poetic translator with a profound and challenging otherness;
in this, at least, they are undoubtedly like 'Homer'. For a poet
translating them, the question is not what you will do with
that otherness, but what it will do with you. An ancient poet
does not uncannily prefigure the brilliance of his or her modern
translators, endorsing from the deep past their sensitivity,
wisdom, and fine feelings. And the point about the ancient
world in a larger sense is not that it resembles (in this way or
that) our own.

We should be very careful, then, about labelling the Homeric
Hymns as 'religious', and believing that word is self-explanatory.
The poems are about Greek gods, it is true, and they pay those
gods various kinds of reverence; but they are not expressions
of religious devotion as that concept is known in modern
European history, and such religious experiences as they figure
have nothing at all to do with the personal enlightenment or
salvation of the narrating poet. At best, the Hymns might serve
their ancient narrators well in bringing a certain amount of
divine sponsorship to bear, whether in the winning of contests
or more general prosperity. The complex patchwork of religious
beliefs which they represent is the very loosest kind of unity,
and is not some kind of ancient 'scripture' on which to found
a theology. Instead, the poets of these Hymns are often in the
business of telling stories, and these stories are narrated with

sometimes extreme levels of sophistication. It is impossible to regain access to the full range of nuance and allusion which the Hymns must have contained; we can, however, still see how frequently, and with what subtlety of effect, they touch the texts of Homeric epic, as well as that other strand of epic literature represented by Hesiod. To a greater or lesser extent, all of the Hymns are poems full of reference, packed with the literary language, the stories, the named divine personalities, and the places known to its audiences from a large body of old, but still living, oral literature.

Assuming that the bulk of the Hymns originate from a period between roughly the end of the seventh century BC and the end of the fifth (which is the modern scholarly consensus), we can think of them as fragmentary records from the culture of professional recitation in which performers travelled between different parts of Greece with their repertoires of epic material. The Ionian coast, the Aegean islands, and the Greek mainland would all be places on the touring circuits of numerous performers, some of whom we know claimed a kind of family connection to their great original by calling themselves *Homeridai*, the Sons of Homer. The very language of the Hymns – like that of the Homeric epics – seems designed for travel, for although it incorporates elements from all the major dialect regions (along with consciously archaic elements), it is not in itself the language spoken in one particular locality. The Hymns also build in a great deal of geographical range, and at a time when few people apart from those involved in merchant shipping would have travelled far from their home towns, this adds a vital dimension.

In part, the awareness of a Greece beyond immediate localities is connected with the whole meaning and understanding of an Olympian pantheon, for which the Hymns are important instruments. Any theology for the culture in which these poems are rooted begins with geography: gods have places of origin (commonly, each god has several), places of special association, and the ability to move rapidly between such locations. Some of the more intensely topographic passages in the Hymns may indeed seem alien to modern tastes, but they must have been challenging and (in a stimulating way) stretching for many ancient imaginations too. Even when translated across huge tracts of time and culture, effects like these can still be real. Few of Chapman's early readership had ever gone much beyond their native counties in England, and this somehow underwrites his superbly confident translation of one detailed Greek itinerary in Hymn 3 (to Apollo):[9]

> [...] all mortalls liue in thy commands.
> Who euer *Crete* holds; *Athens*; or the strands
> Of th'Ile *Aegina*; or the famous land
> For ships (*Euboea:*) or *Eresia*;
> Or *Peparethus*, bordering on the sea.
> *Aegas*; or *Athos*, that doth *Thrace* diuide
> And *Macedon*. Or *Pelion*, with the pride
> Of his high forehead. Or the *Samian* Ile;
> That likewise lies neare *Thrace*; or *Scyrus* soile;
> *Ida's* steepe tops. Or all that *Phocis* fill:
> Or *Autocanes*, with the heauen-high hill:
> Or populous *Imber: Lemnos* without Ports;
> Or *Lesbos*, fit for the diuine resorts;
> And sacred soile of blest *Aeolion*.
> Or *Chius* that exceeds comparison
> For fruitfulnes; with all the Iles that lie
> Embrac't with seas. *Mimas*, with rocks so hie.
> Or Loftie-crownd *Corycius*; or the bright
> *Charos:* or *Aesagaeus* dazeling height:
> Or watery *Samos. Mycale*, that beares
> Her browes euen with the circles of the spheares.
> *Miletus*; *Cous*; That the Citie is
> Of voice-diuided-choice humanities.
> High *Cnidus*; *Carpathus*, still strooke with winde;

---

9   George Chapman, 'A Hymne to Apollo', *The Crowne of all Homers works* (1624), 21.

Naxus, and *Paros*; and the rockie-min'd
Rugged *Rhenaea*.

The translation here both inherits things from the previous
generation in English poetry and passes them on, decisively
altered, into the next. In this, the very otherness of the Greek
is not softened, or made reassuringly familiar; instead, it is the
whole point. The manner of Chapman here will feed directly
into the catalogues of ancient and far-fetched places and names
in John Milton's *Paradise Lost* (1667), but part of it is brought
from the past, and Christopher Marlowe:[10]

    [*One brings a Map.*]

Here I began to martch towards Persea,
Along *Armenia* and the Caspian sea,
And thence unto *Bythinia*, where I tooke
The Turke and his great Empresse prisoners,
Then martcht I into *Egypt* and *Arabia*,
And here not far from *Alexandria*,
Whereas the Terren and the red sea meet,
Being distant lesse than ful a hundred leagues,
I meant to cut a channell to them both,
That men might quickly saile to *India*.
From thence to *Nubia* neere *Borno* Lake,
And so along the Ethiopian sea,
Cutting the Tropicke line of *Capricorne*,
I conquered all as far as *Zansibar*.
Then by the Northerne part of *Affrica*,
I came at last to *Græcia*, and from thence
To Asia, where I stay against my will,
Which is from *Scythia*, where I first began,
Backeward and forwards nere five thousand leagues.

10 Christopher Marlowe, *The Second Part of The bloody Conquests of mighty
    Tamburlaine* (1590), Actus 5, Scaena 3, ll. 127–145.

The ancient breadth of reference in the Homeric Hymn is repeated by Chapman as translator, but its English poetic idiom, the backbone of its diction, was already available to him, in the blank verse of the English stage. In the process, something new and (for Milton, at any rate) viable is added to the language's poetic capacity.

Perhaps, in this respect, things for the ancient Greek authors of these poems were not so very different. Taking, adding, and passing on were all essential parts of the process of composition itself; considered as a whole, all these things could, by common consent, for a time constitute an author called 'Homer'. Like the Olympian gods, Homer had a plurality of origins, and of places in the world, which became more elaborate with the passing of time. And eventually, once biographical thinking became (however slowly) distinct from poetic myth-making, Lives of Homer came to have an appeal. The present volume (like early editions of Homer's Works) includes one such biography, a Life written by someone probably in the late first or early second century AD; someone, moreover, who is passing himself off as the historian Herodotus, from a good six centuries earlier. In this narrative, there are numerous inserted short poems: these became known as Homer's Epigrams, and were duly added to the sum of his Works. Yet they date from long before the compilation of the Life itself, and in all likelihood from long before the real Herodotus. Some are very slight things indeed, others more substantial; yet all of them need the supporting narrative framework to make complete sense. The Life could well have been written partly to explain the poems.

All of this is another way of saying that the existence of 'Homer' is something dependent wholly on Homeric poetry. Just as the fact that the gods Apollo and Hera, Athene and Hermes never existed takes nothing away from the complex and lively reality of the mythology they generated when they were believed in, so the near certainty that there was never a single individual who composed the *Iliad* and the *Odyssey*, the Hymns and the little constellation of Epigrams and minor poems does nothing to render insubstantial the palpable presence of a poet called Homer.

Such a presence can be made solid in poetic translations – as for Chapman, and much later for Shelley, it was undoubtedly touched and proven there. My own task in tackling the Hymns has been to make them, as well as I am able, contemporary poems; and inevitably, this means the kind of contemporary poems I am able to write. So, I expect these versions bear strong marks of my own time and background – the cadence and diction of their English, for example, have a Northern Irish inflection, and their sense of line and form generally accords with the work of somebody whose own poetry has long been (for better or worse) indebted to the resources of both rhyme and metre. On the whole, the versions are 'faithful' (to use the established and interesting metaphor) to the diction and syntax of the Greek. But in making them (as I hope) poems rather than versified cribs, I have been ready to intervene from time to time: not just in compressing and occasionally suppressing epithets, but in formal ways too, sometimes breaking up the longer narratives into formally distinct sections, and turning some Hymns into stanzaic verse. Given all this, it will be obvious that I do not believe myself capable of finding an imitative equivalent, in the metres and rhythms of English verse, for the dactylic hexameter in which these poems uniformly are composed; and I suspect that the efforts expended in finding such supposed equivalents are often a kind of misplaced ingenuity. At all events, I have attempted to turn the Greek into the kind of English poetry I know how to write.

After the Hymns in this edition, I have included the pseudo-Herodotean Life (with the Epigrams), and a couple of appendices in which I have translated lengthy passages from Homer and Hesiod that are of particular relevance to some of the poems. In the Notes, I have supplied a brief essay on each of the longer Hymns, together with a commentary. This will be enough, I think, to point interested readers towards some of the main areas of discussion in the modern study of the Homeric Hymns, and will provide a certain amount of comparative material that will deepen the experience of reading these ancient texts. As far as I could, I have tried to make sure that the main currents of modern interpretation are accounted for; the Notes should also make it clear when I have departed from the original texts, and what has thereby been missed out. Whatever kinds of licence have been exercised in the translations, none has been presumed upon in the commentary material; I have doubtless made mistakes there, but I have not consciously told any fibs on the spurious grounds of a poet's privilege.

It is usually a sign of egotistic eccentricity to change the name of a literary work from something that is already widely known and accepted: hence, this book is what would reasonably be expected, *The Homeric Hymns*. There is a case, all the same, for returning these poems to their remote and many-lived author, and thinking of them as *The Hymns of Homer*. They add, just as generations of readers once thought, to our sense of the *Iliad* and the *Odyssey* by enabling us to experience the full range of possible approaches to their many gods – who are at the same time like and unlike women and men, interested in and scornful of humanity, parts of a real world and still gleefully beyond it: and this experience is everywhere in the poetry, whose movements can be so nimble and so dazzling. Homer without the Hymns is less than Homer.

The Homeric Hymns

Hymn 1

To Dionysus

[four fragments]

A.

                                    ] for
some say, Bull-god, a god from birth,
Drakanos was the place on earth
Semelē bore you to great Zeus;
some say that it was by the side
of Alpheios' deep-running tide;
exposed Ikaros, others; or choose
Naxos, or else claim that the place
was Thebes: wrongly, in every case,
for Zeus found somewhere far from men
to be your proper birthplace when
he hid you well out of the reach
of Hera's pale arms, a place where each
peak of the range is topped with trees,
called Nysa, a far spot that lies
in Phoenicia, almost as far
as where the Egyptian waters are,
where nobody can come by sea,
for there's no harbour that allows
ships with their curly sterns and prows
to ride at anchor; all around
a huge cliff rises to high ground
where splendid and delicious things
grow in abundance [*by fresh springs,*

and where the river cuts a deep
glen in the forest, and flowers keep
back from the rushing water there,
to thrive with only nature's care
not far from perfect grazing land]

*

B.

                    and vines] weighed down
with large grape-clusters of their own [

*

C.

'... [*is what you want: what more*
could you go through, or I deplore
than this? For when Hephaestus left
under his own steam, he was deft
enough, as everyone will know,
to trick you, and leave you a show
for all and sundry then, my dear,
done up and totally trapped here
in devilish straps and locks and chains.
And who could set you free? Around
your middle one great belt is wound,
while he has gone, and set his face
against both pleading and disgrace.
Sister, you have a cruel son;
cripple though he may be, he's one
crafty customer; it's no good
falling at his feet, for he would

still be this wild and furious;
so the one thing left now for us
is to see if he's really made
of iron, for these two sons of mine
are clever enough to combine
to help you – first, Ares is here
to brandish his war-sharpened spear,
and then there's Dionysus too,
with plenty of tricks he can do.
As for Hephaestus, he'd be wise
to keep himself from giving rise
to some quarrel with me, unless
he wants to feel the sore distress
that I can cause, taken from all
sweet pleasures and condemned to fall
again, while Dionysus, this
young lad] ...'

*

D.

'...and in his temples they will raise
statues galore to show his praise,
while for these three things, every three
years people will come in to see
offerings made in sacrifice.'

As soon as he had said this, Zeus
inclined his head and dark brows down,
and the hair blazed out from his crown,
shaking massive Olympus; so
saying, he simply bowed his head.

And now Dionysus, Bull-god,
you who can send the women mad,
look kindly on us all who sing
before we start, and when we bring
our stories to an end, of you:
there is no way to mind a true
song without minding you as well.
So, Bull-god, Dionysus, take
this tribute also for the sake
of Semelē your mother, she
whom people still call Thyonē.

Hymn 2

To Demeter

This is about Demeter, the long-haired goddess
Demeter, and about her child, a skinny-legged
little girl who was just taken away
one morning by Hades, Death himself, on the say-so
of his brother Zeus, the deep- and wide-bellowing God.

She was apart from her mother, and from Demeter's
protecting sword, made all of gold, when he came;
she was running about in an uncut spring meadow
with her friends, the daughters of the god Ocean,
and picking flowers here and there – crocuses and wild roses,
with violets and tiny irises, then hyacinths
and one narcissus planted there by Gaia, the Earth,
as Zeus demanded, and as a favour to Death,
to trap the girl, whose own eyes were as small and bright
as the buds of flowers: it blazed and shone out
with astonishing colours, a prodigy as much for
the immortal gods as for people who die.
A hundred flower-heads sprung from the root
with a sweet smell so heavy and overpowering
that the wide sky and the earth, even the salt waves
of the sea lit up, as though they were all smiling.
The girl was dazzled; she reached out with both hands
to gather up the brilliant thing; but then the earth
opened, the earth's surface with its level roads
buckled, there on the plain of Nysa, and up from below
rushed at her, driving his horses, the king of the dead.

He snatched her up, struggling, and he drove her away
in his golden chariot as she wailed and shrieked
and called out loud to her father to help her,
to Zeus, the highest of high powers;
yet nobody – not one god, not one human being,
not even the laden olive-trees – paid heed to her;
but from deep in a cave, the young night-goddess
Hecatē, Perses' daughter, in her white linen veil,
could hear the child's cries; and so could the god Helios
– god of the Sun, like his father Hyperion –
hear the girl screaming for help to Zeus, her own father:
Zeus, who was keeping his distance, apart from the gods,
busy in a temple, taking stock there of the fine
offerings and the prayers of mortal men.

For all her struggling, it was with the connivance of Zeus
that this prince of the teeming dark, the god with many titles,
her own uncle, with his team of unstoppable horses
took away the little girl: she, as long as she kept in sight
the earth and the starry night sky, the sun's day-beams
and the seas pulled by tides and swimming in fish,
still hoped, hoped even now to see her mother again
and get back to her family of the eternal gods.

From the mountain tops to the bottom of the sea, her voice
echoed, a goddess's voice; and, when her mother heard
those cries, pain suddenly jabbed at her heart: she tore
in two the veil that covered her perfumed hair,
threw a dark shawl across her shoulders, and shot
out like a bird across dry land and water,
frantic to search; but nobody – neither god, nor human –
was ready to tell her what had happened, not even
a solitary bird would give Demeter the news.
For nine whole days, with a blazing torch in each hand,
the goddess roamed the earth, not touching, in her grief,
either the gods' food or their drink, ambrosia or nectar,
and not stopping even to splash her skin with water.

On the tenth day, at the first blink of dawn, Hecatē
came to help her, carrying torches of her own,
and gave her first what news she could: 'Royal Demeter,
bringer of seasons, and all the gifts the seasons bring,
what god in heaven, or what man on this earth
can have snatched away Persephone, and broken your heart?
I heard the sound of her crying, but I couldn't see
who it was; I'm telling you everything I know.'
Hecatē said this, and received not one word in reply:
instead, Demeter rushed her away, and the pair of them
soon reached Helios, the watcher of gods and men.

Demeter stopped by his horses, and spoke to him from there.
'If ever I have pleased you, Helios, or if ever
I have done you a favour, do this one for me now:
my daughter's voice was lost on the trackless air,
shrill with distress; I heard, but looked and saw nothing.
You gaze down all day from the broad sky,
and see everything on dry land and the ocean:
so if you have seen who forced away my child
from me, and who went off with her, whether
a man or a god, please, quickly, just tell me.'
She said this, and the son of Hyperion replied:
'Holy Demeter, daughter of Rhea with her long hair,
you are going to hear it all – for I think highly
of you and, yes, I pity you, grieving as you are
for the loss of your skinny-legged little girl. So:
of all the immortal gods, none other is responsible
than the master of the clouds, Zeus himself, who gave her
to Hades his brother to call his own
as a beautiful wife. Hades with his team of horses
snatched her, and dragged her to the thickening dark
as she cried and cried. But come now; you are a goddess:
call an end to this huge sorrow; be reasonable:
there is no need for such uncontrollable rage.
Hades, the lord of millions, is hardly, after all,
the worst son-in-law amongst the immortals,

and he is your own flesh and blood, your own brother.
As for his position – well, he has what was allotted
originally, when things were split three ways,
the master of those amongst whom he dwells.'

So saying, Helios took up the reins, and his horses
were away all at once, bearing up the chariot
like birds with slender wings. And now grief fastened
– a harsher, a more dreadful pain – at Demeter's heart.
Furious with the black cloud-god, the son of Cronos,
she abandoned the gods' city, and high Olympus,
to travel through rich fields and the towns of men,
changing her face, wiping all its beauty away,
so that nobody, neither man nor woman, when
they saw her could recognise her for a goddess.
She wandered a long time, until she came to the home
at Eleusis of the good man Celeus, master there.

Heartsore, heart-sorry, Demeter stopped by the roadside
at the well they called the Maiden's Well, where people
from the town would come for water; sat in the shade
cast over her by heavy branches of olive,
and looked for all the world like a very old lady,
one long past childbearing or the gifts of love,
just like a nurse who might care for the children
of royalty, or a housekeeper in their busy house.
The daughters of Celeus caught sight of her as they came
that way to draw water, and carry it back
to their father's place in great big pitchers of bronze:
Callidicē and Clisidicē, beautiful Dēmō
and Callithoē, the eldest girl of all four,
more like goddesses in the first flower of youth.
They had no idea who she was – it's hard for people
to recognise gods – so they came straight up to her
and demanded, 'Madam, where have you come from
and who, of all the old women here, are you?
Why is it that you've walked out past the town

and don't go to its houses? Plenty of ladies
the same age as you, and others who are younger,
are there now, in buildings sheltered from the heat,
to welcome you with a kind word and a kind turn.'

When they had done, the royal goddess replied:
'Good day to you, girls, whoever you may be;
I'll tell you what you want to know, for it's surely
not wrong, when you're asked, to explain the truth.
I am called Grace – my mother gave me that name –
and I have travelled on the broad back of the sea
all the way from Crete – not wanting to, but forced
to make the journey by men who had snatched me,
gangsters, all of them. In that fast ship of theirs
they put in at Thoricos, where the women
disembarked together, and they themselves began
making their supper down by the stern-cables.
But I had no appetite for any meal that they made,
and when their backs were turned I disappeared
into dark country, and escaped from those men
before they could sell me, stolen goods, at a
good price, bullies and fixers that they were.
That's how I arrived like a vagrant, and I
don't know what country it is, or who lives here.
May the gods who have their homes on Olympus
send you good husbands and plenty of children
to please the parents; but now, spare a thought
for me, like the well brought-up girls that you are,
and maybe I can come to one of your houses
to do some honest work for the ladies and gentlemen
living there, the kind of thing a woman of my age
does best: I can nurse a new baby, and hold
him safe in my arms; I can keep the place clean;
I can make up the master's bed in a corner
of the great bedchamber, and give all the right
instructions to serving women in the house.'

It was the goddess who said this; immediately
the girl Callidicē, loveliest of Celeus' daughters,
spoke back to her, calling her Grandma, and saying:
'Whatever the gods give, however grievous the hardship,
people put up with it, as they must, for the gods
are that much stronger: it's just how things are.
But something I can do is tell you the names
of men who have power and prestige in this town,
who keep its walls in good shape, whose decisions
count for much, and whose advice is listened to here:
wise Triptolemus and Diocles, that good man
Eumolpus, then Polyxeinus, and Dolichus,
and our own dear father of course, all have
wives kept busy with the care of their houses;
not one of them would take a dislike to you
and turn you away from the door – they would welcome
you in, for there *is* something special about you.
Stay here, if you will, and we'll all run back
to tell our mother, Metaneira, the whole story,
then see whether she'll suggest that you come
to ours, and not go looking for another home.
She has a new baby in the house now, a son
born later in life, hoped for and prayed for:
if you were to take care of him, and see him through
to manhood, you would be the envy of any
woman, so well would that childcare be paid.'

Demeter simply nodded her head, and the girls
filled their shiny pitchers up with fresh water
and carried them away, their heads held high.
Soon they were at the family home, where they told
their mother all they had seen, all they had heard.
She ordered them to hurry back, and request this woman
to come and work for a good wage. So then
like deer, or like young calves in springtime,
happy and well-fed, running around in the fields,
they pulled up the folds of their long dresses

and dashed down the cart-track: the long hair,
yellow as saffron, streamed back over their shoulders.
They found Demeter where they had left her, by the road,
and they led her then towards their father's house
while she walked a little way behind, troubled at heart,
her head veiled, and with the dark dress fluttering
this way and that over her slender legs.

They got back to Celeus' house, and went in
through the hallway, where their mother was waiting,
seated by a pillar that held up the strong roof,
with her child, the new son and heir, at her breast.
The girls ran straight to her: slowly Demeter placed
a foot over the threshold, her head touched the rafters,
and around her the entire doorway lit up.
Astonishment and draining fear together shook
Metaneira; she gave up her couch to the visitor
and invited her to sit. But Demeter, who brings
the seasons round, and brings gifts with the seasons,
had no wish to relax on that royal couch, and she
maintained her silence, with eyes fixed on the floor,
until Iambe came up, mindful of her duty,
and offered a low stool, which she had covered
with a sheep's white fleece. The goddess
sat down now, and with one hand she drew
the veil across her face; and there she remained,
sunk in her quiet grief, giving to no one
so much as a word or a sign, sitting on there
without a smile, accepting neither food nor drink
for an age, as she pined for her beautiful daughter,
until Iambe, resourceful as ever, took
her mind off things with jokes and funny stories,
making her smile first, then laugh, and feel better,
and Metaneira offered her the cup she had filled
with wine, sweet as honey: but she shook her head
and announced that, for her, it was not proper now
to take wine – instead, she asked Metaneira

to give her some barley-water and pennyroyal
mixed up together: the queen made this, and served it
to the great goddess, to Demeter,
who accepted it solemnly, and drank it down.
Only then did Metaneira begin to speak:
'Madam, you are welcome here; all the more so
for coming from no ordinary stock
but, I'd say, from the best – for your every glance
is full of modesty and grace, you have something
almost royal about you. But what the gods give us,
hard though it is, we mere human beings
endure: all our necks are under that yoke.
You are here now, and whatever is mine shall be yours.
This little boy – my last born, scarcely hoped for,
granted me by the gods only after much prayer –
nurse him for me now, and if you raise him
to be a healthy, strong man, then any woman
at all will be jealous to see you, so great
will be the reward I give you for your work.'
Demeter replied: 'Accept my greetings, good lady,
and may the gods be kind to you. I will indeed
take care of this fine boy of yours, as you ask.
I shall rear him, and neglect nothing: sudden sickness
will never harm him, and never will some witch
of the forest, who taps roots for magic or poison,
touch a single hair of his head; for I know
stronger sources to tap, and I know the remedy
for all such assaults: a sure one, unfailing.'

Then with her two arms, the arms of a goddess,
she drew the baby in close to her own bosom,
and its mother smiled at the sight. In the big house
from then on Demeter looked after the son
of Celeus and Metaneira, while he grew up
at a god's rate, not eating solids, or taking
milk, but fed by her with ambrosia, as if
he were indeed a god, born of a god;

she breathed gently over him and kept him close,
and at night, unknown to anyone, she smuggled him
into the burning fire, like a new log of wood.
He was thriving so well, and looking so much more
than a human child, that both the parents were amazed.

And the goddess Demeter would have delivered him
from age and from death, had not Metaneira
been up one night and, without so much as
giving it a thought, from her own bedroom
looked into the hall: in sheer terror for the child
she screamed, and did her best to raise the alarm,
seeing the worst and believing it; she called out
to her little boy, half-keening: 'Demophoön,
my own baby, this stranger is hiding you
in the big fire, she's the one making my voice shrill
with pain, Demophoön, my darling, my child.'

She cried all this out, and the goddess heard her.
Furious that instant, mighty Demeter
took the child – their last born, scarcely hoped for –
and with her own immortal hands she brought him
out of the fire, set him gently on the floor,
then, brimming with anger, turned on Metaneira:
'You stupid creatures, you witless and ignorant
humans, blind to the good as well as the bad
things in store for you, and no use to each other:
I swear to you here, as gods do, by the rippling
dark waters of Styx, that I would have made
this child of yours immortal, honoured, a man
untouched by age for eternity; but nothing now
can keep the years back, or keep death from him.
There is one mark of honour that will always be his:
because he once slept in my arms, and lay in my lap,
all the young men at Eleusis, at the set time
each year, as their scared duty, will gather
for the sham fight, and stage that battle forever.

For I am Demeter, proud of my own honours
as the bringer of joy to the gods, and of blessings
to mortal men. Everyone now has to build me
a spacious temple, with its altar underneath,
by the steep walls of your city, where a hill
rises just above the Maidens' Well. The rites
will be as I instruct, when I teach you the ways
to calm my anger, and be good servants to me.'

And with that, instantly the goddess changed form –
her height, her whole appearance – shuffling away
old age, so that sheer beauty blazed and spread
in and around her; from her robes a gorgeous perfume
drifted, and from her immortal flesh there came
pure light, with the reach of moonbeams; her hair
flashed over her shoulders, and the entire house
was flooded with a sudden brilliance of lightning
as she stepped out through the hall. Metaneira's
knees went from beneath her, and for an age
she sat there speechless, not even thinking
to pick that dear child of hers up from the floor.

When his sisters heard the boy starting to cry
they jumped straight out of their beds, and one
caught him up in her arms, and held him close,
while another stoked the fire, and a third
dashed on bare feet to take hold of her mother
and help her away. As the girls huddled round him,
trying to comfort him and dab his skin clean,
the baby wriggled and fretted, knowing full well
these nurses were hardly the kind he was used to.

That whole night long, shaking with fear, the women
did their best to appease the great goddess.
When dawn came at last, they told everything
to Celeus, exactly as Demeter had instructed,
and he, as their ruler, lost no time

in calling the citizens together, and giving them
the order to build the goddess her temple
and to put her altar just where the hill rises.
They listened to him, and they did all that he said,
so that a temple rose up, as the goddess required.
When the job was done, and the people stopped working,
they all went home; but golden Demeter
installed herself in her temple, apart from the other gods,
and stayed there, eaten up with grief for her daughter.

She made that year the worst for people living
on the good earth, the worst and the hardest: not one
little seed could poke its head up from the soil,
for Demeter had smothered them all; the oxen
broke their ploughs and twisted them, scraping
across hardened furrows; and all the white barley
that year was sown in vain. She would have destroyed
every single human being in the world
with this famine, just to spite the gods on Olympus,
had not Zeus decided to intervene: first
he dispatched Iris, on her wings the colour of gold,
to give Demeter his orders, and she did as he asked,
covering the distance in no time, and landing
at Eleusis, where the air was filled with incense.
She found Demeter wearing dark robes in the temple,
and spoke to her urgently: 'Zeus, our father
who knows everything, summons you back now
to join the family of the immortal gods:
come quick, don't let his command be in vain.'
But her pleas had no effect at all on Demeter:
then Zeus sent out all of the gods, one by one,
to deliver his summons, bringing the best of gifts,
with whatever fresh honours she might desire;
but Demeter was so furious then that she
dismissed every speech out of hand, and told them all
that she would neither set foot again
on Olympus, nor let anything grow on the earth,

unless she could see her beautiful daughter once more.

When he heard this, Zeus, the deep- and wide-bellowing God,
sent Hermes with his golden staff down into the dark
to talk to Hades there, and ask his permission
to lead Persephone back up from the shadows
and into daylight again, where her mother
could set eyes on her, and so be angry no longer.
Hermes agreed to do this: he hurried away
from his place on Olympus, down into the earth's
crevasses and crannies, down, till he reached
the king of all the dead in his underground palace,
stretched out at his ease, and by his arm a trembling
bride, who pined still for the mother she had lost.
Coming up close to him, the god Hermes began:
'Hades, dark-haired lord and master of the dead,
my father Zeus orders me now to take away
from Erebus the royal Persephone, back
to the world, so that Demeter, when she sees
with her own eyes her daughter returning
may relent, and give up her implacable grudge
against the gods – for what she now intends
is terrible, to wipe from the face of the earth
the whole defenceless species of mortal men
by keeping crops under the ground, and then starving
heaven of its offerings. In her rage, Demeter
will have nothing to do with the gods, and she sits
closed in her own temple, apart, holding sway
there over the rocky citadel of Eleusis.'

Hades listened, with just the hint of a smile
on his face, but did not disobey the express
order of Zeus the king, and he spoke at once:
'Go, Persephone, go back now to your mother,
go in good spirits, and full of happiness,
but don't feel too much anger or resentment.
You know, I won't be the worst of all the gods

to have for a husband, brother to your father Zeus;
and here you could be the mistress of everything
that lives and moves, have the finest of honours
among the gods, while for all those failing to pay
their dues by keeping you happy with sacrifice,
proper respect and generous gifts, there will be
nothing in store but punishment forever.'

Persephone jumped straight up, full of excitement,
when she heard what he said; but Hades, looking
around him, and then back over his shoulder,
gave her the tiny, sweet seed of a pomegranate
for something to eat, so that she would not stay
up there forever with the goddess Demeter.
Then Hades got ready his gold-covered chariot,
hitching up his own horses, and in stepped
Persephone, with the strong god Hermes beside her,
who took the reins and the whip in his hands
as both of the horses shot forward obediently
out and away, making good speed on their journey,
untroubled by the sea, or by flowing rivers,
or grassy glens, or freezing mountain tops:
they sliced thin air beneath them as they flew.

When they came to a stop, it was in front of the temple
where Demeter kept vigil; and, at the sight of them,
she ran forward wildly like someone possessed.
At the sight of her mother, Persephone leapt out
and into her arms, and hugged her, and she wept,
and the two of them, speechless, clung hard
to each other, until suddenly Demeter
sensed something wrong, and broke the embrace.
'My darling,' she said, 'I hope that down there
you didn't eat anything when he took you away?
Tell me, and tell me now: for, if you didn't,
you can stay with me forever, and with the gods,
and Zeus, your father; but, if you did eat

anything at all, then you'll have to go back
underground for the third part of every year,
spending the rest of the time at my side: when
flowers come up in spring, and bloom in the summer,
you will rise too from the deep mists and darkness –
to the amazement of men, as well as the gods.
But how did Hades abduct you? What tricks
did he use to bring you away to the dark?'
'Mother,' Persephone answered, 'I will tell you it all.
When Hermes came for me on the orders of Zeus,
to take me out of Erebus, so you could see me
and abandon your vendetta against the gods,
I jumped for joy; but then Hades, unnoticed,
gave me the seed of a pomegranate to eat,
and made me taste it: it was sweet like honey.
I'll explain, just as you ask me to, how he
snatched me away in the first place, when Zeus
planned everything to bring me down under the earth.
We were playing together in an uncut meadow
– me and all my friends – and gathering for fun
handfuls of the wild flowers that were growing there:
saffron and irises, hyacinths, and young roses,
lilies gorgeous to look at, and a narcissus
that bloomed, just like a crocus, in the soil.
While I was taken up with that, from nowhere
the ground beneath me split apart, and out
came the great king of millions of the dead
who dragged me, as I screamed, into his gold-
covered chariot, and took me down into the earth.
Now you've heard what it hurts me to remember.'

That whole day long, they were completely at one:
each warmed the other's heart, and eased it of sorrow,
the two of them brimming over with happiness
as they hugged one another for joy again and again.
The goddess Hecatē came to them and joined them;
still wearing her veil of white linen, she caught

Demeter's little daughter over and over
in her arms, and became her companion forever.

Only then did Zeus, the deep- and wide-bellowing God,
send down to speak to Demeter her own mother,
Rhea, to reconcile her with her family.
On his behalf, she could offer whatever new honours
were needed, and guarantee that Persephone
would stay down in the darkness for only a season,
the third of a year, and the rest with her mother
and all of the gods. Rhea hurried to the task,
reaching the fields near Eleusis at Rarion
where harvests once were abundant, but now
no harvest could come up from the cropless plain
where Demeter had hidden away the white barley,
though afterwards, as the spring went on, it would
thicken and move with long corn, and the furrows
would be filled in due course with cut stalks
while all the rest was gathered up into sheaves.

Here the goddess first came down from the trackless air
and she and Demeter greeted one another with joy.
Rhea delivered her message from Zeus, and the promises
he made for Demeter, and for Persephone,
urging her daughter, 'Now, child, you must
do the right thing, and not venture too far
by keeping up this grudge of yours against Zeus:
let food grow again for people on the earth.'
Demeter could say nothing against this: she allowed
crops then and there to come from the fertile ground;
she freighted the wide world with flowers and leaves.

She went then to the men in power – Diocles,
Triptolemus, Eumolpus, and Celeus himself,
the people's leader, to give them instruction
in her liturgy and rites: all of the mysteries
neither to be questioned, nor departed from,

and not to be spoken about for fear of the gods,
a fear so great as to stop every mouth.
Whoever has witnessed these is blessed among men:
whoever has not been inducted, whoever
has taken no part in them, can expect no good
fortune when death fetches him to the darkness.

Once she had revealed all of this, Demeter
returned to Olympus and the company of the gods;
there she and Persephone, holy and powerful,
live beside Zeus himself, where he plays with thunder.
Anyone whom they favour is deeply blessed,
for they send the god Wealth to his own hearth
dispensing affluence to mortal men.

You who protect the people of fragrant Eleusis,
rocky Antron, and Paros surrounded by the sea,
Lady Demeter, mistress, bountiful goddess,
both you and your lovely child Persephone,
favour me for this hymn, give me a living,
and I will heed you in my songs, now and always.

Hymn 3

To Apollo

Let me recall in order everything
in the story, and let me leave out no
detail as now I set myself to sing
of the long-ranging, lethal god Apollo
who can make even the other gods spring
up from their seats in alarm when, just so,
he strides through Zeus's hall with a drawn bow.

As that bow flashes all across the room
his mother Leto, from her throne beside
Zeus, the god of thunder-clouds and doom,
gets up, makes sure his bowstring is untied,
then shuts the quiver, takes the bow from him,
with her own fingers from his strong and wide
shoulders, before she hangs it up in pride

of place on a pillar of his father's house,
high on a peg made out of solid gold;
she leads him then to an illustrious
seat of honour, where his hands can hold
the precious goblet which his father Zeus
fills up with nectar, calling out a bold
toast to Apollo: the gods do as they're told,

drinking to him, and only then quite daring
to sit back down. Leto just smiles, because
she's so very pleased with herself for bearing

a son like this, so strong, who when he draws
his bow is stronger still. Leto, now wearing
your pride rightly, great goddess, pause
to take our worship and our mute applause –

Apollo's mother, and the mother too
of Artemis, both of them glorious
archer-gods; Artemis you gave birth to
in Ortygia, the island famous
for quails; and the great god Apollo you
bore while leaning against the mountainous
long promontory on Delos that's called Cynthus,

under a palm tree, near the running streams
of the stony river Inopus. No praise
is new to you; but then, what kind of hymns
could do you justice? Phoebus, where you blaze
down on us, it's the entire world that teems
with all the places and the thousand ways
to summon you, wherever the light plays:

whether far inland, where green grasses feed
the heifers, or out along island shores;
or where clifftops and rocky crags succeed
each other on the heights, from which there pours
river on river, to where the rivers lead,
those seaside harbours, steps down from the floors
of mountain ranges, where the salt sea roars.

Shall I tell the story first of how Leto
pushed against Cynthus with its twists and bends
of rock, to give you birth where she'd meet no
witnesses but black waves, that from both ends
of that island grip it, and don't let go,
and rose for her that night where the shore winds
around Delos, beneath shrill-singing winds?

Starting from there, now you rule all mankind.
Past all the people that there are in Crete,
and every last inhabitant you'd find
in Athens; Euboea, famous for its fleet;
Aegae, Iresiae, and the little island
of Aegina; Thracian Athos; the sweet
high places on Pelion, far from heat;

or Samothrace, and Ida's shaded heights;
Peparethos, surrounded by the sea;
Imbros, so well set-up and set to rights;
Lemnos, sunk under fog; the fair and free
Lesbos, where Macar, happy man, delights
to live; Scyros, Phoceia, Autocanē;
and Chios, the loveliest in its degree

of all the islands, where Mimas and Corycus,
rough summits, face it from across the waves;
steep Aisagea; then Claros, luminous;
Samos, where water rushes down and raves
across the stone; Mycalē's mountainous
highlands; Cos and Miletus, where the graves
and city are of an ancient tribe that lives

there still, the Meropes; those black and sheer
headlands on Cnidos; Carpathos awash
with gales and winds and breezes everywhere;
Naxos and Paros; and where breakers crash
against stony Rhaenaea as they rear
up from the sea: to all these places, wish-
ing to give birth, Leto came and went in a flash,

to see if any of them would submit
to becoming her new son's holy birthplace.
Yet each one trembled at the thought of it,
for none, however rich, would dare to face
the prospect, worried what they might get

if they took on, even with a good grace,
Phoebus Apollo and his tricky case.

None, that is, until Leto found her way
to Delos, and made the island her request,
letting it hear the words she had to say:
'If only you, alone amongst the rest
of the islands, Delos, would consent to play
host to my son Apollo, and put his best
temple up on your land, to make it blessed!

As things are, who is bothering with you?
You're poor alike in cattle and in sheep;
you have no harvests to look forward to,
or trees whose heavy branches are bent deep
with fruit; yet if you now provide this new
god Apollo a temple, you're sure to reap
the benefits when, from everywhere, people

come with their gifts of livestock, and the smell
of roasting fat fills the air all around –
from then on, foreigners will keep you well
able to feed your own here, where the ground
gives you so little.' Delos, pleased with it all,
replied: 'Leto, daughter of the renowned
Coius, let me say I like the sound

of being the place where Apollo is born,
and indeed it's all too true that nobody
thinks well of such a desolate, forlorn
place as I am, so this would be a way
of making myself famous; yet I'm torn
by doubt, for there's one problem I can see
– I tell you openly and honestly:

they say that this Apollo will turn out wild,
and not be slow to throw his weight around,
whether in heaven, or where earth is piled
deep with the grown grain; that's why I sound
anxious – in case he can't be reconciled
to this little stony island, so with one bound
escapes, and kicks huge waves over the ground

to sink me, and leave me inundated,
almost as soon as he first sees the sun,
drawing the salt water across my head
the minute he decides he'd rather run
off to some other country, and there instead
have his new temple, beautifully done
for him in a sacred grove, the finest one,

while the octopus and the black-pelted seal,
who haunt places a long way off from man,
make their homes in me. That's why I feel
I need to ask you, goddess, if you can,
to swear a binding oath, and make the deal
secure between us, as our common plan:
Apollo's temple, here where he began,

will be forever a place of pilgrimage,
oracular for all men – do you swear to this?'
At once, Leto was happy to engage
herself, and swore: 'Now be witnesses
to me Earth, and the high, wide stage
of Heaven; witness, too, where the abyss
gurgles and chokes it down, the River Styx

(this the most dreadful promise gods can make):
Delos is where Apollo's temple will be
forever, where his own altar will take
offerings, and his grove have tree on tree
heavy with perfume.' Leto could not break

this oath, and Delos now rejoiced to see
herself as Apollo's birthplace and sanctuary.

But then for nine days, and for nine long nights,
Leto went into labour, and the pain
was beyond anything that comes by rights
with normal childbirth; choosing to remain
beside her through the stabs and the sharp bites
of every birthpang, there was a whole train
of the greatest goddesses come from heaven –

Ichnaean Themis, Rhea and Dionē,
Amphitritē, whose cry mixed with the cries
of Leto, howling all night like the sea,
and many more as glorious as these,
but not the pale-armed goddess Hera: she
stayed put in Zeus's palace, where the sighs
and shouts of that long labour could not rise

for Eileithyia, the birth-goddess, to hear
(she kept her hidden far up and away
on Mount Olympus, right under the sheer
gold of the highest clouds, in her dismay
and jealousy that Leto might soon bear
within another night or another day
so matchless and powerful a baby boy.)

The others then dispatched Iris to bring
Eileithyia down to the island, and promise her
an enormous necklace, nine whole cubits long,
made out of golden threads, with golden wire
across which all its elements were strung,
but to make sure that not a single murmur
reached Hera, who would stop things then and there.

Heeding all this, with steps like the fast wind,
Iris sped off, and in next to no time
had left the other goddesses behind
and come to the precipitous, sublime
mountain of Olympus, where from one end
of the huge hall she called, and at the same
moment, right up to its front door, came

Eileithyia to hear every last word
of her sisters' entreaty and promises;
and in the very instant that she heard
all this, and Leto's terrible distress,
she agreed to go: the two together, paired
like rock doves, fearful that each sound is
being caught somewhere, making less and less,

slipped away then, and very soon arrived
at Delos, where the second she set foot
on dry land, Eileithyia contrived
to start things moving: so, as Leto put
both arms around the palm tree, and jack-knifed
her knees down where the softest grasses shoot,
the earth beneath her, for all that it stayed mute,

started to smile; all of a sudden then
out and into the world and the world's light
Apollo came: that moment, every one
of the goddesses raised up to full height
great whoops of victory; when that was done,
Apollo, they poured water pure and bright
all over you, and they swaddled you up tight

in dazzling linen cloths wrapped round with gold.
This baby needed no breast-milk, instead
Themis with her own hands served him untold
power in nectar, and in all the good
of pure ambrosia; Leto rejoiced to hold

in her arms now, safe and divinely fed,
a strong son who would be the archer-god.

But just as soon, Phoebus, as you had tasted
immortal food, you started to pull and tear
those cords of gold, their fastenings all wasted
as you broke through them: 'The bent bow and lyre',
Phoebus Apollo said then as he breasted
the last tight linen band, 'I here declare
my symbols; and to humans everywhere

I shall pronounce the will of Zeus the King.'
That said, he set his feet upon the ground
and left all the goddesses wondering
to see him walk; while Delos, at the sound
of the god's voice, was bright and glistening
with new spring flowers appearing all around,
pleased that Apollo's homeland would be found

forever on these islands and near shores:
Cynthus, all rock, deserted, and a free
run of the peopled districts were now yours,
Phoebus, the lord of long-range archery,
your temples there in plenty, and holy arbours,
and the remote, high mountain territory
from which fast rivers tumble to the sea.

Yet you keep Delos closest to your heart,
where the Ionians in thousands come
together, in long trailing cloaks, and start
processions to your sacred stadium,
children and wives and all, to watch the art
of boxers, dancers, in your honour; some
singing to you themselves in a great hymn.

Anyone who came across them would swear
these Ionians, got up in their best,
were gods, and not people; all of them there,
the men good-looking, and the women dressed
to kill in the very finest they could wear,
and treasures they brought with them, sailing west
in a fleet whose every ship was new and fast.

And this as well – another wonder, whose
memory won't ever die – the great choir
of girls from Delos, every one Apollo's
servant: their songs about him first, then more
about Leto, and Artemis with her arrows,
women and men long gone, and ancient lore
whose telling people everywhere adore.

These girls even know how to imitate
exactly voices of the visitors,
their accents, and the babble they create
all speaking at each other as strangers;
nobody hearing them would hesitate
to say it was himself he heard, and hears,
so brilliant a mimic gift is theirs.

But now may Apollo, and Artemis too,
be good to me; and you girls who can boast
of living here, remember me when you
are asked by some new pilgrim to this coast
from far away, tired out with travel, who
has sung the best of all the singing host
that visit you, and delighted you the most:

tell him, all of you, it was a blind man
who lives on Chios, where there's little more
than stones, whose songs were once, and still remain
the best performed beside this holy shore;
and I will spread your fame as far as I can,

through towns and cities, swarming places where
I praise Apollo, whom the goddess Leto bore.

Lydia and Lycia, great Lord, belong to you,
and the sea-city, Miletus, is yours;
yours alone is the sea-splashed Delos too:
in fine, sweet-scented clothes you take your course
as Leto's son to Pytho's rugged shores,
holding the lyre that makes under your hand
such perfect melodies sound and resound.

From there, fast as a thought, Apollo flies
up to Olympus, Zeus's palace home,
where he meets all the other companies
of gods in the very place where they have come
to sing: their tunes and his golden plectrum
on the lyre-strings mix and mingle; before long
the Muses make response with their pure song,

about what heaven gives and what men suffer,
for all the gods' gifts helpless, ignorant,
their lives short, and with nothing there to offer
against a sure decay; while at the front,
leading the dances wherever they want,
the Graces and the Hours, Harmonia, Hebe,
and Zeus's own daughter, Aphrodite,

hold hands in moving; and there with them, one
who's far from plain, and far from short and shy,
but tall, and glorious to look upon –
Apollo's sister Artemis, in full cry,
whose arrows rattle as she dances by;
there too the god Ares is to be found,
and watchful Hermes, who killed Argus the hound,

as Phoebus Apollo plays music on the lyre,
dancing in time to it, with high steps and fast,
while casting radiance like one white fire
all round him where his feet go, and every last
thread of his garments flickers, blazing past
Leto and Zeus where they sit wondering
at their son, who leads gods when they dance and sing.

Apollo, far-ranging Apollo, what kind
of poem can I write to you, a god
for whom a thousand stories come to mind?
Your liaisons on their own might fill the odd
epic, for there was no path left untrod
by you that led to more than just a kiss
from girls like Azan's daughter, Coronis,

who dumped handsome Ischys, Elatos' son,
to be with you; or Phorbas, Triopas's boy,
whom – just as you caught Erytheus – you won
racing on foot, with no tricks to deploy
other than speed: you could utterly destroy
Triopas and Leucippus in their state-of-the-art
chariots, leaving them far back and apart.

But maybe the best story I could tell,
Apollo, lord, is this saga of how
you travelled across land and the sea-swell
to find a proper place you could endow
forever with your oracle, allow
people to make the journey there and bring
tribute and prayers to the archer-king.

From Olympus north into Pieria
you came first, where the earth has turned to sand
at Lectos, came to the people of Ainia,
then straight on through the Perrhaebeans' land;
on south again, until soon you would stand

at Iolcas, the last stop before Cenaios
where the boats for Euboea cross and re-cross,

and then you walked on the Lalantine plain,
but you found nothing to make you want to build
your temple there, or plant lane after lane
of trees around the sanctuary; you willed
yourself then over the narrow, light-filled
strait of Euripus, till you stood upon
the holy green mountain, Massapion.

From there you soon came to Mycalessos
and near it Teumassos, swathed round in grass;
not far to the site of Thebes – all grown across
at that time still with a thick, tangled mass
of bushes and wild trees, for then you could pass
Thebes (a holy place now) and not be aware
of a single human being who lived there.

And then, mighty Apollo, you made your way
to Onchestus, and Poseidon's sacred grove,
where a colt that was tamed just the other day
will draw its breath, almost too tired to move,
from pulling a carriage, and the man who drove
it there, experienced as he is, mustn't balk
at jumping from his chariot to walk.

The other horses, having got rid of him,
rattle an empty vehicle along
the track, till they start to go crooked, skim
the ditch, veer off and crash; grooms from among
the locals, as dutiful as they're strong,
take care of them, but they leave out of town
those broken cars, empty and upside-down,

obedient to the rule, time out of mind,
as they still pray with the original
words to the god, leaving a wagon behind,
where forever he will have the first call
on it as lord and master of them all,
the god Poseidon in his holy place
where wreckage stands, as in a stopped-still race.

From there, mighty Apollo, you made your way
to Cephisus, the quick river that feeds
Lilaea's soft, clear waters as they play
through Ochalea, where its banks of reeds
turn to great wheat-fields, and from there it leads
to Haliartus, bedded in green grass,
the next place your divine footsteps would pass

until you reached Telphousa; there, the plain
and level site struck you as suitable
for a good temple set in sovereign
gardens of yours, and so you went to tell
the spirit of that place what was your will.
'Telphousa,' you said, 'this spot looks to me
perfect for my capacious sanctuary,

my oracle, where people will flock in
always, bringing me offerings of the best,
from as far as the Peloponnesian
farms, and the mainland, and all of the rest
of Greece, from the small islands where they nest
in the waves; and this is where I'd deliver
unerring speech, prophetic truth, forever.'

Phoebus Apollo, with these very words,
started to lay foundations in the ground,
broad and straight lines of them going forwards
to claim the land; Telphousa turned around,
saw them, and quickly in her anger found

a way to address this temple-building lord
for whom stones rose, as of their own accord:

'Phoebus,' she said, 'great wonder-worker, king,
there's one point I'd want you to bear in mind
now you're so seriously considering
erecting such a wonderfully designed
temple here, where the entire world can find
your oracle, and come in droves to give
you offerings from the places where they live;

I'll say it, and ask you to think about it:
the noise of those fast horses will bother you,
and the constant row, when you could do without it,
of mules being watered – more than just a few –
at my holy spring, always coming through;
then the incessant clamour, rough and loud,
of an enormous and inquisitive crowd,

more keen to see the latest racing gear
on the expensive chariots, and be in
amongst the panting thoroughbreds, than peer
at treasure heaped up, back from all the din,
behind bars in a temple: if you'd begin
to take advice from me – needless to say,
it's just advice, and you must have your way,

since you're my better, and the one in charge –
you would do well to plant your sanctuary
at a place called Crisa, couched beneath the large
mountain Parnassus; there you wouldn't be
bothered by traffic, or the cacophony
of hooves as they go past, and there your fine
altar would be a hushed and splendid shrine,

so all the more, people would bring to you
offerings, the finest ever brought along,
which you'd accept with pleasure as your due,
their god now, great god of the Paean song.'
Apollo thought these reasons of hers were strong
and changed his mind, and so Telphousa kept
the place for herself, with the god side-stepped.

You left her, Phoebus, and you went straight on
to a settlement belonging to the Phlegyae
(a bad lot, wild men who have always gone
against God's laws) at the bottom of a valley
with the marshes of the Cephisus nearby,
and left there sharpish, up a stony ridge
until you saw over the highest ledge

Crisa, beneath Parnassus white with snow,
on a spur of land facing towards the west,
with a hollow, rough glen stretching out below
and a great cliff above. Here was the best
site, one by far surpassing all the rest,
and instantly Apollo set his mind
to building his temple, gorgeously refined,

in that very place; so again he gave the speech
exactly as before, to say he would
establish his sanctuary here, where each
and every Greek would make the neighbourhood
rich with their best tributes of wine and food
forever, and where he himself would tell
prophetic truths from his high oracle.

That done, Apollo laid foundations out,
broad and straight lines of them going forwards
to claim the land: over them, the two stout
sons of Erignus made good the god's words
by setting the huge threshold-stone towards

the doorway – Trophonius and Agamenes,
dear to the gods, well up to works like these.

Then tribes of workers in their hundreds came,
builders and carriers, experts with stone,
who cut great blocks, measuring each the same
for the temple walls, and set them one by one
until the enormous structure was full-grown,
a wonder of the world, a place whose name
would live forever in songs' and stories' fame.

A stream runs clear nearby: it is the spot
where Zeus's son levelled his mighty bow,
took deadly aim, and with a single shot
struck there and finished off, and left to rot
the serpent Pytho who had brought men low,
a bloated monster gorging on the flocks,
a plague for everyone, a blight, a pox.

It was this hateful and repulsive snake
who once, when Hera asked her, had agreed
to become a foster-mother, and to take
care of Typhaon for the goddess's sake –
a foul creature, to make the whole earth bleed,
to which Hera had given birth in spite,
jealous of Zeus's bringing to the light

of life glorious Athene, whom he bore
from his own head: that was when Hera flew
into a rage, and decided to take no more;
addressing the assembled gods from the floor,
she let all of her anger crackle through:
'Hear from me, gods, goddesses, every one,
about the huge dishonour being done

to me this minute by the god of cloud:
Zeus himself, to whom I have been a wife
without fault, now decides from all the crowd
of gods in heaven, the one of which he's proud
the most is this, to whom he's given life
himself, Athene, with her face all eyes,
to whom just now the whole attention flies.

Of course, the gods take a far different view
of Hephaestus, lame Hephaestus, hobbling,
the son that I conceived and gave birth to
on my own: I took one look at him, and threw
him straight from heaven like an unworthy thing
into deep ocean; and yet from the water
silver-footed Thetis, Nereus' daughter,

along with all her sisters, rescued him –
she might have done us all some better favour.
You nasty piece of work, Zeus, with your grim
intricate plots and plans, your dark and dim
intentions, what gave you a twisted savour
from giving birth to Athene on your own?
For a mother, wouldn't your own wife have done?

Born that way, don't you think that she would still
have carried your name well from end to end
of heaven? Look out, I warn you, for what will
come of all this before I've had my fill
of getting even: for now I will attend
to the task of conceiving another son
all on my own, so with no damage done

to your honour, or to my own good name,
when I forsake your bed, and far from here
spend time with other gods, free from this shame.'
At that, enraged and confident in blame,
Hera turned round, and made her contempt clear

by leaving all of them, then with the flat
of her palm pressing the ground where she sat

over and over solemnly in prayer:
'Earth and broad Heaven, listen to me now;
and all you Titan gods, existing there
in the world beneath of dread and nightmare,
enormous Tartarus, from which you endow
eternal gods and men alike with life;
all listen now to Hera, Zeus's wife:

send her a child, and let her conceive
that child without him, by herself alone,
and make that offspring strong enough to leave
him far behind, with ample power to heave
him over, just as he himself had done
with Cronos, a young god able to take hold
of and topple the dead weight of the old.'

With this, the very soil that gives things life
shifted beneath the pressure of her hand;
seeing it move, she knew they'd not been deaf
to her request, the powers of night and strife
underground, who gave her to understand
that everything she asked for would come true.
Then Hera's spirit swelled with what she knew,

and from that moment, for an entire year,
she never once went into Zeus's bed,
and never to the place kept for her, near
his ornate high throne, where she used to hear
everything that was being planned or said,
his smallest troubles, sitting at his side
and thinking through the things he would decide.

So she spent time in her own sacred space,
her temples full of prayers and offerings,
Hera, heaven's queen, keeping her high place,
in her look nothing but beauty and grace,
until the months brought round the day that brings
a year's climax, and the season to its end
with the child she had asked dark powers to send,

Typhaon, who resembled neither men
nor gods, a ghastly creature, horrible,
given to the immortals as a bane;
the goddess Hera took him up and ran
with him to Pytho, who could then fulfil
her own bad nature in the evil act
of being for him the mother that he lacked.

Pytho destroyed whoever she could find,
and brought with her a day of certain doom
to any among the crowds of human kind
whose paths she crossed – that is, until the time
that Lord Apollo made his arrow zoom
fast and unstoppable from the golden bow,
perfectly targeted to lay her low.

And there she crashed, rolling across the ground,
bitten and tortured by appalling pain;
she panted, gasped; she turned her length around,
but all that came out was the dire refrain
of fury hissing, over and over again,
as her body jerked and shuddered in the wood
until the last breath came, a breath of blood.

Over the prone shape then Apollo spoke:
'Here, on this soil that feeds the race of men,
is where you'll rot away, never to choke
the life out of the living world again,
and where people will bring me offerings, when

once more they have the good fruits of the earth
instead of murder, constant fear, and dearth.

Nothing can shield you from disgusting death:
neither Typhaon, nor the vile, accursed
Chimera can win you a single breath;
here you must lie, and let your body burst
with putrid matter, stinking with the worst
of all the dead, as nothing but more spoil
for the hot sunshine and digesting soil.'

He said this as the darkness closed her eyes;
and then the holy power of the sun
rendered her down to be the place she dies
forever in – Pytho, a rotten pun,
where the people even give Apollo one
title of Pythios, to mark the spot
where sun transformed a monster into rot.

The minute he was able to turn his thought
back to the journey that had ended here,
the sly piece of deception which was wrought
on him by a water-spirit, bright and clear,
dawned on Apollo, who then, in a rare
fury returned at once to that last place
where he and Telphousa came face to face.

'Did you ever think', he said, 'you'd get away
with tricking me like that, just so the fine
pure waters here would always rush and play
as sacred to your name, and not to mine?
From now on, Telphousa, time will assign
me a title alongside yours, to be
senior to you in perpetuity.'

In a great downpour of cascading stone,
the god Apollo made the mountains move,
smothering her waters; and with that done
put his own altar in a shadowed grove
at her spring's source: and there the people prove
his power still, praying to him by the name
Telphousios, for the nymph stifled in shame.

Apollo's next job was to find the right
men who could work for him as ministers
in rock-bound Pytho; thinking how he might
discover them, he looked where the sea stirs
dark-flashing, and caught sight of mariners
in a fast ship, crowded along the deck:
fine-looking men, who were all sailing back

from Cnossos, King Minos' city on Crete,
of the same line that serves Phoebus today,
performing his every sacred rule and rite,
and making known to all who come that way
whatever Apollo would have them say
when he shakes the sweet laurel in a glen
beneath Parnassus, to tell truths to men.

They were on business, and they held a course
for Pylos, and the people who lived there,
but suddenly, with an unearthly force,
the god Apollo leapt from sea to air
and straight onto the deck, choosing to wear
for now the terrifying shape and skin
of an unnaturally huge dolphin.

If any of the sailors, curious,
came up too close, they would be thrashed away
by the wild creature's blind and furious
strength that could make the very timbers sway
and groan; so in pure horror and dismay

they kept their distance, and they made no sound,
touching no sails to turn the ship around,

the dark-prowed ship that sped on as before,
with the original rigging taut and tied,
a brisk south wind speeding it all the more
with Cape Malea on the starboard side,
then those Laconian shores where the waves ride
landfall like jewels in the distance; soon
they reached a place made sacred to the Sun,

and called Taenarum, where the woolly sheep
of the god Helios can graze their fill,
a pretty town, where they wanted to stop
and watch for what this strange and terrible
creature would do – find out if it would still
lie there on deck, or maybe simply free
itself by jumping back in the fishy sea.

But what their rudders told the ship to do
meant nothing now, for it went sailing on,
holding a course where they could stand and view
the rich Peloponnese as it sank down
and out of sight behind; meanwhile the one
thing powering them was the lord Apollo's breath
as it steered them easily from underneath.

The coast came back in view: first Arenē,
then Argyphaea, the Alpheios' ford
at Thryon; Pylos then, and little Aipy
full of houses; Chalcis next, and toward
Crounoi and Dymē; everyone on board
then saw beautiful Elis slip away,
Elis, where the Epeians rule to this day.

Time passed, and as it neared Pheia, the ship
bounded along in a god-given breeze.
Out from the clouds appeared Ithaca's steep
summit, Doulichion, Samē, and the trees
of Zacynthus: when it had passed all these,
Zeus himself sent a good strong western wind
to bring the ship securely on around

the mainland coast, and into the great gulf
that leads to Crisa, where the land divides
with the Peloponnese almost cut off.
So they were sailing eastwards, on both sides
of them the shore, Apollo and Zeus their guides,
right on to Crisa, its vineyards high in the sun,
and pebbly bay, which now they crunched up on.

Immediately, Apollo shot away
in a sprinkle of sparks and burning shreds of light,
like a bright star that outshines the mid-day,
making the skies flash up to heaven's height;
he took himself past lines of tripods, right
into the inaccessible and dim
holy place that was kept sacred to him,

where with the force of divine miracle
he made a brilliant fire spring up and burn,
so that its strong and sudden glare could fill
all Crisa, to make wives and daughters turn
shrieking from the god, and that way learn
the fear of him – and into each he sent
an onrush of dread and astonishment.

From there, Apollo flew back to the ship,
moving as quickly as a racing mind,
and he took on the broad and burly shape
of a young man, whose long hair fell behind
his head across strong shoulders: as they lined

the deck, where again they could freely walk,
he faced the sailors, and began to talk:

'Who are you, strangers? Which way have you come
over the unmarked pathways of the sea?
Have you business here, or are you just on some
random voyage, and set on larceny,
betting your whole lives on what comes your way
out on the ocean, bringing as you go
to other people nothing but more woe?

But why are you just lounging there on board,
and not getting yourselves down to dry land,
storing away tackle and rigging-cord
on that black ship of yours? I understand
that worn-out travellers, who will have manned
their craft for weeks in the sea's solitude
aren't slow to come ashore looking for food.'

This gave the Cretans some more confidence,
and their head-man spoke out: 'Sir, we give you
our warmest greetings – all the more so, since
your shape and stature, and what you say too,
raise you above most men: may gods send true
happiness your way. But I must ask
you some simple questions as a first task:

What place is this? And what people live here?
I should explain we never thought to land
on these shores, for we were trying to steer
the regular course to Pylos we had planned
from our native Crete – but then, sir, our hand
was forced, and some god took us here astray,
not the road home, but quite another way.'

Now it was the god Apollo who replied:
'You lived in tree-lined Cnossos, gentlemen,
at one time, but you never will abide
in that fair city in your homes again,
or see your wives there: from now on, the plan
is for you all to spend your lives with me
and tend my rich and famous sanctuary –

for I am the son of Zeus; I am the god
Apollo, and I led you across the sea
here, meaning you no harm – meaning instead
to place you in my temple, which will be
known to the world, and where, through me,
you'll know the gods' intentions, all of you
honoured forever in the work you do.

So work now, as I tell you, and be quick:
take down and fold away your sails, before
moving the ship on land into dry dock;
take out your own possessions, with any more
ship's tackle, and build an altar on the shore:
stand round it, when you've taken all these pains,
and offer in its fire white barley-grains.

Because I leapt from out of the sea-mist
onto your deck, taking a dolphin's shape,
when you are praying to me now, you must
pray to the dolphin-god, god from the deep,
and let your altar ever-after keep
the name Delpheios, recognisable
from everywhere, to be a landmark still.

So eat your dinner here by the ship's side,
and make the gods an offering of wine:
once all your hunger has been satisfied
you must get up and join your steps with mine
on a journey where your voices will combine

to sing the Paean hymn, until you come
to the great temple that must be your home.'

They heard this, and followed his every word:
the sails and sheets were all folded away
and the tall mainmast lowered down toward
its wooden crutch, slowly by each forestay;
they jumped down next right into the sea-spray
and hauled their ship high on the sandy beach,
then set it up on props, securing each;

then they built a small altar on the shore
and lit a flame there, into which they threw
white barley-grains, eager now all the more
to do what the god had told them to do,
and standing in a circle, the whole crew
prayed round their altar, sharing out the food,
and poured wine to the gods from where they stood.

As soon as they had eaten and drunk their fill,
they started out; and going at the head
was Zeus's son, Apollo, who leapt uphill
weightlessly: he was playing as he led
them all the lyre which kept time to their tread,
while close behind him those good men of Crete
sang the Paean, following his light feet

(just like the Cretan Paeans, which the Muse
makes people everywhere remember best),
and soon, with the ground light beneath their shoes,
they got up high to where, like an eagle's nest,
Parnassus hid the spot that so impressed
Apollo as a dwelling-place, the site
for worshippers to come to, day and night.

He showed them everything then: first the great
temple, and then its holy inner shrine.
This put them in an awestruck, nervous state,
until the Cretans' leader gave a sign
that he would hazard speech with this divine
master: 'My lord,' he said, 'because you thought
it the best thing, finally you have brought

us here, far from our loved ones and our friends,
a long way from our country; but sir, how
are we to live, and us here at the ends
of the earth? We beg you, think about this now:
not a field for wheat, nor a meadow for a cow,
nor anything to help us, while we give
the whole world service, with the means to live.'

Apollo smiled as he made his reply:
'You muddled men, who always seem to want
more worry, and to meet trouble half-way:
for all of these anxieties that haunt
you the remedy is simple, and I grant
your question an answer – keep it to heart:
from now on, I advise you all to start

having at hand a good sharp working-knife,
ready to slaughter offerings of sheep
that come your way, in a supply for life,
when the processions climb a dozen deep
up here to bring me gifts. See that you keep
good watch over my temple, and you show
a welcome to people as they come and go.

However, you must hold to my straight way:
one insolent act, one bad word out of you
– which men are far too ready to do or say –
and I'll make sure that you receive your due
chastisement, and let other powers through

to be harsh rulers here; now all is said,
your calling and duty lie clear ahead.'

*And so, at last, I pay my own
homage to you, who are the son
of Zeus and Leto; and for this
song, and other songs like this,
in memory I keep you a place.*

Hymn 4

To Hermes

1. His Birth

Now, Muse, is the time to sing
all about Hermes, the son
born to Zeus and Maia, king
in Arcadia and Cyllenē
where the flocks gather and run;
busy god, who sprints away
on the messages of heaven.

Maia bore him, Maia who
swept her hair back as she swept
Zeus off his feet when the two
met in a love-nest she kept
secret, that shy beauty's home,
deep in shadows, her own cave
far from where the gods might come
prying over cloud and wave.
In the dead of night, Zeus would
make love to her: it was there,
breathing deep in her long hair
all the while, the god made good
his escape from Hera, who
slept and slept the long night through:
he kept his liaison then
hidden from all gods and men.

Slowly great Zeus worked his will:
so, just as the tenth new moon
hung itself above the hill,
he led out into the light
Hermes, baby god, and soon
wonders, rarities galore
started happening by right
for the child that Maia bore –

clever, streetwise, full of guile,
cattle-driver, thief by night,
lurker at the house-gates while
people sleep, herder of dreams,
miracle-provider for
gods in heaven: and it seems
he was able, well before
noon on that day, the fourth day
in the month when Maia bore
him, to take in hand and play,
striking music from each wire,
his own instrument, the lyre.
That too was the time he stole
cows – not just from anyone:
from Apollo's own control
long before the day was done.

2. *The Tortoise*

No sooner had he bounded out
 – whoosh – from between his mother's legs,
than Hermes left his cradle behind
with all its ribbons, toys and tags,
and got himself out and about,
crossing the threshold of his cave
already on a mission to find
Apollo's cattle – newborn, brave.

And as he left his high-roofed home,
what was the first thing he should come
across but a tortoise, and in this
he found himself a wealth of luck:
for Hermes, as you know, it was
who first performed the clever trick
of transforming that creature to
a thing you can put music through.

He met it at the courtyard gate
where, with a slow sashay and roll,
chomping its way through its own weight
in grass, the tortoise took a stroll;
at the sight, Zeus's gifted child
laughed aloud, and said as he smiled,
'Here's the first thing that I caught sight of
 – a token not to be made light of –

that means good luck. Tortoise, hello:
you're one born party-animal,
I know, and always on the go;
where did you get that spot-blotched shell,
half plaything and half ornament,
you carry so lightly, so well,
through the mountains? It's time you went
indoors with me, as a heaven-sent

companion, where you'll be some use
when you make me the very first
to have the good of you – I choose,
you see, not to be doing my worst
('Better at home', as the poet says,
'than risking trouble out of doors'):
alive, one of the defences
when bad luck never rains but pours,

and dead – if you should die some day –
a lovely singer in the house.'
With this, he took his toy away
inside, cradling it in both hands,
where his first action was to toss
it upside-down, then with a grey
iron blade begin to prise and hoke
the life out of it, stroke by stroke.

As a thought crosses someone's heart,
cutting fast through his frets and cares,
or as the lights begin to dart
from a quick glance, so all at once
Hermes united choice and chance,
word and action, taking up pairs
of reed-canes, which with skill and strength
he had cut down to the one length,

and fixing them through holes he made
in the tortoise's plated back,
he stretched over that little rack
a piece of ox-hide; then he laid
in two arms, and a piece that went
between them; these he flexed and bent
gently to hold the seven strings
of sheep-gut by which a lyre sings.

Once he had made it, Hermes took
this new instrument in his hand,
and found a plectrum then to strike
out a scale from the strings that spanned
its soundbox: all the time it rang
the notes out, at a whim he sang
whatever words came first to mind
(as lads on a night out will find

plenty of new words for old tunes):
he sang of Zeus and Maia, how
the two of them would bend and bow
together whispering, taking turns
to call each other secret names;
of his ancestry (noble, it seems),
his mother's wealth, her home, its staff,
cauldrons, tripods – part-song, part-laugh.

But as he sang and sang away
to himself, thoughts began to stray:
into his holy baby-bed
he set the scooped and hollowed lyre;
hungry for meat, meat by the joint,
putting his mind now to entire
mischief and deception, he led
his own way to a vantage-point,

a place thieves go to in the night,
up to no good there, out of sight.

3. The Sandals

By this time, the Sun
with his horses and chariot
was on his way down
below the level land
into the ocean;
and now Hermes had got
himself at a fast pace
as far along the planned
route as Pieria
and its bolt-hole heights;
Pieria, the place
where gods would put to graze
on the perfectly green grass
their own immortal prize
cattle: and it was these,
fifty of them by rights
not his, the god Hermes
drove away from the herd,
leading them off-road
and into trackless sand
where he changed the tracks they made.
As full of cunning now
as he would ever be,
he turned their footprints round,
making their hooves all go
the wrong way – you would see
fore-hooves pointing backward,
hind-hooves to the front –
and driving them, he went
ahead with his own back turned.

When he came to the sea-shore
where black sand smoothed and churned,
Hermes made for himself

a pair of sandals – strange,
unthought-of, wonderful –
his touch faint as a sylph's:
myrtle-twigs galore
wicker-bound with whole
branches of tamarisk,
springy and thin and brisk
handfuls that he tied
around the light, long-range
shoes he had gathered straight
from Pieria. So the great
god Hermes prepared
to travel far and wide
like a man who is geared
up now for the long road.

4. A Farmer

It was then that somebody saw him:
an old farmer, who was tending his
vines as they came into blossom,
at work that evening, caught sight of
Hermes bustling and hurrying
towards the plain, hotfoot from
grassy Onchestus. The first to
speak then was Maia's glorious
child, who said: 'You there,
old fellow, you with your back bent
from digging and digging this vineyard,
you can count on a bumper vintage
this year, as long as you don't see
what you've seen here, and don't hear what

you've heard just now, and keep quiet,
the better to mind all of your business.'

With that he drove on, saying
no more, his strong and bulky cattle.

5. *The Fire*

Mountain on mountain, sunk still in the dark;
valleys between them where the least sound echoed,
then level grounds, flowery as any park:
Hermes drove the beasts through here on his journey.

Night-time was his friend; but the greater part
of it had passed now, and the rest was passing:
before long, a new working day would start,
now that the royal moon had reached her zenith.

This was the hour when Zeus's noble son
brought to Alpheios' streams the broad-faced cattle
belonging to Apollo – every one
of them a stranger to the yoke – then into

a roomy cattle-shed with a high pitched roof,
in front of it water-troughs and a huge meadow;
he fed the noisy cows there on the hoof,
then herded them together to the building

while they still chewed clover and galingale
damp with the morning air; then Hermes gathered
branches and sticks in bale after bale
to try out all that wood for proper firewood.

The first thing was to carve a length of bay
down to a point with his blade good for whittling,
then turn it against wood, and twirl away
till up beneath his hand the sparks came floating,

for Hermes made himself the pioneer
of flame conjured from little more than kindling.
He caught up dry logs that were lying near
and tumbled them down into the fire-hollow,

where flames got bigger with the rising heat,
and while the fire roared, thanks to the god Hephaestus,
Hermes went in to fetch two cows for meat
and dragged them by their long horns, curled and twisted,

with main force out the door, then slammed them flat
down on the earth, where they snorted and bellowed;
he leant into them, and from where he sat
he rolled them over, having pierced their backbones.

No sooner was that job done than he got
to work on butchering the rich and fatty
joints of beef, and then skewering the lot
on wooden spits, the easier to roast it:

blood-blackened sausage-links of tender tripe,
great hanks of flesh, and steaks from rump and sirloin
(the other pieces lay in their own slop
there at his feet, where they had just been scattered).

He stripped the hides, and stretched the two of them
out over a big rock, all rough and jaggy,
and there they are still, frozen against time,
in solid form to outlast the long ages.

Then Hermes slid the portions of cooked meat
from each stick down onto a great smooth platter,
twelve of them, and each serving with a neat
place given it by lot in the whole order.

Immortal as he was and above such things,
the roasting smell, fatty and rich and fragrant,
that wafted from those twelve meat-offerings
made glorious Hermes covet his own portion,

but not for a moment did his steadfast will
allow him to taste even the slightest morsel:
instead, he took up meat and fat and all
and stashed them in the roof as his theft-trophy,

then fetched more sticks to feed them to the fire
that now consumed the rest of the two cattle,
their heads, their hooves, remains of their entire
carcasses; and as soon as he was finished

the god threw his pair of sandals away
into the deep eddies of the Alpheios,
put out the fire, and smothered into grey
its last few embers while the moon was shining.

6. The Return

By the time the cockerels readied
themselves to stand and crow,
already Hermes had struck
out on the long road
that took him back, back
all the way to Cyllenē
and the dizzying mountains there:
on the whole of that journey
not one encounter
with man nor god, and even
the dogs, who can often
sense these things, all kept
quiet as he passed them.

God had made him sleekit,
and he came home like the mist
in autumn, or the autumn wind
as it sidles through a closed
door, in at the keyhole;
walking, he made no sound
you would make on that floor
as he returned, deeper
and further into the cave,
to his own little cradle
where he drew back over
himself the cot-blanket
and was a baby again,
playing with the bedclothes
across his knees, but with one
hand keeping close at his side,
on the left, that special lyre.

7. Mother and Son

Maia didn't fail to spot him – one god notices another –
and she wasn't holding back: 'You're a cute one, aren't you,
away out half the night somewhere, and you walking
the roads as bold as brass? Well believe you me,
you'll be going out that door trussed up like a chicken
when Apollo finds you, and you'll be lucky then
if you can get loose while he carts you through the country.
Away you on: it's well seen now that your father
put you into the world to be a pain in the behind.'

Hermes was ready for her, with some crafty answers:
'Mummy,' he said, 'why are you trying to scare me
like this, as though I were really nothing but a baby
who knows no better, some kid checked by a cross word?
Look at me: I'm more than ready now to get started
on the kind of project that would see the pair of us
set up forever. I know you'd be perfectly happy
for us to remain here, with neither offering nor prayer
to our names – but no, that just isn't going to happen.
Rather than keeping house in the deep-down hollows
of a cave, this pointless existence, don't you agree
it would be far better to live at ease with the other gods,
seeing them day after day, and talking about this and that
surrounded by luxury, in our own wealth and splendour?
As for what's owed to me, it's my settled intention
to make a beeline for a station as high as Apollo's,
and if my father should do something to prevent me
then I'll fashion myself – and well you know that I'm able –
into the robbers' robber, the first and foremost of thieves.
Now if the son of great Leto really is after me,
I can give him something more serious to think on,
for I'll walk straight in to his temple at Pytho
and make off with his gold, his best cauldrons and tripods,
his polished-up iron, and all of his fanciest outfits:

you'll soon see, if you want to.'
They were still talking
together like this, Zeus's son with his mother
the lady Maia, when from heaving deep Ocean
Dawn came up, bringing her light to men everywhere.

8. Onchestus

Apollo, meanwhile, had made his way
to Onchestus, and that famous grove
held under land-battering sway
by the god Poseidon; above
the track, already working, slow
but sure in his little row of vines,
there was our friend the farmer: so
Apollo used his best designs
to learn something from the old man.

'You, sir, clearing down the brambles
in grassy Onchestus,' he began,
'I'm here from Pieria on my rambles
in search of cattle from my herd,
all of them female with twisty horns,
for the black bull was only spared
because he was grazing the far field
and all four watchdogs were taking turns
following, keeping their orange eyes
on him (as men will synchronize
attention sometimes), so both bull
and dogs, strangely enough, were left
behind while further from its full
height the sun dropped, and some theft
took place – for the cows disappeared

from their soft meadow, their home field.
Tell me, old fellow, have you heard
anything, or kept your eyes peeled
for a stranger driving cattle down
this quiet back road out of town?'

Answering him, ready to talk,
now the old farmer took the lead:
'It's a hard thing, it is indeed,
to mind all that your eyes have seen
and tell it; and there's plenty walk
the road here every day in life –
you wouldn't know where they had been,
with all the badness in them rife.
But now, there would be others too
come past here, they'd as likely do
you a good turn: to tell the one
sort from the other, thon's a quare
job right enough. I was near done
tending the steep slopes yesterday
as the sun was setting over there,
when I saw what I'd nearly say
was a wee boy – I saw hilt nor hair
after then, but I think a boy –
and him driving beasts with a switch
up and down, like it was a toy;
but here's the thing: I thought they went
backwards as the wee fella sent
them on their road fornenst the ditch.'

So said the old man: Apollo
that very instant was on the go.

9. *The Tracks*

He looked up, and saw a bird with spread wings:
  Apollo knew this was a bird of omen
that told him the great robber had been born,

  the child of Zeus, who was the child of Cronos.
A son of Zeus himself, he made haste then
  to take the road as far as holy Pylos

in search of his stolen and shambling cows,
  the purple clouds all spread over his shoulders,
covering them like a cloak, as he sped on.

  Before long, far-ranging Apollo noticed
the cattle-tracks, and suddenly burst out
  with 'What? What's this? These prints, these muddy
          markings,

certainly belong to my prize longhorns,
  yet they are pointing back towards the meadow
of asphodel where all of this began,

  and here beside them, these other odd footprints:
they don't look like a man's or a woman's steps;
  they don't belong to grey wolves, bears or lions,

and not even the centaur, with his mane,
  makes tracks like these when he leaves his big hoof-marks
behind him, monstrous, after he escapes:

  weird tracks on one side of the claggy pathway,
and weirder ones still on the other side.'
  With this the great god, son of Zeus, soon hurried

on till he came to Cyllenē's high woods
  and to the cavern there, deep-sunk in shadows,
where lately the nymph gave Zeus a new son.

  The mountain-sides breathed out with a mild perfume
while flocks of dainty-legged sheep cropped grass;
  there great Apollo went on, and descended

to the dark cave with its threshold of stone.

10. The Arrest

Hermes knew at once who had come inside –
Apollo, robbed of his cattle, full of rage –
and so his body shrank itself to hide
in the cot-blanket; just as at the stage
when hot embers need ashes' coverage
they're lightly buried to last the night, so
as soon as he caught sight of Apollo

Hermes' frame and his limbs grew less and less:
his head was smaller, and his hands and feet,
until he was what anyone would guess
a new-bathed baby, talcumed dry and sweet,
as innocent a thing as you could meet,
ready for bedtime – but awake as well,
beneath his arm that lyre of tortoiseshell.

Not for one moment was Apollo fooled:
he recognized the nymph and her dear son
as lovely Maia and Hermes, the clothes pulled
over this child to help him pass for one,
and he searched high and low before he'd done

all through the house; he took a gleaming key
and opened up the store-cupboards, all three,

full of nectar, ambrosia, and gold,
full of silver, and dresses of bright white
and purple dye, luxurious and bold,
a nymph would wear, and all the things that might
be in gods' houses. Once he'd brought to light
everything in the darkest corners there,
Apollo fixed young Hermes with a stare:

'You in the cradle, either you tell me
here and now what has happened to my cows,
or else the two of us are going to be
at loggerheads – believe me, what follows
from that would be none of your minor rows:
I'll grab you, then I'll fling you far away
to pitch-dark Tartarus, and there you'll stay

in the thick shades, helpless for evermore,
when neither father nor mother sets you free
to see the light again, but in the sore
shadows your power's lost with your liberty,
and the only subject people that you see
to lead nowhere in almost complete dark
are the small souls who never made their mark.'

With subtle words Hermes made his reply:
'Great son of Leto, what is it you mean
by all this threatening? And to imply
your cattle might be here: can they be seen?
I've neither heard nor spotted them, nor been
privy to the least word on where they are:
to treat me as your source is going too far,

and really, do I look like a strong man
who could make off with cattle? Not at all:

the only thing that I'm able to plan
is sleep, with mother's milk, and a nice shawl
round me after a warm bath; let's just call
this little outburst our secret, for who
among the gods would ever think it's true

that a newborn could take himself outside
straight through that door and right on to the land
that cattle graze? You're talking so far wide
of the mark: look how soft my feet are, and
how hard the ground is, then you'll understand
I was born just yesterday; perhaps instead
I should swear a great oath, on my father's head?

For I can tell you truly, here and now,
I'm not responsible; I never saw
anyone else come near a single cow
of yours to drive it off against the law,
whatever your cattle are like, for I can draw
conclusions only from the story I've heard,
although I'm willing to credit every word.'

With that, he raised his eyebrows and looked round
the room, as he whistled a tuneless tune
as though what he'd just heard was empty sound
and no more. But the god Apollo soon
answered him, laughing: 'Well, you little goon,
it won't be long before you're breaking in
to people's houses, leaving many a one

without a single stick of furniture
to sit down on, a junior conman,
and you'll be giving headaches, that's for sure,
to almost every shepherd or herdsman
who sleeps out on the slopes, for when you can
you'll steal away all of their cows and sheep
if you feel peckish. Now, if you want sleep,

I'll give you sleep, and sleep once and for all,
unless you get out of that cot, and come
with me, a shifty creature of nightfall,
into the daylight of opprobrium
amongst all gods as thieving, troublesome.'
And saying that, in no mood now to play,
Phoebus Apollo bore the child away.

11. *The Signs*

At this point, strong Hermes
made his mind up:
out onto the warm breeze
he sent a sign
from where, high in
his arms, Apollo held him:
a sharp *crip-crup*,
a not-to-be-held-in
rude belly-roar
out the back door;
then a huge sneeze.
Straight down to the floor
Apollo dropped him then,
but got to his knees
to look the little man
in the face, keen as he was
to be pressing on,
and joshed with Hermes:

'Zeus's and Maia's son,
small enough to swaddle,
this pair of signs
will help me, don't worry,

to find my stout cattle
wherever they've gone,
sure as the thunder-rattle:
just you lead on,
and away we'll both hurry.'

12. Olympus

It didn't take Hermes long to be up
and away, but he worked his two arms out
of the baby-clothes, and clapped hands to his ears
before he spoke to Apollo again:
'You are the worst tempered of all the gods,
always on my case, tearing strips off me,
a real pain in the ass – and all for what?
Because you're so upset about your cows!
Cows? I've had it with the whole tribe of them.
I didn't take yours, didn't see them stolen,
these famous cows I never hear the end of:
put it to trial before Zeus himself.'

By now, each one of them had said to the other
all that he had to say, still just as far
from settling the matter. To be fair,
Apollo wasn't in the wrong to arrest
Hermes over the cattle; and Hermes
was trying to pull the wool over his eyes,
but when he found Apollo just as full
of sense as he himself was full of tricks,
he took a direct route, fast through the sands,
leading the way with Leto's son behind him,
until the two of them, both Zeus's children,

got themselves to the summit of Olympus,
to their father, and the scales of justice there.

Olympus was covered in snow and sunshine
where gods were congregating after dawn;
Hermes, and Apollo with his silver bow
took up position at the knees of Zeus,
until he, the high thunderer, spoke first,
asking his splendid-looking elder son,
'Phoebus, where are you shepherding this fine
catch from, this newborn infant with the build
of a herald? Now here's a serious thing,
I'm sure, to bring before the gods' assembly.'

Far-ranging Lord Apollo gave his speech:

'Father, you are about to hear a tale
of far from casual interest. Now, you
say all the time that I am on the trail
of things to pilfer – but this boy, this new
find I've made is a bad one through and through:
I caught him on the heights of Cyllenē
where I had made my long, laborious way.

He has more nerve, this boy, more bare-faced cheek
than any man, or any god, who steals
from people on the earth: this very week
he stole my cattle, and took to his heels
with them along the coastal road that reels
out to Pylos, away from the loud sea,
driving them further and further from me.

As for the tracks they left – those tracks were twice
freakish, amazing, some bad spirit's work,
for there in the black soil, by some device
their prints went backwards into a soft murk
towards the asphodel meadow, to shirk

any pursuit; while he, on his feet and hands,
without leaving the path had crossed the sands,

impossible fellow, still rubbing out
the weird prints, as though he moved on thin
branches of oak, and not legs. Round about
the sandy stretches where he must have run
his tracks were still quite clearly to be seen,
but when he came on to the stonier places
neither he nor the cows left any traces.

According to a certain mortal man,
he was seen driving on towards Pylos
broad-fronted cattle; he put them in a pen
well out of notice, and then back across
the roads like lightning in the dirt and moss
laid a false trail; next thing, in the deep gloom
of a black cavern that he calls his home

he was tucked up, invisible as night,
rubbing his eyelids like a sleepy-head
where even an eagle with the sharpest sight
wouldn't have spotted him there in his bed.
'I haven't seen the cows,' is what he said,
'I've heard nothing of them, and couldn't tell
you where they are even if you paid me well."

Having said this, Phoebus Apollo took
his place again; Hermes was ready now
to give his own defence-speech for the gods
to hear, and so he spoke to Zeus directly
as judge and chairman in the immortals' court:

'Father, all that I'm going to tell
you now is just the simple
truth; and indeed, I'm so truthful
that I don't even know
how to lie. So,
just as the sun was rising today
Apollo here forced his way

into my house, looking (he said)
for those cattle of his;
he brought nobody, no gods as witnesses;
he threatened me instead,
telling me how he was going to throw
me down below
to bottomless Tartarus –

me, a child born yesterday,
and him in the full bloom
of his strength – he can't deny
knowing that, and he can't say
I have the sturdy build of some
cattle-rustling thief:
just look at me, it's beyond belief.

You can take my word – and after all
you say you are my father – I didn't,
so help me, drive home his cattle;
I never even went
one step over the door,
and that's the truth I'm telling you straight.
I honour Helios, in whose sight

we all are,
just as I honour
each and every god, and as a son
I love you, and I think you know
by this stage I am not the one

to blame for this; but just to show
my good faith, I will swear you now

this great oath: by the glittering gates
of heaven, never shall I pay
him any compensation – not after
that house-search of his that grates
with me still – however deft or
strong he is; you, though, can say
you help the younger ones get by.'

Hermes said this, looking around to check
it had gone well, and all the while he kept
the blanket folded over his left forearm:
he wasn't about to cast that to the floor.
Zeus, though, started to laugh good-naturedly
at the spectacle of his naughty son
making this plausible yet ridiculous
account of what had happened to the cows.
He told both parties then to work together
as equal partners in a search, and Hermes
to be the guide in it, the go-between,
and show – with no further deceitful purpose –
Apollo where his fine cattle were now.

Then Zeus the son of Cronos made a sign
with his head, and Hermes immediately
agreed, convinced without another word
(for Zeus's will is readily accomplished).

13. The Cattle

And so they lost no time, these two
fine sons of Zeus, until they came
to Pylos, where the stream runs through
its sandy soil of that very same
river, the Alpheios: there were
the green fields and the steep-roofed shed
where the cows had been taken care
of through the night. Now Hermes led
the way down a stony defile
and herded into broad daylight
those handsome heads of cattle, while
Apollo saw, off to the right,
the two hides stretched on a high rock
and asked Hermes straight out then, 'How
on earth did you pull off that trick,
expertly slaughtering those two
cows – you, born and grown up in a tick?
I'm not one to be easily
astonished, and yet even so
I wonder how powerful you'll be
if you have further still to grow.'

Apollo started twisting strong
handcuffs for him from sally rods,
but these went shooting before long
back to the soil beneath the god's
feet, joining up and twisting round
each other till they looped and ran
over the cows on their meadow-ground
as part of wily Hermes' plan,

who glared at the overgrown field,
satisfied now it was concealed.

14. The Lyre

The time had come for Hermes, now Leto's son
  powerful as he was, grew willing enough
despite all that had happened to be won

  over, as if completely off the cuff
to take out onto his left arm the lyre,
  tuning it with a plectrum until the buff

tortoise-body started to sing higher
  at his fingers' touch. Delighted at the sound,
Apollo chuckled and smiled as the desire

  to hear more closed upon him and gained ground,
finally inundating his whole heart;
  he listened to the music as Hermes found

the confidence to stand close by and start
  singing, singing with a glorious voice,
with the sweet lyre in its supporting part,

  a hymn, beginning with praise for the joys
of Mnemosyne, the Muses' mother, who
  had made him her especial care and choice;

then Hermes, himself the son of Zeus, went through
  in song the deathless gods in their right form
and order, ranks and alliances all true,

  a master of the instrument on his arm.

15. The Agreement

By now, Apollo was desperate
with the desire for more, and said,
'What you've been able to create,
you slaughterman, you clever-head,
is worth my fifty cows and more:
I think that something can be done
to settle things amicably here.
But tell me this, resourceful son

of Maia, was it since the hour you
were born that you found you could do
these marvellous things, or did maybe
some god, or even a mortal man,
instruct you in the mystery
and teach you such a profound song?
For never have I heard this plain
a voice so original and strong,

and I declare that never before
did god or man learn it, apart
from you – this captivating art
of Zeus and Maia's tricky son.
What is this skill? And, even more,
what brought the inspiration on?
How did you get the knowledge? For
the music here makes three things one,

bringing together happiness
and love, and love's sweet drowsiness:
you see, I am a fan as well
of those dancing Muses who dwell
on Mount Olympus, who have to do
with all songs and all instruments,
yet none of the accompaniments
at young men's feasts when the turns go

round to the right is a match for this;
now truly, son of Zeus, I'm lost
in wonder at how well you play.
However small you seem, it is
obvious that you have the most
brilliant things to give; so just
you listen to what your elders say:
before long, fame will come your way,

acclaim from gods will come for you
and for your lovely mother too.
Listen to me; I'll tell you true:
I swear by this spear in my hand
I'll give you a high place to stand
over immortals, that will bring
you fortune, wealth, and everything
your heart desires: I'll follow through.'

Hermes replied then, cannily:
'Apollo, what you ask is fair
enough; not in the least do I
begrudge your wanting now to share
this skill of mine. I'd like to be
your friend in all I think or say –
as you well know, for already
you know all things from where you stay

in the front rank among the gods
for strength and stature: Zeus's love
blesses your piety, and loads
you down with honours of all kinds.
They say that one gift from above
(for Zeus gives such as these) which finds
you over all gods, past their reach,
is the gift of prophetic speech.

Now, the fact is you can have
any knowledge you want, and if
your heart's set on the lyre, then give
yourself free rein, go ahead and play:
accept it from me; party away.
Be my friend, and don't be so stiff;
perhaps you'll pay, for what you learn,
a little respect in return?

So here's the lyre, and you can be
a fine musician if you hold
her gently, setting her voice free
in the notes' high talk, both bold
and clear; and take her out with you
for feasts, dancing, hullaballoo,
whether by night or day, mistress
and focal point of happiness.

Touch her softly, and treat her right:
whoever makes intelligent
demands of her, and knows the slight
intimate moves, wins her consent:
then there's no end to the delight
she'll give; but if you're rough with her,
the music will be broken and bent,
a sound nobody wants to hear.

She's yours, Apollo; now I will
take these cattle away to graze
pastures down from the highest hill
to the flat, paddock-dotted plains.
The cows and bulls will mate; I'll raise
calves in plenty, male and female:
you're fond of wealth, but there's no call
for you to get worked up again.'

Hermes gave him the lyre; Apollo gave
in return a brightly shining goad
and with it custody for good
of the whole herd. Notes on the stave
rose up from under Apollo's hand,
with Hermes' consent, as they fanned
resounding out, bright and alive,
for the voice of the singing god.

16. The Oaths

They took the cows back then to the asphodel meadow
and they set off together, with the lyre's accompaniment,
to Mount Olympus, and its top-covering of snow.
Zeus was pleased now, and he joined them in friendship:
Hermes could love unreservedly the son of Leto,
just as he does still; Apollo possessed his new tokens,
chiefly the lyre on his arm, and he played it expertly;
while Hermes, in need of some fresh musical skill,
invented the pipes for himself, with their far-piercing notes.

Even so, there was more that Apollo needed to say:
'I worry, Hermes,' he began, 'that such a sharp operator
as you might steal the lyre from me, or even my bent bow,
since Zeus has licensed you to pilfer goods on the earth.
But if you take the step of swearing the great oath
of heaven, either with your head, or else by the turbulent
water of Styx, never to do this, I shall be satisfied.'

Hermes nodded the promise, and affirmed it solemnly, never
to steal what belonged rightfully to Apollo
and never to breach the defences of his temple.
Apollo gave his approval, and he swore friendship

to Hermes above other gods, and above mortal
men fathered by Zeus:
                              'I will always abide
by this, and to honour you fully, I will present
you now with this triple-headed staff made of gold:
it is the magic bearer of wealth and prosperity,
a guardian against evils, and the guarantor
of all those lucky events and words I can claim
to know from the mind of Zeus. But prophecy itself,
my dear boy, is not a gift destined for you
or indeed for any other god; I have already sworn
a second strong oath, that no god apart from me
shall ever know or give voice to the intentions of Zeus.
I can damage any man, and can profit any other,
turning the tribes of people in what direction I choose:
whoever listens well to me, or pays attention
to birds of true omen, their cries and their flight-paths,
will do well out of it, and I'll not lead him astray.
But anyone determined to push things too far,
to read past what's intended, and so outsmart heaven,
will have travelled for nothing, though I take all that he brings me.'

17. Bee-girls

He dropped his voice. 'Another thing,
Hermes, that you should know:
there are three girls, they're sisters, who
live deep down in a hollow
under Parnassus – whitening
dust covers their heads
like barley, and they have wings.
As a boy in the cow-sheds
I learned how they could operate
a wholly separate
system, and my father took
no notice: they go flying
all over the place, to look
for honeycombs, and when
they consume these, they issue
prophecy by the book,
with every word of it true.
If they fly off again
full of the golden honey, then
you know they are benign
and will pronounce; but once deny
them that sweet food
and instantly things go awry:
they buzz in confusion,
and asking them will do no good.

I tell you this exclusively;
consult them, and amuse
yourself just as you choose:
even some mortal man, maybe,
well instructed by you
will know to listen to what you say.
Such things as these will stay
with you, Hermes, just like the cows

with their twisty horns,
all of them your own concerns,
mules in the field, horses,
roaring lions and wild boars
with their bare tusks;
dogs and sheep; all that flourishes
on earth, and the land's tasks:
Hermes to the fore
over livestock everywhere,
and Hermes alone
the messenger who can go down
to Hades; who, without
a gift will give back nothing,
not the smallest thing.'

18. Hermes

So the lord Apollo showed
how much he loved Maia's son;
Zeus immediately bestowed
blessings, and Hermes went on
moving between gods and men:
seldom bringing profit, he
goes through the night randomly,
tricking folk when they can't see.

*

*Hermes, this salute from me,
for your sake, is for the sake
of the other songs I'll make.*

Hymn 5

To Aphrodite

Tell me, Muse, tell me the story
of a goddess dressed from top to toe
in gold, the goddess Aphrodite
from Cyprus; of what she gets up to,
how she has given gods irresistible
urges, how she has brought to heel
the whole crowd of men upon earth
and the birds in the sky, with all
of the creatures on land, or those beneath
the waves – Cythereia, call her,
Cythereia covered and
covered with flowers in garlands.

*

There are, in fact, three
goddesses whose wits
this great Aphrodite
can't fuddle: first
Athene, the glitzy-
eyed daughter of Zeus
who goes for the fiercest
battles, and chooses
war over love
every time, all for
the sheer
buzz of the action;

she likes to approve
the hardware, and give
a full education
to makers of war-buggies,
bronze-workers, craftsmen,
and all kinds and degrees
of tender-skinned women
to whom, from the start,
she taught the true art
(quick thought, and quick fingers)
of labour indoors.

Then there's Artemis,
the goddess whose arrows
are lines of light, and whose
clear voice carries
as far as the arrows:
Aphrodite can't touch her,
for all her wiles and smiles,
since she's so much
enamoured already of bows,
targeting the wild
beasts who haunt the foothills,
a lover of tree-shadows
and the open-air dancehalls
that are loud with the singing
and shouting of hunters.

And those powers of hers,
of Aphrodite's, could get
no hold on one other
goddess, the spirit
of the hearth, Hestia,
who was the first-
and last-born of that crooked
god Cronos, and so
gorgeous that even Apollo

and Poseidon made their play
for her, though she would have
none of it, and rejected them both
in the most final way,
swearing a deep oath
while she touched with her five
fingers the very head
of Zeus the father, to stay
a virgin forever and always,
and pay no heed
to lovers, or love, at all.
Rewarding her, Zeus
gave Hestia a great
privilege, her place
to be right at the heart
of each and every house,
to take the dripping fat
from solemn offerings,
jealous of honour
among divine beings,
and worshipped, revered
by men everywhere.

*

Not one of these could she get to, not one
could she wheedle or outwit; but of all
the rest, nobody has ever slipped away
from Aphrodite – no god, no mortal man –
and even Zeus, who toys with thunderbolts,
the greatest god, the one with most to his name,
had his good sense turned by her, and his sharp
wits blunted whenever she felt like it:
she was able to get him together, no problem,
with the women on earth, make him forget
all about Hera, who is sister and wife to him,
among immortals by far the best-looking

as well as the best-born, the child of Rhea
and wily Cronos; when he married her, Zeus
was thinking straight, and made the best of matches.

Zeus decided at last that he would give
Aphrodite herself the hots for a human being
and get the two of them in bed together,
so that in future she wouldn't be so quick
to laugh out loud, in front of gods and goddesses,
at those she had managed to couple with mortals,
making gods the fathers of human offspring
and mating goddesses with men who will die.
So he afflicted her, all at once, with powerful
longing to have for herself the man Anchises
– who was wandering, just then, on the higher
slopes of Mount Ida, picking a way between
the little streams as he took care of his cattle,
and more than fit-looking, not unlike, in fact,
a god himself: the minute she saw him there,
Aphrodite wanted him, wanted him badly,
and that was the one thing in her mind now.

                              *

So back she went, back to Cyprus,
to the incense and the perfumes
that hung in all the rooms
of her own temple at Paphos,
closing its great doors behind her
so that her servants, the Graces,
could properly attend to her:
they poured a bath, then they coated
those perfect surfaces
of her body with fancy oil –
the kind that is ambrosial,
exclusive to the gods – and kitted
her out in the very sexiest gown,

fragrant, and sheer against the skin.
Dressed up in gold, Aphrodite
hurried from Cyprus over to Troy,
cutting a path straight through the sky
and the high clouds that marked her way.

She came down on Mount Ida's
watered slopes, the home of beasts,
and she made her way in haste
to where his farmer's hut was
on the mountain; at her side
came a whole obedient parade
of grey wolves, hungry-eyed
lions and bears, and fast-footed
leopards, deer-predators
fawning on Aphrodite now.
It pleased her to see them all,
so into their minds she put
hot desire, unstoppable,
and they bedded, two by two,
each other then and there
in the grown-over shadows
of their hidden lairs.

She arrived where herdsmen pitched
permanent camp, and found there
Anchises – the match
of anyone for god-given beauty –
all on his sweet own
in the yard: he was off-duty,
for the rest were spending the day
minding their cattle down
in the green fields while he,
apart from the crowd,
was left to just hang around,
strumming away
to amuse himself on a lyre,
and playing it loud.

*

So there she was, from nowhere, standing in front of him,
  Aphrodite the daughter of Zeus;
she didn't want to frighten him, or dazzle completely
  those big puppy eyes, so she made herself
into a tall girl, busty and pretty, like a bride in waiting.
  Anchises looked at her, and looked
in pure amazement, looked and took in all of
  that face – beautiful – and that
figure, her long curves under the glittery dress,
  and a fancy shawl the colour of fire,
twisted gold earrings, a bracelet snaking over her arm,
  necklaces that lightly overlapped,
with their tiny links flashing across her white skin,
  and most of all, like a full moon,
the gemstone suspended glowing between her breasts.

Turned on as he was, Anchises spoke
politely to her as he looked her full in the face:

'Mistress, Lady, O goddess for certain –
accept, please, this welcome; though which one you are
  among all of the holy immortals,
down now in this homestead, I can hardly tell:
  you are Artemis maybe, or Leto,
or the goddess Aphrodite brilliant with gold,
  noble Themis, or far-sighted Athene;
unless perhaps you're one of the Graces, come here
  from keeping company with the gods,
and known themselves as immortal; maybe you're one
  of the nymphs haunting the woods
and coppices on this enchanted mountainside,
  its river-springs and its green grasses.
Whoever you are, though, I shall build you an altar
  in some high-up, conspicuous place,
and make offerings there in every due season.

So do, please, think kindly of me:
let me make myself the best man in all of Troy;
   send me a flourishing family of my own,
and grant a long lifetime that brings me
   happy and rich to death's door.'

'Anchises,' said the daughter of Zeus himself,
   'I'm no divinity, so why do you,
the finest-looking man on this earth, call me
   a goddess? I am no such thing:
I'm human, and a mortal woman gave birth to me;
   my father you might well have heard of,
King Otreus, who rules over all of Phrygia.
   I know your language as well as my own,
for a Trojan nurse reared me in the palace
   who served in those days my dear mother,
and that's how I understand what you say.
   Just this minute, though, I was taken
up in the sky, and out of the dance I was in
   with dozens of brides and brides-to-be,
as a big crowd was watching our fancy footwork;
   snatched up by Hermes, no less,
who flew me over hundreds of worked fields,
   then across unworked, unmapped land
where all the ravenous beasts have their hideouts,
   while not once could I feel my feet
so much as touching the black, damp soil;
   but he whispered to me that Anchises
would soon be my husband, and father my children.
   He showed me the way here, pointed you out,
then all of a sudden Hermes was back in heaven
   with the entire family of the gods,
and I was heading straight for you – and all of this,
   I guess, is as it had to be.
So here I am, down in front of you on my knees,
   asking in the name of Zeus
and in that of your fine parents – for they must be

pretty special to have produced you –
to take me, a virgin, a girl with no notion
  yet about love or how it's done,
and show me to your father and your good mother,
  your brothers too, there at home,
where I'll fit in as perfectly as you could desire.
  Send somebody now to Phrygia
to give this news to my own people, and they'll
  send you back gold and fine cloths
which you can accept as the best of dowries.
  Once all that's done, throw a party
for us to astonish the gods and people alike.'
  The more she spoke, the more Aphrodite
inflamed him, and he jabbered out, hot with desire:
  'If you are mortal, if a mortal
woman gave birth to you, and the king Otreus
  is your father, as you're telling me,
and if you came here escorted by the messenger-
  god Hermes, then yes, yes, you'll be
mine to have forever; and nobody, mortal or not,
  would be able to stop me
taking you to my bed – not even Apollo himself
  firing his baleful arrows
straight at me, piercing me through: for I'd rather
  die, and go under the earth
to Hades, than never once have made love
  to this woman who looks like a goddess.'

                    *

He took her by the hand,
and smiling, Aphrodite
kept her eyes turned
down towards the ground,
as though she couldn't see
the bed she was going to,
a low couch piled high

with fresh linen, and then
arranged on top, a few
hides of lions and skins
of bears Anchises killed
on the crags and steep hills.
As they got to the bed
the first thing that he did
was take gently from next
her skin the jewellery,
gold threads from round her neck,
the ear-rings set with gems,
and from her forearms, glittery
bracelets, expensive items
going the way of her dress
and silk-light underwear
that he placed with tenderness
on a sliver-studded chair.
Then, by the gods' will,
by the gods' will and fate,
but not knowing at all
for certain the true state
of things, Anchises made
love, just as a man does
to a woman, to a goddess.

*

About the time when herdsmen on the hills
lead back their cattle and their flocks of sheep
out of the flowering pastures to the farm,
she let Anchises fall asleep at last,
utterly spent, while she put on her clothes.
Dressed up again, the goddess stood full-height
in the little hut, her head touching the ceiling,
with light now shining from her lovely face
as Cythereia, and only then she woke
her lover from his sleep to talk to him.

'Get up,' she said, 'get up, my Trojan prince:
what are you doing, lying there asleep?
Tell me, do I still look as good to you
as lately, when you first set eyes on me?'
Wakening slowly, Anchises turned himself
towards her voice, keen to respond; but when
he saw in front of him the gorgeous eyes
and steady head of the goddess Aphrodite
he was terrified, he turned his gaze away
and, for good measure, hid that handsome face
of his behind the blanket; as best he could,
he started to address her formally.
'The minute I saw you, goddess, I saw
no mortal woman – it was you who lied
to me about that. I beg you, however,
now in the name of Zeus, his sacred name,
not to leave me living as half a man,
but be merciful, and spare me the fate
of wasting away that comes to all those
mortal men who make love to immortals.'

*

'Anchises,' said the goddess, 'there's
no need to worry, or to dread
whatever I, or the gods indeed,
might do to you – those awful fears
are needless for the best of men,
who may count on goodwill from heaven.
Already, inside me, your seed
is quickening towards the child
from whom will come an entire line
of Trojan kings: he will be called
Aeneas, and that very name
will speak forever of my shame
in letting the heart rule the head
and entering a mortal's bed.

But still, it's interesting, no?
that of all human beings, those
whose looks and nature come the most
near to the gods have belonged to
your family: first, as you know,
the blonde-haired boy called Ganymede
for his good looks was taken up
by Zeus, to pass round nectar-cups
in the gods' palace, and succeed
there as a heartthrob barman, kept
busy pouring immortal drink,
lovely to look at, and adept
at broaching the great casks of gold
so that divinities can sink
as much of the stuff as they can hold.
His father wasn't happy, though,
when in a whirlwind blowing through
from nowhere, he watched his son go
where no one on this earth can know:
the boy that Zeus loved, he loved too.
He dropped into the deepest grief,
but Zeus took pity on him then,
and in return for his dear son
he furnished compensation
to give the man joy and relief
in the form of horses, a team of them,
the finest racing thoroughbreds
to call his own, and keep at home.
As far as the young Ganymede's
fate was concerned, Zeus sent on news
by way of Hermes, that he was
beyond the reach of death or age
and like the gods now, the gods' page.
Once he heard this, the father took
heart, and he soon gave up his tears;
from then on, with a brighter look
on his face, he rode at all hours

those horses of his, and their hooves,
like a storm punching from above,
made the earth shudder where they moved.

Another time, the goddess of Dawn
fell for a relative of yours,
Tithonus – like you a handsome man,
well up to standard for the gods –
and off she went to ask of Zeus
this favour: that Tithonus should
not die, but live for evermore.
Zeus simply gave one of his nods,
meaning that her wish was made good;
she might have thought harder before
she phrased the actual request,
for Dawn neglected to spell out
that he should not, like all the rest
of you, get older with the years,
fuller of aches, fuller of tears,
those ineradicable signs
that leave you with no cause to doubt
the end your very flesh divines.
As long as he was young and strong,
then in the best of his middle years,
he loved the goddess hard and long
and lived, relieved of costs and cares,
with her out at the earth's far edge
– flower-lighted, early-rising Dawn –
and had no more to brood upon
than love, without a thought of age.
One day by the side of Ocean, she
looked at her lover's face and head,
his stubbly chin, locks flowing free
in the sea-breeze: and she saw, instead
of colour there, the first grey hairs.
It was the worst of all her fears:
she sent her husband straight to bed

and cared for him like an invalid,
feeding him on the gods' own food,
ambrosia, to do him good,
and giving him, while she kept him there,
a makeover, new clothes to wear.
But when, eventually, old age
was starting to bear down on him
and he had reached that hateful stage
when each and every tired limb
gives up, and will not budge again,
she did what she thought best to do:
the goddess left him all alone
in that room, and put the doors to
forever, the huge shining doors.
Although his little voice still pours
itself out to the very dregs,
Tithonus' strength is gone; no power
returns as hour follows hour
to those dry, twisted arms and legs.

That's not a fate I'd choose for you –
among immortals to live through
day upon day forever; yet
if you could stay as you are now,
your face young and your body straight,
my husband, I would not allow
my thoughts to wander in regret,
or sorrow to fold over me
its heavy layers: but over you
old age will wrap itself, and cling
closer for all you try to do
to tear it off; and age will bring
you what it brings to other men –
exhaustion, and a blighted life,
filled up and over-filled with grief –
age, from which even the gods, when
they glimpse it, turn their eyes away

in sheer revulsion; and now they
will call me names, make fun of me,
as soon as ever they hear tell
of us, and of how shamefully
I acted when today I fell
into this bed with you. They'll pay
me back for tricks I used to play
on them, when they would go in fear
of all that I might do or say
to hoodwink them, and gently steer
gods into crazy love-affairs
with mortal girls: now I won't dare
open my mouth in front of them
to mention this – this utter shame,
unutterably stupid, my
rash moment, and its legacy,
inside me, beneath what I wear:
a child already growing here.

And as for this baby of ours,
when first he sees the light of day
the nymphs, who in their mountain-bowers
live in seclusion, far away
on the sacred heights, and neither are
immortal nor quite human, will
take him safely into their care.
They have much longer lives than yours:
for sustenance they eat their fill
of the gods' delicacies; all
enjoy their open-air adventures
when they step out with divinities –
for eager every time to please,
they make love to satyrs, to Hermes
himself even, where cool moss paves
recesses of the mountain caves.
As soon as they are born, tall firs
or oak trees grow from the good soil:

such height and beauty as are theirs
up on the mountains make them seem
like living temples; men recoil
from taking axe or saw to them,
yet in the end death pays its call –
those fine trees wither where they stand,
the bark rots round them, branches fall,
and when they finally break apart,
for the nymphs too the end's at hand,
as one by one their souls depart
to go forever from the light.

These nymphs will have full oversight
for five years of the boy, and when
that time is up, they'll bring him here
to you; laying eyes on him then,
you'll look with wonder at your son
and see the god in him, then bring
the child back home to windy Troy,
and after that, should anyone
ask of you who your little boy
has for a mother, answer them
exactly as I tell you now:
say that a nymph with eyes as bright
as the buds of flowers, who lives in some
deep mountain wood, gave birth to him.
But if you ever once allow
yourself to tell the truth, and boast
stupidly that you've gone to bed
with a goddess, and made love to her,
to Cythereia, then you're lost:
for then, tougher and angrier
than you can imagine, Zeus will cast
a thunderbolt straight through your head,
and leave only the smoke behind.
You've been told now: keep that in mind;

don't mention me, not once; just you
remember what the gods can do.'

*

With that, the goddess shot away out of sight
to walk in high heaven, invisible as the winds.

*

Queen of Cyprus and the green fields of that island,
here is my homage; for now I have started from you
I shall go on, I know, ready for the next thing.

Hymn 6

To Aphrodite

What I shall do is sing
all about Aphrodite,
   her beauty shining
   out, holy to see,
and her head ringed with gold,
who owns every stronghold

on Cyprus that the waves
go round, and where the West
   Wind, who receives
   those waters, tossed
her over the ocean home,
cushioned on its soft foam;

where the Seasons, with their
headgear all glittering,
   took her to their care
   happily, to string
thin perfumed clothes over
her shoulders, and cover

her forehead with a crown
– minute gold filigree –
   and then hang down
   worked findrinny
from her pierced ears: and round
her tender neck they wound

fine chains of gold, the kind
they would wear themselves, when
    dressed up to attend
    the gods' dances in
their father's house; so they,
with her finery on display,

led Aphrodite on
to the immortals, who
    were utterly won
    over, and drew
closer to take her hand,
each one wanting to land

her as his wife, and take
her home with him, so great
    was the heartache-
    ing glamour that
glowed out from all around
Cythereia, violet-crowned.

I too salute you, see
your deep and long-lashed eyes,
    and the smile for me
    that says the prize
in this contest is mine,
and mine it will remain.

Hymn 7

To Dionysus

Now from my memory and into all
    of yours will come this story of the great
son of Semelē, Dionysus, tall
    at the ocean's edge like a young man, looking straight
out from a jagged headland or sea-wall,
    his thick dark head of hair blown back in spate
by the same wind that flapped a crimson-red
cloak out across his shoulders, flapped and fled.

Soon enough, men on a trim-fitted ship
    came at full speed over the dark sea-swell –
Etruscan pirates, whom fate had set up
    for this – and the very minute they could well
make him out, all they had to do was tip
    each other the wink, and up they jumped and fell
on him, bundling him straight on board,
as every minute their greedy spirits soared.

He looked to them like the prince of some royal line,
    and what they wanted was to bind him fast
with heavy chains and handcuffs of stiff twine;
    but these were not enough – they simply cast
themselves from his hands and feet without a sign
    of effort from him, where he sat and passed
his time smiling at those captors, his two
wide-open eyes the deepest of deep blue.

When their helmsman saw what was going on
   he yelled out to them, 'Lads, what god is this
you're trying to tie up here and imprison?
   Our ship, foursquare and sturdy as it is,
cannot contain him, for he must be one
   of them - yes, yes, he must be either Zeus
or the god Apollo of the silver bow,
or else Poseidon, since he doesn't show

the least sign of being like mortal men,
   more like the gods who keep their palaces
on Olympus - so let's put him back then,
   back on dry land, and gently too, for his
anger might make him call out from their den
   the winds, who when they come break to pieces
even the strongest vessels that must train
their sights on the eye of a vast hurricane.'

Once he said that, the captain cut up rough,
   calling out 'Mister, just you keep an eye
on the wind's direction, help us get enough
   sail hoisted here to set us on our way.
This fellow we've taken is the right stuff
   for men to make a profit from - I'd say
he's bound for Egypt, Cyprus maybe, or
the lands beyond the North Wind's rush and roar -

farther perhaps, who knows? For in the end
   he'll tell us about his friends and what they have,
his family as well, to whom we'll send
   our terms for ransom, now that this one brave
stroke of good fortune has brought him to hand.'
   When he had finished this, the captain gave
the order for them to raise the mainmast
and stretch the mainsail out to sea at last.

The wind blew full-on into that great sail,
   and they tightened the rigging from both sides,
but miracles came too with the blowing gale
   for them to see: first off, there were whole tides
of wine on the decks, wine you couldn't fail
   to love the taste of, its bouquet that hides
but still half-breathes the gods' ambrosia:
the sailors were amazed by what they saw.

On the sail-top next, all along the mast,
   a hefty vine started to twist and grow,
and coming from it, weighing it down fast,
   bunch upon bunch of huge grapes hung below;
ivy with berries too, flowers trailing past
   and over places where the oars would go,
each one now like a garland or a wreath,
disguising the dark ship that lay beneath.

Seeing all this, the crew started to shout
   to their helmsman to turn the ship around
and head for shore; the god turned himself out
   that instant as a lion who could bound
to the higher deck, roaring: he put a stout
   rough bear in their midst then - a dreadful sound
when it reared up, raging - the lion too
on the upper deck just glared them through and through.

Every man there raced to the stern, and kept
   close to the helmsman who had shown such good
sense, then stood beside him as they wept
   with fear; and that was when, hungry for food,
straight onto their captain the lion leapt,
   and they, hoping that somehow still they could
avoid a worse fate, jumped into the sea,
all of them in one single company,

where they became dolphins. But the god took
    pity on the helmsman, and held him back
to make him lucky, saying 'I like the look
    of you, good seaman; you're safe from attack.
For I am Dionysus, born when Zeus hooked
    Cadmus' girl, and loudest roarer in the pack.'
Semelē's son, there's neither song nor story
can be complete without your grace and glory.

Hymn 8

To Ares

Ares, crushingly strong, heavy in the chariot, gold-helmeted,
    hefty-hearted shield-bearer, saviour of cities, bronze-
    armoured, iron-fisted, never-tiring, powerful with the
    spear, cornerstone of Olympus,

Father of Victory in every just war, helper of Right, tyrant
    over rebels, leader of righteous men, crowned king of
    true manhood, driver of the fiery-red globe through
    the seven tracks of space, where your burning horses
    keep you forever high up in the third orbit; friend to
    mortals, giver of youth and strength,

Hear me, and come down blazing into the head, turn lies
    away from the heart to help me chase away badness,
    the yearning for devilment, the short step into war's
    death-coldness:

Blessed one, bring me the courage to sidestep fights with
    enemies, all dire conflict, and to live always under the
    best orders of peace.

Hymn 9

To Artemis

Sing, Muse, sing about Artemis now,
  virgin god, Apollo's sister, brought
up at his side; sing about how
  many arrows shoot out from her bow,
how she makes her thoroughbreds go
  down for water where reeds are caught
up in the strong and steady flow

  of Homer's river, the Melēs, where
she drives a wagon of solid gold
  through Smyrna to the tier-on-tier
vineyards of Claros: there she, the bold
  far-ranging archer, is waited for
by Apollo at the temple door,
  a silver bow in his own hand.

Artemis, I begin with you, and
  from this song carry on to more.

Hymn 10

To Aphrodite

Her name is Cythereia, she
  was born in Cyprus: I
    will sing all about her.

Gifts as fine as honey
  is sweet are what she brings
    to people everywhere;

always she smiles, and on
  that lovely face of hers
    new blossom breaks.

Goddess, the queen
  of fertile Salamis,
    queen of all Cyprus, here

is my homage – give
  me this much in return:
    wonderful poetry

in which to remember
  you now and forever
    after, with every word.

Hymn 11

To Athene

Pallas Athene first, guardian
of the city, terrifying god,

to whom, with Ares, the works of war
mean most – the fighting, the laying waste

of whole towns, and horrible shrill sounds
that clash – watching the great army as

it leaves, and watching it returning:
bring us the happy life, good fortune.

Hymn 12

To Hera

Of Hera on her throne of gold,
borne by Rhea to be the queen
of every god, with her untold
beauty such as was never seen
before, the wife, and sister too,
of Zeus, with his great deafening
thunderbolts that exact the due
awe even immortals must bring
to his strength and her glory through
high Olympus – of her I sing.

Hymn 13

To Demeter

The first thing to do
is to name you,
Demeter, holy god, and your
daughter, like you a pure
beauty, Persephone;
long-haired god, this is the way
I greet you:
save our city, say
this song can come to meet you.

Hymn 14

To the Mother of the Gods

Sing this for me, Muse, with your far-travelling voice
and your descent directly from Zeus himself:

sing about the mother of all divinities
and every last person on earth, about how
much she loves the shrill sound of a fife-band
and the clapper-clamour of hammering lambegs,

how she adores mountainous echo-chambers
and valleys full of trees, with all the sounds there
of wolves that howl amongst ferocious lions;

and in that same song may all goddesses
be honoured with you, the mother of the gods.

Hymn 15

To Heracles the Lion-hearted

Heracles shall be my subject, who is
far and away the greatest to have been
once mortal on this earth, a son of Zeus
(when he hid beneath black clouds to love Alcmēnē
in the town of Thebes, between the dances there);
who long ago, under orders from a king,
Eurystheus, had to travel far and near
over the earth's unutterably long
distances, and the whole length of the sea;
who did many bad things, but suffered more;
and who lives now set up in luxury
on snowbound Olympus, in the best of cheer
thanks to slim Hēbē, long-legged, always young,
and his to possess: master, Zeus's son,

bring me your brilliance, bring me good fortune.

Hymn 16

To Asclepius

I want to start this song
with the healer of all ailments,
Asclepius, the son
of Apollo, who was born
on the Diotian plain
to a princess, Corōnis,
child of Phlegyas the king:
Asclepius, great boon
to all mankind, and
soother of their pains,
master, this is how
I find the words for you,
and how I come to you
in supplication
with just a song, this song.

Hymn 17

To the Dioscuri

You singing, Muse, you
with your voice as clear
as glass, as clear as air,

singing about the twin
sons of Tyndareus, who were
fathered by Olympian

Zeus, for Leda gave
birth to them in the shade
of Taygetus' heights

after she made love
in secret to him
one dim night

made all of clouds:
I name you aloud,
Castor, Polydeuces,

Tyndareus's boys,
the fast horses'
drivers and riders.

Hymn 18

To Hermes

When Hermes is the theme
– the ruler of Cyllenē
and Arcadia's green
sheep-pastures, the same

Cyllenian Hermes
who once put down
that *mauvais chien*
Argus, and who flies

on the gods' business – then
the place to start is where
Atlas' daughter, Maia,
gave birth to him:

beautiful, but shy,
she liked to keep apart
from where gods consort,
and lived out of the way

in the deep deep shade
of her own cave-house;
and it was there that Zeus
would visit when they made

love over and over
again, where they could not
be seen in the hot night,
and no one could discover

the pair of them, no one,
while Hera with her white arms
was herself in the arms
of sleep, in a sweet swoon.

Hermes, good giver
of favours, go-between
from heaven for all men:
keep my welcome forever.

Hymn 19

To Pan

Tell me, Muse, all about Hermes' dear child,
his taste for noisy parties, or his two
horns and his goat's feet: how in the wild
woody places his favourite thing to do
is join the nymphs there, scamper-dancing through
the trees, who love to tread upon the brink
of high, sheer drops while they call on this true
god of all shepherds, shaggy Pan, the link
between rock-paths, cold summits, and the hills' ice-rink.

He loves to rove and ramble to and fro,
deep in thick stands of rushes sometimes, then
sometimes down to the rivers where they go
gently along; or else he strides between
tall crags of stone, making his way again
up to the highest spots, from which he sees
flocks grazing far below; across the plain
white of the snowline he can run: on these
lower slopes too, he tracks beasts through their territories.

At other times, alone towards nightfall,
the sharp-eyed god goes up from the hunting ground
and pitches there a shrill and sudden call,
raising his own high spirits with the sound
of music, notes from reed-pipes spilling round
him everywhere, so that even the bird
who sings all day when springtime flowers abound,

as though she poured lamenting word on word,
could not, compared with him, make her honey-voice heard.

The mountain nymphs at his heel sing their song
as they dance onwards at a frantic pace
past the black trickle of a mountain spring,
and cliffs near to the mountain-top replace
each clear note with its ghost, as echoes race
down and around: the god himself slips through
the dancers' circles, maybe shows his face
right at the centre: but then with a few
hoof-beats he's off again, headed for somewhere new.

A cloak of spotted lynx covers his back;
he loves the nymphs' clear singing, and his heart
swells in the cool meadows, where most would lack
the skill to say where different perfumes start
and stop – the crocus and the flowering tart-
sweet hyacinth, and the still-wet field-grass;
the nymphs' song meanwhile, with translucent art,
praises Olympus, praises every class
of god there, and one whose speed no god can surpass –

Hermes, heaven's first messenger to all,
who came to Arcadia, the rivery land
where countless flocks are kept, and where he still
is the Cyllenian god, having his grand
temple there; for it was there he planned
to make Dryops' sweet daughter his to keep:
god though he was, he had to turn his hand
to minding all her father's daggy sheep,
serving a mortal man, his desire ran so deep.

In time he made love to the girl, and she
in the home they shared bore Hermes a son –
his goat-feet and two horns a sight to see,
his uproar and loud laughter never done –

so that she took to her heels there and then
in fear of his baby face and its bizarre
full beard, its look of otherworldly fun;
but Hermes cradled the young avatar,
his happiness enormous, spreading near and far.

He lost no time in ferrying the child
to where the gods all live, keeping him warm
with skins of hares that lately had run wild
on the hillsides; holding his bundle firm,
he sat down beside Zeus without alarm
and, in full view of all, displayed his son.
Bacchus and every god there felt pure charm:
for that, they called him Pan. Now I have done,
help me, lord, in this song and every other one.

Hymn 20

To Hephaestus

Muse of the pure note, your next song
will be about Hephaestus, known
for his genius, who along
with the god Athene has shown

to men the secrets of great works –
men who before had lived in caves
like beasts, where nothing brilliant lurks;
his famous skill forever saves

them from this, and they live at ease
year in, year out, untroubled now,
in their own houses as they please:
Hephaestus, may the song appease

you in this place; may you allow
us wealth for prayers such as these.

Hymn 21

To Apollo

Phoebus, a swan still on the wing
knows how beautifully to sing
all about you; and that same swan
as soon as it has settled on

the fast Pēneios' river-banks
keeps up its song of praise and thanks:
and first and last, the poet too
with his tuned lyre tunes words for you.

Hymn 22

To Poseidon

Here the first great god that I
mention is Poseidon, mover
of the earth, the unpastured sea;
ocean god, presiding over
broad Aegae and Helicon.
Earth-shifter, the gods assigned
you a twofold part, the one
horse-taming, the other to find
safety for ships; I salute
you Poseidon, carrier
of the world and absolute
god with black and streaming hair:
keep your heart in charity
with those sailing on the sea.

Hymn 23

To Zeus

Zeus the best, the most powerful
of all gods, far-sighted king,

who shapes to perfection
everything, who talks in private

to his discreet
consort Themis, leaning

across beside him, listening:
highness, majesty, son

of Cronos, far-sighted king,
look kindly on us all.

Hymn 24

To Hestia

Hestia, where you take care
for Apollo's sacred place,
holy Pytho, from your hair
shines pure oil: now to this house,

with a mind to help us, come,
come with wise Zeus at your side,
come, and by your favour from
songs here let no beauty hide.

Hymn 25

To the Muses and Apollo

Of the Muses, and of Apollo and Zeus
 – for from the Muses and from the far-ranging
Apollo people on the earth have skill
to be poets and players on the lyre,
while men are rulers by the will of Zeus –
let me begin to sing: the happy man
is the man the Muses all love, so that from
his lips flows their continual sweet voice:
children of Zeus, I greet you now, that I
always may have your favour for my song
and justify that blessing many times.

Hymn 26

To Dionysus

With a glossy trail of ivy through his hair
I picture Dionysus, hear his voice:
he roars as a wild beast roars from its lair,
son of Semelē, who was Zeus's choice
of mate; given once to the wood-nymphs' care
by his great parent, to be nursed away
from view in the glens high on Nysa's side
where he grew up, complete in every way
and numbered with the gods, his father's pride,
in a cave of healthy and sweet-smelling air.

It's all been told before: when they had done
their job, and brought the young god to his strength,
Dionysus would stay out of the sun
by walking to and fro for the whole length
of tree-grown valleys, on his head a crown
of bay leaves, and silver-green ivy leaves;
the nymphs would follow, adding to the din
he makes from shouts and music, as he weaves
grapes and vines: Dionysus, let me win
your blessing as the years pass, one by one.

Hymn 27

To Artemis

She pours down arrows as the sky pours rain;
even their slender shafts are made from gold;
the stags and does perish in her domain;
her pack of hunting dogs do as they're told:

the goddess Artemis, whom I praise now,
with her girl's shape perfect and untouchable,
Apollo's own sister. I will tell how
up on the breezy heights she moves at will,

pacing the mountains' quiet shadow-roads
until she draws a shining bow, and shoots
arrow on arrow, and the place explodes
with noises of panic, trees torn from their roots,

as frightened beasts make the bare summits quake
with their howls and commotion from dark woods,
and then all of the earth begins to shake,
and the sea with its fish churns up and floods,

but she, unfazed by any of this, where
she turns destroys each animal she sees,
her heart hardened against their loud despair,
killing them with their entire families.

*

Once she has done this to her heart's content,
Artemis the arrow-pourer, calm of mind,
her hunting passion for the moment spent,
goes on to a great palace where she'll find

Phoebus Apollo in the thriving town
of the Delphians, her own brother: there
the Muses and Graces dance up and down
perfectly under her control and care.

She unties the cord from each end of her bow
and hangs it up then in its proper place,
the bent-back weapon, with its shafts below,
till she steps forward with a glowing face

and the richest of clothes against her skin,
to lead the dances, while the others sing
in voices that are deathless, and begin
a hymn to Leto, the goddess who could bring

into the world such children as these are
who leave even the other gods behind,
standing above the rest of them so far
both in the life of action and of mind.

*

Now I sing praises of you both, the two
children of Zeus and thin-ankled Leto,
in this, and in my other songs also.

Hymn 28

To Athene

Pallas Athene is the great god I praise:
her deep stare full of knowledge, and her heart
perfectly hardened into all its ways;
beautiful virgin, mistress of the art

of keeping safe a city, strong as stone,
for whom Tritonis was the fountainhead
where wise Zeus gave birth to her on his own,
out of his glorious skull, from which she led

her way to life in complete battle-gear,
gold over gold, flashing against the light.
All of the gods who saw this, far and near,
were dumb with awe, for Athene jumped right

down in front of Zeus himself, straight out
of his own head, brandishing in her hand
a sharp and ready javelin: with a shout
so dreadful that it shook the entire land

up to Olympus, Athene roared her strength
and the earth echoed back that awful sound;
the ocean heaved its depths, and the waves' length
crashed over coastlines, whipping up and round,

until all of a sudden the leaping sea
was held back down, and Hyperion's son
stopped his fast horses in their tracks, while he
waited an age, till Athene had begun

to take off from her shoulders the brand-new
armour of a god; and wise Zeus at this
moment too could celebrate. I greet you
now, daughter of Zeus, for the work I do
here is yours, as all my other work is.

Hymn 29

To Hestia

Hestia, you are in every tall house
whether it belongs to the gods in heaven
or to men who walk the earth, and there

you have a place of ancient privilege
where you enjoy your honours as of right;
no one will start a party without you

and an offering of wine made sweet with honey
to Hestia, first and last; and you, Hermes,
the son of Zeus and Maia, divine messenger

with a staff of gold, sender of blessings,
be good to us, and work with Hestia
who is close to your heart, for each of you

dwells in the fine houses of earth-bound men,
so perfectly attuned to one another
that you can follow through, with all the strength

of a sharp mind, every good action there.
Daughter of Cronos, Hermes with your staff:
I greet you both, now and in other songs.

Hymn 30

To the Earth, Mother of All

I will sing about the Earth:
she is the oldest of all;
deep-grounded, she gave birth
to everything, and still
she feeds the world, dry land
and sea, and birds in the sky
from an always open hand:
Gaia, what comes to be,

crops and fruit and offspring,
depends on you, your say
over what time will bring
to life, or take away
from it for mortal men;
and true prosperity
can happen only when
you decide to supply

someone with fertile ground
and livestock in the fields,
so that good things abound
– all that the land yields –
in his own house, and he
is looked up to in a town
well-ruled, with its lovely
women, its wealth, renown:

the boys there in their high
spirits are full of life,
and little girls dance by
with herb-robert and loosestrife
through the damp morning grass;
holy god, abundant
god, this is how it is
for those to whom you grant

your favours, and so I
come to you, the gods' mother,
wife of the starry sky,
asking for no other
return now for my song
than such a life as this,
remembering you long
in its kept promises.

Hymn 31

To Helios

Calliopē, Muse,
    daughter of Zeus,
you should begin your singing now
about Helios, dazzling bright,
and about how he was brought
to birth by Euryphaëssa, who
    bore him to the son
of earth and the starry sky, Hyperion:

he married her,
    his own sister,
known for her dark-looking eyes,
this Euryphaëssa; they had
beautiful children, like Eōs
with her arms of the dawn's rose-shade,
    and Selēnē
whose shaken hair is moon-glow and moon-ray,

then Helios,
    untiring as
any god, and in the gods' mould –
he brings out light for heaven and earth
wherever his horses have trailed
across the sky, and from beneath
    his gold headgear,
all force and purpose, his two eyes burn clear

        while everywhere
        around him flare
    sharp rays of light, near blinding,
    and the cheek-plates of his helmet blaze
    around his head, still kindling
    the gleam of his radiant face
        far and wide,
as round his body the breath of the wind

        ravels and flaps
        the glowing tips
    of a great gown over his frame,
    with stallions beneath him, who
    eventually he leads home
    through the sky, and then into
        Ocean's deep places
to loose them from their golden harnesses.

        I praise you, lord,
        and come forward
    now to ask your favour, if you
    will give comfort and a good life;
    since I've begun with you, I'll show
    next how well mortals could behave
        whose actions were
such as gods wanted men to see and hear.

Hymn 32

To Selēnē

The next thing to do,
    Muses, for you
experts in the truest poetry,
Zeus's own offspring, is to tell
about the near-invisibly
winged Moon, whose far and beautiful
    disc in the sky
cradles the whole earth while the night goes by

and from whose face,
    deathless in space,
the shape emerges, gleam on gleam,
of things in order; lampless air
suddenly shines, and the rays seem
to be her glittery crown of hair
    when from the sea,
where she has bathed her body, Selēnē

drives her strong
    horses along;
in her dress made out of pure light,
a full moon, or a harvest moon,
she urges the thick-maned colts straight
on, and she wheels the orbit on,
    till at her height
she is beaming down from heaven in all men's sight,

with her cool flame
a sign for them,
and a great marker. Long ago,
Zeus was her lover, and in time
their union had a child to show,
for she bore Pandia to him,
Pandia, whose
beauty was all that any god might choose.

Lady, goddess,
long-haired mistress,
Selēnē with your pale arms,
beginning from you, I shall sing
of men who took half-divine forms,
whose stories all the poets bring
with them when they come
like good servants, to call the Muses home.

Hymn 33

To the Dioscuri

Muses, you with your made-up, big-lashed eyes,
go on to tell us about Zeus's two sons,
Tyndareus's family, both the children
of willowy Leda – Castor, the horse-tamer,
and Polydeuces, his flawless twin brother:
she had made love to Zeus beneath the summit
of Mount Taygetus, behind his screen of clouds,
and bore these boys to be the saviours
of earth-bound men who have taken to the sea
in their fast ships, whenever winter storms
trample the cruel stretches of grey waves:
then sailors call out loud in their distress
to the twin sons of Zeus, offering them
white lambs for sacrifice on the high stern;
as the storm-blast and the huge sea-blast start
to take the ship under, then suddenly,
hurrying there with beating eagle-wings,
the pair of them are seen, and at that moment
they put a stop to the gale's vicious force
and calm the waves back down to a clear sea;
at their glad signals of deliverance
the mariners who see them all rejoice
to have reached an end of fear and misery.

I praise you both, remembering you in my songs,
Tyndareus's boys, riders of fast horses.

On Homer
His Background, Life, and Times

(Pseudo-) Herodotus

1. Herodotus of Halicarnassus has written this study of the background, life, and times of Homer, and has made every possible effort to arrive at the best-informed account.

When ancient Aeolian Cymē was founded, different peoples from all over Greece came together there, and one of those who arrived from Magnesia was Melanōpos, the son of Ithagenēs and grandson of Crēthōn. He had little to bring with him, for he was a man of very modest means. But once established in Cymē, this Melanōpos got married to the daughter of Omyrēs, and from the marriage he had one child, a girl, to whom he gave the name Crētheis. Melanōpos and his wife lived out the rest of their days there; the daughter, though, Melanōpos gave to a man he knew well, an Argive called Cleanax.

2. What happened some time after this was that the girl started seeing a young man secretly; and soon she was pregnant. To begin with, this escaped notice; but when Cleanax finally saw what had happened, he was furious. He called the girl in to see him, and blamed her for everything; he told her, too, that she had brought shame on herself in front of the whole town. He had decided on a plan for her: at that time, the Cymaeans were starting to establish colonies around the gulf of the Hermos, and one colony was named Smyrna – by Theseus, who wanted to create a memorial in honour of own wife, whose name was Smyrna. (This Theseus was one of Cymē's Thessalian founders, a descendant of Eumēlus the son of Admētus, and a very rich man.) Cleanax put Crētheis with a Boeotian man, Ismēnias, who was his very closest friend, and was to be one of the first colonists.

3. A while after all this, Crētheis went out with a number of other women to a religious festival that was being held at a river near Smyrna called the river Melēs; she was then at her due date, and she did in fact give birth there to our Homer – who was not born blind, but fully-sighted. She gave the name Melēsigenes to her baby, taking it directly from that of the river. At that time, Crētheis was still with Ismēnias, but later on she left his household and took up manual work to support herself and the child, taking jobs from various employers as and when they were offered, and providing for her son's education as best she could.

4. At this time there was a certain man in Smyrna by the name of Phemios, a teacher of writing, music, and the other arts to boys. Since he lived on his own, he took on Crētheis as someone to process and spin all of the wool that he received as payment for his services as a tutor. She started to work for him, with great efficiency and agreeableness, so that Phemios became more and more pleased with her. In the end, he came to her with the proposal that she should move in with him; and as well as many other things that he hoped might persuade her, he made her the promise that he would adopt her boy as his own son, and that once he had taken his rearing and education personally in hand, Melēsigenes would be certain to become an accomplished young man: he could see that the child was quick and intellectually gifted. This was enough to persuade Crētheis to say yes.

5. The boy was by nature extremely able, so with the benefit of a good, careful education he soon put himself ahead of others his age; and as time passed, and he came to adulthood, he was the match for Phemios himself in terms of learning. This was how things were by the time Phemios died, leaving everything to his adopted son; and not long afterwards, Crētheis too passed away. This left young Melēsigenes to set himself up for a tutor. Once he was in business on his own, people began to take notice of him, and he won admirers amongst both the locals and those

from further afield. Smyrna was a commercial hub, from which a great deal of grain was traded, with large quantities of it being brought in for export from all over the surrounding area; so, when the foreigners had finished their dealings for the day, a good many used to come and sit in on Melēsigenes' classes.

6. Amongst these foreigners, there was at that time someone from the country around Leucas, called Mentes: he was what was then accounted a cultured man, and one who knew a great deal, and he had come to Smyrna with his own ship to purchase grain. He talked Melēsigenes into shutting up his tutoring business and joining him on his voyages, on the promise of a steady wage and all that he needed to live. He told him that now, while he was still young, was the time to get out and see other countries and other cities than his own. I myself suspect that he was swayed by this last consideration above all, for it may be that even at this time he was starting to think seriously about trying his hand at poetry. He closed his school accordingly, and set sail with Mentes. Wherever he visited from then on, Melēsigenes took in everything about the locality and found out a lot by asking: no doubt he was all the time keeping written records.

7. On a return voyage from Etruria and Spain, they put in at Ithaca; and it was here that Melēsigenes first developed an eye ailment, one that was very severe. Mentes had to sail on back to Leucas, so he left him to be taken care of by someone in Ithaca – his trusted friend Mentor, the son of Alcimos – whom he urged to tend him carefully. When he returned again on the next trip, he said, he would take Melēsigenes back on board. Mentor gave his patient excellent treatment: he had ample means with which to do so, and his reputation on Ithaca for honesty and generous hospitality was second to none. It was here that it happened Melēsigenes began to research and collate the stories told about Odysseus. The inhabitants of Ithaca still maintain that it was at this time, while he lived among them, Melēsigenes became blind; my own conclusion,

however, is that he in fact recovered there, and it was only later, when he was in Colophon, that he permanently lost his sight (the Colophonians have corroborated this).

8. Mentes did indeed take Melēsigenes with him when he returned to Ithaca from Leucas, and for a good while after that he kept him as his companion on his travels by sea. It was when Melēsigenes arrived in Colophon that the eye disease came back, and this time he was unable to get the better of it, so that it was there he became completely unable to see. He left Colophon and came to Smyrna again as a blind man; and it was in this state that he made his first attempts at the composition of poetry.

9. A little while later, in Smyrna again and with little to support himself, Melēsigenes made up his mind to go to Cymē. He travelled across the plain of the Hermus until he came to a colony of Cymē, founded only six years after Cymē itself, called Neonteichos [Freshwall]. The story goes that it was here he came into a cobbler's shop, and spoke these, his very first verses of poetry: [*Epigram 1*]

> All of you people who live
> in streets that go high up above
> each other in Hera the bride's
> steep city, by these lower sides
> of tall, thick-wooded Saidēnē:
> take thought now for the needy,
> for somebody homeless and friendless
> where all of you enjoy endless
> water that tastes like the cool
> drink of the gods, from a full
> deep river, the Hermus, clear-
> bubbling as it gushes sheer
> down from the mountain, a thing
> free-given; and Zeus's own offspring.

(Saidēnē is the mountain that overlooks both Neonteichos and the river Hermus.) The name of the cobbler who owned this shop was Tychios; on hearing these verses, he took it in his mind to give shelter to this creature, for he felt sorry for a blind man who was reduced to begging. He told him to come on into the workshop, and said he was welcome to a share of whatever he had; so in he went. He used to give poetry readings for the people sitting with him there in the cobbler's shop – *The Theban Expedition of Amphiaraus*, along with the Hymns to the gods that he had composed. And he became celebrated amongst those who heard him, partly for this and partly also for the witty comments he could make on the things being said around him.

10. So from now on, Melēsigenes stayed about the town of Neonteichos, making some sort of livelihood from his poetry. Right up to my own time, the townspeople there could still show you the spot where he would sit and give recitations: they held the place in great reverence on that account. A poplar tree stood there, and this they said had been growing on the spot since the time Melēsigenes came to live amongst them.

11. Nevertheless, a little while after then, when he was feeling short of cash and finding it hard to keep body and soul together, he made up his mind to be off to Cymē to see if he could do any better there. Just as he was ready to get on his way, Melēsigenes recited these lines: [*Epigram 2*]

> May these my two feet carry me to the good people's town
> where hearts and sense are of the best; and let them not slow down.

So, leaving Neonteichos he came by the easiest route (through Larissa) to Cymē; and it was here, the Cymeans maintain, that he composed the famous inscription for Midas son of Gordiēs – the one that is to this day carved on his memorial stele:

[*Epigram 3*]

> I am the girl made all of bronze
> who stands guard over Midas' grave:
> while water flows as it flowed once,
> and the trees' highest branches wave,
> while rivers fill up, and the sea
> brings in its tides around the shore,
> while the sun rising makes dark flee,
> and the bright moon shines in the dark,
> where he is wept for more and more
> on Midas' tomb I keep the mark
> forever, and for all to see.

12. At Cymē, Melēsigenes would sit with the older men in their clubs and recite the poetry he had composed; he also pleased greatly those who heard his conversation, with the result that they were soon his admirers. Since the Cymeans were so keen on his work, and because he had brought his audience so close to him, Melēsigenes put certain proposals to them, saying that he would make their city everlastingly famous if they were prepared to put him on the public payroll. The men liked the sound of this, and advised him to go and make his case at the city council directly to those in power; they said that they would certainly give him their support. He did what they suggested, and while the council was gathering he entered the chamber and asked an official to bring him into the meeting. This the man agreed to do, and when the time came he led him in. Standing in the midst of them, Melēsigenes delivered the same speech about his support which he had previously given in the clubs. Having said his piece, he left the chamber again and took a bench, while inside the councilors deliberated about the right response to give to his request.

13. The fellow who had brought him in was in favour, as were those councillors who had had the chance to hear him perform in the clubs; but the story goes that one of the councillors was

opposed to his application: he made a number of points against it, but his main problem was that, if the city decided to lay out its resources in this case for blind people – the word he used was *homēroi* – then in no time they would have a whole host of useless dependents on their hands. (Hence it was that the name Homer came to take the place of Melēsigenes, alluding to his disability as the people of Cymē referred to it with that word of theirs for the blind, *homēroi*. 14. Thereafter, foreigners too began to use this name whenever they mentioned him, and it spread that way.) So, the argument of the Chairman of the council concluded that no state support should be offered to Homer; and somehow or other, the rest of the council was minded to go along with this. An official came out of the chamber and outlined to the waiting poet the reasons that had been given for opposing his application, and the negative decision which the council had now reached. When he heard this, Homer was very annoyed, and he spoke these verses: [*Epigram 4*]

What kind of Fate exactly
did Zeus take it into his head
  to allow to have for its breakfast
me, no more than a wee lad
still at the mammy's knee?

Where Phrikōn's people, the whole
crowd of them, riders of fast
war-horses burning for battle,
built Zeus that fortified city
he demanded close to the sea,

Smyrna on Aeolia's shore,
and a clear brilliant river,
the Melēs, running right through it –
that's where I landed:
before I knew it, from there

the Muses, God's daughters,
were leading me with them
out again across the water
to this other fine place,
this city of men,

and with every intention
of me singing the praises
of all of its people, the same
people who then
gave the thumbs-down, stupidly,

to a poet's voice, said no
to the gift of a good song;
there's one of them, though,
that did me this wrong
by speaking against me

who'll soon enough know
the cost of his actions.
But I may just thole,
and tell my poor heart
to take life on sufferance.

Now, though, all I'll say
is that I've got two feet
with no reason to stay
here in Cymē's streets,
and blind as I am

I shall leave as I came
with my pride intact,
and take the direct
road out of this town
to some other home.

15. After this, Homer left Cymē and went to Phocaea, but not before he had placed a curse on the Cymaeans that no great poet should ever be born there to bring glory to their town. Once he got to Phocaea, he made a living in the only way he knew, reading his poems to people as they sat in the drinking clubs. In Phocaea at this time there was a fellow called Thestorides who taught boys reading and writing – not at all a decent man. When he got to hear about this poet Homer, he sought him out, and said that he would give him hospitality, take him in and feed him, in return for his having the poems he composed put in writing, and an undertaking to supply Thestorides with any new poems as they became available. Homer listened to all this, and he decided that it was something that had to be done, since he was in sore need of the most basic things.

16. It was while he lodged with Thestorides that he composed the *Little Iliad*, the work that begins:

> I sing now of Ilion, and of Dardania with its horses,
> over which Greeks suffered so much, bondsmen of Ares.

He also produced the poem called *Phocais*, which the people of Phocis say that Homer wrote when he was with them. Just as soon as Thestorides had got the *Phocais* and all the other poems safely written down, he started to plan how he could take himself away from Phocaea, planning to pass the poetry off as his own. He then began to neglect Homer, who in these verses addressed him directly: [*Epigram 5*]

> There's many a thing, Thestorides, to take men by surprise;
> but nothing stranger than the thought that deep in one man lies.

Thestorides did leave Phocaea, and went to Chios, where he opened a school. He did well for himself there, getting plenty of praise for the poems which he performed as if they were his own. Homer carried on in Phocaea in the same way as ever, scraping a living from poetry the best he could.

17. It wasn't long until some men arrived in Phocaea on business from Chios, and when they heard the same poems from Homer that they had already listened to often in Chios from Thestorides, they told him that a teacher of reading was performing these very pieces, and getting plenty of success on that account, back where they came from. Homer realized that this must be Thestorides, and all that he wanted then was to get himself to Chios as soon as he could. He went down to the harbour, but he was unable to find there any vessel sailing for Chios; there were, though, some men who were getting ready to embark for Erythrae to collect timber. Homer was willing to make Eurythrae the first leg of his journey, so he approached the sailors and asked them to take him on their ship, giving them many good reasons to agree to his request. They decided to say yes, and told him to come with them onto their trading vessel. Homer thanked them all warmly, and got on board. Once he was settled, he spoke the following verses: [*Epigram 6*]

> Strong mover of the world, Poseidon, hear me
> where you rule over sacred Helicon;
> give a fair wind and a safe passage home
> to these sailors who steer and work the ship.

> When I come to the foot of craggy Mimas
> grant that I meet there true and righteous men,
> and then let me punish the wretch who duped me,
> who outraged Zeus, god of the host and guest.

18. When the journey was done and they made landfall near Erythaea, Homer spent the first night in the shelter of the ship; in the morning, he asked for one of the sailors to guide him into the town, and this was duly done. Making his way though the countryside near Erythraea, which for him was very rough and steep, Homer improvised these lines: [*Epigram 7*]

> Earth, holy mother, giver of all,
> giver of ease and peace of mind,

how smooth you are for some, how level
the course you grant them; but behind
there are others who stumble and fall,
the ones that you don't like, who find
their way broken, hard and unequal.

When he got to the town of Erythrae, Homer asked around
about an onward passage to Chios. Someone who had known
him in Phocaea bumped into him, and Homer asked this man
to help him find a ship that would take him to Chios.

19. There was no ferry that went from the harbour, but his
acquaintance took him to the place where the fishing boats put
in, and he found there some men about to set off for Chios.
Approaching them directly, he asked them whether they might
take Homer along with them: but they gave him not so much
as a word of reply, and went straight on their way. There and
then, Homer spoke these lines: [*Epigram 8*]

You sailors who go far over the sea,
out where no other men would want to be,
who share the sorry lot, without a word,
of the shearwater, that timorous sea-bird:

have some respect now, find it in your hearts
to obey Zeus, god of guests, who rules on high.
Sin against him, and the payback that starts
at once is dreadful, not to be passed by.

Just after the sailors had put out, an adverse wind blew up and
they were forced back to shore, to the very place they had set
sail from, where they discovered Homer still seated by the
water's side. As soon as he knew they had been driven back in
this way, he said to them: [*Epigram 9*]

Good people, the wind has gone against you now,
but if, even at this late stage, you take

me with you, this adverse weather will break,
your journey can resume, and a fair wind blow.

The fishermen now regretted having refused to take him
before. They said that if indeed he wanted to come with them
they were not going to leave him behind, and they told him to
come on board. So they got underway again, and sailed until
they put in by a promontory.

20. The fishermen got on with their work, and that night
Homer stayed on the nearby beach, before getting up and
walking inland in the morning when, after wandering a good
way, he reached a place by the name of Pitys, the place of pines.
As he was resting there that evening, something fell down on
to his head: it was the fruit of the pine-tree, which some people
give the name of a snail-shell, and others call a pine-cone. At
this, Homer pronounced some extempore lines: [*Epigram 10*]

There is another pine
drops down a finer fruit
than yours, up where the wind
rattles from head to foot
trees on the top of Ida,
where the god Ares will stand
with his sword by men's sides:
Kebrania's army then
will seize it as their own.

(This was at the time when the Cymaeans were getting ready
to take over Kebrania near Mount Ida; a great deal of iron is in
fact produced there.)

21. So up Homer got, and he walked on following the sounds
of goats feeding in the fields. Once some dogs started to bark at
him, he shouted back at them: the goatherd, whose name was
Glaucus, heard his voice and came running up to him, calling
off the dogs and driving them away. He was puzzled for some

time about how a blind man could have got to this place all on his own, and about what he might want here. He came up to Homer and asked who he was; how had he made his way to these deserted, pathless places, and who or what was he in search of? Homer told him the whole story of what he had gone through, and won his sympathy – for Glaucus, it would appear, was not an insensitive man. He took Homer and guided him to his hut, where he got the fire going and cooked him a meal, and setting it right in front of him invited him to eat.

22. While they were having their dinner, the dogs outside barked at them (something they often did), and Homer spoke these lines to Glaucus: [*Epigram 11*]

> Glaucus, you're the watchman here; I'll give you a wee tip:
> dogs should have their dinner first at the yard gate, then you slip
> back for your own – that way's better, for dogs can hear
> strangers approaching, or a savage beast that comes too near.

When he heard this, Glaucus was delighted at the advice, and not a little amazed by Homer. Once their dinner was over, the two of them fell deep into conversation, with Homer telling everything about his wandering life and the various towns and cities he had known. Glaucus listened to this, completely fascinated; only when it was bedtime did he cease.

23. The next day, Glaucus decided that he would go to see his master to inform him about Homer. He handed the job of pasturing the goats over to another slave, and left Homer there in the hut, with the promise that he would return soon. He went downhill to Bolissus (which is quite close to where they were), found his master, and gave him a full account of Homer that made much of his arrival as an extraordinary thing, and then asked him what was now to be done. The master, though, believed very little of what he said, and he called Glaucus stupid for taking in and feeding disabled beggars. He told him, even so, to go and bring this stranger to meet him.

24. Glaucus went back to Homer and told him this; he advised him that he should agree to go, since he could do well out of it. Homer wished to set out, so Glaucus took him and led him to his master. As soon as this Chian began talking to Homer, he found him to be intelligent and full of knowledge, and he persuaded him to remain there and take care of his children's education (for the Chian had sons of that age). He gave them to Homer to educate, and Homer accepted that employment. It was at the Chian's house in Bolissus that he composed the *Cecropes*, the *Batrachomyomachia*, the *Psaromachia*, the *Heptapaktike*, the *Epikichlides*, and all the others of his lighthearted poems, and one consequence of this was that he now became well known in this city too for his work. It didn't take long for Thestorides to discover that he was there, and without any delay he made for the harbour and left Chios.

25. As time went by, Homer asked the Chian to bring him to Chios itself, and at last he arrived in that city. He established a school, and there he started to teach boys poetry. Homer seemed to the Chians to be a very clever fellow, and many of them became his fans. Once he had the wherewithal, he got married to a local girl, who went on to bear him two daughters – one of these ended her days still single, and the other he gave in marriage to a man of Chios.

26. When he set himself to composing poetry, Homer found ways to show the gratitude he felt. First, in the *Odyssey*, he expressed his thanks to Mentor the Ithacan for taking care of him so well in Ithaca when his eyesight was failing, by giving his name to a companion of Odysseus: in the poem, when Odysseus sets sail for Troy he leaves his household in Mentor's hands as the best and most trustworthy of the Ithacans. In many other parts of the poem also he paid tribute to him by making Athene, whenever she entered into dialogue with a character, assume the form of Mentor. He repaid his debt, in the *Odyssey* as well, to his own teacher Phemios for the care and education he had been given – especially in these lines: [*Odyssey* 1:153–155]

The herald then put into Phemios' hands
a wonderful lyre – Phemios, who stands
out from all others for his singing voice:
on that lyre he struck up a glorious noise.

He also calls to mind, in these other lines, the owner of the ship
with whom he sailed out and saw so many different towns and
countries, whose name was Mentes: [*Odyssey* 1:180–181]

I can call myself the good Amphialos' son,
Mentes; I govern each and every one
of the Taphians, those lovers of the sea.

He also expressed his gratitude to Tychios the cobbler, who
took him in at Neonteichos when he came into his shop,
putting him into the *Iliad* in these lines: [*Iliad* 7.219–221]

Ajax was close, and came holding his shield
like a great tower – a bronze shield made from seven
layers of hide that Tychios fashioned for him,
Tychios from Hylē, the best of leather-cutters.

27. With all this composing of poetry, Homer's fame spread
through Ionia, and word of him was reaching mainland Greece.
Living in Chios, known for his work and with many people
coming to hear him, plenty of those who encountered Homer
urged him next to try the mainland. He was open to this idea,
and he did have a great liking for travel.

28. When he took stock of the fact that he had composed a
good many lines of poetry that offered fulsome praise to Argos,
but none that honoured the city of Athens, he set about adding
lines to the *Iliad* to extol Erechtheus, and he inserted these into
the Catalogue of Ships: [*Iliad* 2:547–548]

The people of Erechtheus the large-hearted,
whom once Athene the daughter of Zeus
nourished, and whom fertile grain-fields bore.

Also these verses, in praise of the Athenians' leader Menestheus, who he said was the finest commander of both cavalry and infantry: [*Iliad* 2:552–554]

> Peteos' son took charge of them, Menestheus,
> whose like no one on earth has ever been
> for marshalling cavalry and men with shields.

Also in the Catalogue of Ships, he put Aias the son of Telamon along with the men of Salamis: [*Iliad* 2:557–558]

> Aias led out twelve ships from Salamis
> and brought them where ranks of the Athenians stood.

Into the *Odyssey* he placed these verses, to the effect that Athene, after speaking with Odysseus, took herself to the city of the Athenians, thus honouring it above all others: [*Odyssey* 7:80–81]

> She came to Marathon, and the broad spaces
> of Athens, into Erechtheus' strong house.

29. With these additions to his poetry made, and all else got ready, he embarked on his voyage to the mainland, but on the way he put in at Samos. It happened that just then the locals were keeping their festival of Apatouria, and one of the Samians, who saw Homer's arrival and recognized him from Chios, went to his clansmen and told them about the poet, making much of him. The clansmen said to bring Homer to meet them, so he found him and said, 'Dear sir, now that the city is celebrating Apatouria, my clansmen want to invite you to join us in the festivities.' Homer said that yes, he would be happy to do this, and he set off along with the man who delivered the invitation.

30. On the way, Homer encountered a group of women at a crossroads who were engaged in some sacrificial rites to Kourotrophos; the lady in charge, who didn't like the look

of him at all, called out, 'Here you, away from the sacrifice!'
Homer took this rough speech to heart, and he asked the man
who was escorting him who it was who had spoken to him,
and to what god exactly was her sacrifice being made? He
explained that this was a woman carrying out the rites of the
god Kourotrophos. Having listened to the explanation, Homer
came out with these verses: [*Epigram 12*]

> Listen to me, Kourotrophos, listen to my prayer:
> make this woman turn away from young men's love,
> keeping them out of her bed; Kourotrophos, there
> let her try for pleasure the old men with white hair
> whose strength has rubbed and rubbed itself away to prove
> impotent, now it goes straight from ardour to despair.

31. When he reached the assembled clan and was standing in
the doorway of the hall where they were holding their dinner,
some versions of the story say that a fire was already burning
inside, but others claim that one was lit only after Homer had
pronounced these lines: [*Epigram 13*]

> Sons are a man's crown, walls well-fortified
> a city's; horses glorify the plain
> and ships the ocean, going far and wide;
> possessions make a home more grand, and when
> kings sit in state there is a spectacle
> for all to see: but a finer sight still
> is the hearth-fire burning in a house again.

He stepped in then, and sat at his ease to share dinner with the
men of the clan. They in their turn paid respect to him, and felt
great admiration for his work. Homer made his bed there for
that night.

32. On his departure the following day, certain potters, who were
firing delicate earthenware in a kiln, caught sight of Homer;
they called him over, and (since they had heard all about what

he could do) they asked him to sing for them, saying that they
would give him in return some of their pottery and other things
which they had. The verses Homer sang for them were these,
which go under the title of 'The Kiln': [*Epigram 14*]

> Potters, if you are going to pay
>   me something for this song,
> I'll ask Athene to come this way
>   and place her hand along
> the kiln: may the black-figure cups
>   and dishes be true black,
> finished to please whoever sups
>   from them and pays you back
> in the markets and in the streets,
> giving us both good balance-sheets.
>
> But if you have it in your minds
>   to start to cheat and diddle:
> whoever tries that on soon finds
>   I'll call up every divil
> who blights the kiln – Smash-up and Breaker,
>   Over- and Under-bake,
> Warp-the-Clay, and then Crack-maker,
>   all of them set to take
> trade down with them to a new low
> when their own bad gifts they bestow.
>
> I'll say to them, come in, come in
>   to your houses full of fire;
> the kiln is yours, and that foul din
>   is the weeping potters' choir;
> just as a horse's jaws will munch
>   on oats, so may the kiln
> swallow up little pots, and crunch
>   them to powder within:
> Circe, the daughter of the sun,
> drug these potters every one.

Let Chiron next, and the whole crowd
    of centaurs come with him
(both those that Heracles allowed
    to escape, and the rest of them
he slew), then may they strike the works
    to make the kiln fall down,
with groans from each potter who lurks
    behind, while I look on
with laughter at the mischief made
where all of those rough spirits played.

Anyone who peers in to see
the damage, may his features be
scorched red forever – let him learn
to behave well, or else to burn.

33. Homer stayed for the winter in Samos, and at every full moon he would pay a visit to the most prosperous households there, receiving something for his performance of these verses, which are called 'The Laden Branch'. (He would always have some of the local children with him on these occasions, guiding him on his way.) [*Epigram 15*]

Here we come now, to the house of a man
of great power and great note, a prosperous man.

Open for us, doors, and in comes wealth
with ease and happiness, plentiful wealth.

May your grain jars be full to overflowing
while bowls of rich bread dough are overflowing,

and give us a share now of your finest barley,
sesame seeds mixed in with the finest barley.

A carriage will bring your son's bride to the house;
mules with hardy hoofs will bring her to this house,

and may she stand, at the loom where she weaves,
on a floor of pure amber as she weaves.

Every year that comes, I shall return;
just like the spring swallow, I shall return.

We are barefoot at your porch, so bring us something;
for Apollo's sake, dear lady, bring us something.

Give, if you want to; if not, we won't wait here,
for we didn't come to your house to move in here.

These lines were for a long time afterwards recited by the young people in Samos, whenever they went out collecting for Apollo's feast.

34. When the spring came, Homer left Samos to journey to Athens. He set sail with local men, and was soon diverted to Ios: they did not put in at the town itself, but dropped anchor just off a headland. It was then that Homer, just as they were rowing in, started to feel unwell; and as soon as they made landfall, he lay down on the shore, all his strength going. The crew remained there for a few days, owing to some difficult weather, while people from the town would come and meet Homer, and were greatly struck by him when they listened to what he said.

35. One day, when the sailors and a few townspeople were sitting with Homer, some fishermen sailed in at the place. They disembarked from their fishing boat, approached the group, and said this: 'Come here, good strangers, listen to us and see whether you are able to tell the meaning of what we are going to say.' One of those present told them to go ahead, and they then said: 'What we have taken, that we have left behind; and what we did not take, that we carry.' Some people claim they spoke this in the form of a verse:

We've left behind the ones we caught;
the ones we missed are what we've brought.

Nobody there was able to solve this riddle. The boys then explained that when they were out fishing they were unable to catch anything, but when they sat down on dry land they had cleaned themselves of bugs, and all the lice that they caught they left right there, but all they couldn't catch were going home along with them. When he heard this, Homer spoke the following lines: [*Epigram 16*]

> For you were born from just such fathers' stocks,
> no landholders, no grazers of rich flocks.

36. As a result of the illness from which he was suffering, it came about that Homer died on Ios. This was not, as some people maintain, on account of his having been unable to solve the boys' riddle, but purely from the natural cause of his infirmity. When he died, he was buried there by the shore on Ios by those he had sailed with and by the folk from the town who had met him. A long time afterwards, the elegy that follows was inscribed over him, by which time his poetry had travelled far and wide, and become universally admired. The piece was not composed by Homer himself:

> Here earth has covered over the sacred head
> of godly Homer, creator of heroic men.

37. From what I have said already, it is clear that Homer was neither an Ionian nor a Dorian, but from Aeolia. He offers his own proof of this. A poet of this magnitude, when he depicts things commonly done, is likely to look for either the best ways possible, or to return to the customs of his native place. You can judge of Homer, therefore, simply by paying attention to his writing. Whenever he describes acts of religious sacrifice, he either finds the most approved form, or has recourse to that unique to his homeland. He writes this, for example: [*Iliad* 1:459–461]

> And first of all they drew back the beasts' heads,
> then slaughtered and then skinned them, cut the bones
> from their thighs and wrapped them up in fat
> twice-folded, with the raw meat laid on top.

In these verses, nothing is said about the use of the loin-cut in rites of sacrifice: and it is the Aeolians, alone among all the Greeks, who do not make a practice of burning the loin. Again, in the verses that follow, Homer shows that he is an Aeolian, and has full entitlement to make use of their particular customs: [*Iliad* 1:462–463]

> The old man then on pieces of split wood
> burnt entrails, and poured over them clear wine
> while young men at his side held in their hands
> forks with five tines.

It is only the Aeolians who use five-tined forks to roast entrails; all other Greek people have forks with only three. Even the word for 'five' here is Aeolian – *pempe*, rather than the usual *pente*.

38. I have now given a full account of Homer's ancestry, his death, and the life he led. As far as the dates of Homer are concerned, these can only be reckoned properly from the following information. From the campaign against Troy led by Agamemnon and Menelaus, it was a hundred and thirty years until the settlement of Lesbos with cities (there were no cities there before). After the colonization of Lesbos, it was twenty years until the founding of Aeolian or Phrikonian Cymē; and eighteen years after Cymē, the Cymeans founded Smyrna – this was when Homer was born. Between this date and Xerxes' crossing of the Hellespont in his invasion of Greece, when he crossed to Europe from Asia, it was six hundred and twenty-two years. From that point, it is easy for anyone who wishes to do so to measure the dates by referring to the list of all the archons of Athens. Homer was born after the Trojan War itself by one hundred and sixty-eight years.

Appendices

Appendix 1

Demodocus' Song: *Odyssey* 8: 266–366

So next the poet struck up on his lyre
a polished song about the hot desire
there was between Ares and Aphrodite;
how in the very palace of the mighty
Hephaestus, her husband, they went to bed
in secret, and gave lovers' gifts, and shed
all sense of shame together there; but soon
Helios told Hephaestus what he'd seen
when he shone down upon them making love,
and now that there was nothing left to prove
Hephaestus took to heart that dreadful tale
and slunk into his workshop with a bale-
ful mind: he set up on the anvil block
his huge anvil, started to forge and knock
together chains and links of chains that would
never be slipped or broken, fast for good.
When he had finished making in sheer hate
for Ares the components of this great
trap, he went to the chamber where his bed
was waiting; over the bedposts he spread
all round a ring of chains, and then he slung
more from the ceiling-beams, so there they hung
as fine as spiders' webs, invisible
even to gods' eyes, high up on the wall,
so craftily had he designed his snare.
When everything needful to prepare
the trap was put in place, he made it known

that he'd be off now to visit his own
favourite place on earth, the well-
trigged out Lemnos, that famous citadel.
Ares, who drives his team with reins of gold,
was keeping a sharp eye out, and the bold
god lost no time, as soon as he caught sight
of Hephaestus going away for the night,
in slipping back into the palace where
he could make good his mastering desire
for the crowned goddess Cythereia; she
had just returned from keeping company
with her great father Zeus, and while she sat
just taking her ease at home, Ares let
himself in, and he took her hand in his
and whispered, 'Darling, there's no time like this
for us to have some fun here in your bed,
now that Hephaestus has it in his head
to leave the country, and has likely gone
on one of his trips to those rough-spoken
Sintians who live on Lemnos.' When she heard
all this, she went along with every word
enthusiastically, and so the two
of them did just what they wanted to do
and fell into bed. No sooner had they done
this than the many chains dropped, one by one,
that clever old Hephaestus had fixed up,
binding them both from bottom to the top,
so they could neither move nor sit upright:
and each of them, where they were trussed up tight,
was well aware there could be no escape.
Now to their sides came the familiar shape
of the hirpling god, who had turned straight back
from his road to Lemnos, for he changed his tack
when Helios his watchman brought him word.
He went to his own quarters so much stirred
to fury that he stood at the front door
shaking with anger, and let out a great roar

for gods to hear: 'Zeus, father, all of you
blessed immortals: what you have to do
is come here now, and you will see a sight
for sore eyes – one that's laughable all right,
but past all bearing: the visible proof
that Aphrodite, under my own roof,
full of disdain for me, for being lame,
has been playing fast and loose at the game
of love with no-good Ares, just because
he's fit and capable in all he does
and I'm a cripple – but for that, I'm not
to blame, for it's the parents who begot
me, and I wish they never had. Now, though,
you can all see them where they are on show,
those lovers who leapt into my own bed,
however much I want to hide my head
in grief from that sight. But no matter how
much they may be in love, I doubt if now
they'll want to lie together in this way
much longer: they will not let sleep delay
them – but my trap will, with its chains,
until her father pays me back those gains
he had from me when I was courting her,
whose face was really the face of a cur,
his pretty daughter, pretty and untrue.'
While he said this, gods began pushing through
to his palace and its porch of bronze: first came
Poseidon, who can shake the world; the same
instant busy Hermes was close at hand;
Apollo too, who works over sea and land,
came quickly; but goddesses stayed behind
in their own homes, abashed by what they'd find
if they should join their brothers, who now stood
in the porch, those divine patrons of the good,
laughing their socks off when they saw the tricks
wily Hephaestus had managed to fix.
With a glance at his neighbour, one would say

to another, 'Look how bad deeds never pay:
the slow ones catch the quick sometimes, just as
Hephaestus here, slow and all as he is,
caught up on Ares, quickest of the gods
living on Olympus, against the odds
although he's lame, with his mechanic arts;
and now's the time that Ares' payback starts.'
They spoke like this to one another, then
the lord Apollo, who is Zeus's son,
said to his brother, 'Hermes, giver and guide,
wouldn't *you* like to be lying beside
Aphrodite, in gold there on the bed,
even though chains should bind you foot and head?'
Hermes replied, 'Apollo, if that could be,
then the strongest of chains and padlocks, three
times as many as these, might wind me round,
and goddesses and gods see me enwound,
so long as I could sleep with Aphrodite.'
At this, the gods all laughed together – only
Poseidon didn't join in, and he kept
pleading with Hephaestus, that most adept
of all craftsmen, to let Ares again
go free, asking him to undo each chain.
'If you do this, I promise you I'll pay
in my person all that's due in the way
of ransom, by these gods; just let him go.'
But the lame god Hephaestus wasn't slow
to give him his answer: 'Mover of the earth,
Poseidon, you should know that it's not worth
your while to ask this: for all promises
made for the untrustworthy, such as these,
mean nothing; after all, how could I place
you in fetters and hope I could save face
in front of these gods, once he has been sprung
both from my trap and his debt all along?'
'Hephaestus,' Poseidon said straight away,
'if Ares shirks his debt, then I will pay.'

'I won't, and neither should I,' said the lame
god, 'refuse your offer, all the same.'
With that, he undid the strong bonds, and those
two lovers, set loose from constraints so close,
jumped up at once: Ares ran off to Thrace,
while Aphrodite fled to her own place
in Cyprus – Paphos, her special retreat,
her temple, with its altar smelling sweet:
the Graces cleaned her there, and they poured oil
exclusive to the gods, ambrosial,
over her soft skin; and at last they dressed
her in breathtaking clothes of the very best.

Appendix 2

The Battle of Typhaeos and Zeus (Hesiod, *Theogony* 820–868)

But when Zeus drove out of the sky
the Titans, then enormous Earth
mating with Tartarus, thanks to
gold Aphrodite at her work,
bore Typhaeos, her youngest son,
whose hands grasp tightly what they hold
and whose feet, as a god's feet, move
with supernatural stamina;
a hundred heads of a hundred snakes
came from his shoulders, their black tongues
darting and flicking, a dreadful monster,
and from the eyes on every head
fires spattered under all the brows,
so everywhere he looked, the flames
from head on head kept bursting out,
and voices from those loathsome things,
the heads, made their unspeakable
noises on every side – sometimes
such sounds as only gods could bear;
sometimes a great bull's bellowing
at full strength; sometimes a lion
with all its heart devoid of pity;
sometimes like a wild pack of pups,
beyond belief shrill; and sometimes
nothing but hissing, so that from
deep down the high mountains echoed.

A deed that is undoable
that very day might have been done,
and over men and gods alike
he would have lorded it, had not
the father of all gods and men
taken quick notice, and begun
to sound his thunder loud and long
so that the whole earth fearfully
sounded it round again, with all
of broad heaven and the deep sea,
Ocean and buried Tartarus.

As he came at them, from his steps
tremors passed through great Olympus
and all the world began to moan.
The sea, as dark as violets,
shrunk from the shock the two of them
made as they clashed – the lightning bolts
and thunderclaps, the flames that beast
mixed with tempests and crazy storms:
the land boiled, and the sky and sea;
around headlands and over them
beneath the battering gods, big waves
walloped until from everywhere
an unchecked quaking soon took hold.
Hades, down where he rules the dead,
felt fear then, and in Tartarus
the Titans, put under in hell,
stuck close to Cronos in the dire
deafening noise and battle-roar.

When Zeus brought his whole strength to bear
and took up his weapons of war,
thunder and lightning, the flashing bolt,
then from Olympus with one bound
he struck Typhaeos from every side,
scorching each repulsive head

on that unnatural prodigy.
Once he had laid into him with
hard blows, Typhaeos went down lamed
and under him the vast earth groaned.

Fast and intense as lightning, fire
shot from the god, from the mountain dark,
to strike him: and again the earth
took the entire shock of great flame,
starting to melt the way tin melts
when craftsmen heat it in their pots,
or as iron, toughest of all things
in the good earth, at Hephaestus' hands
melts when it meets on wooded heights
the advancing flames: in just this way
his keen fire melted down the earth
as Zeus slung Typhaeos away
to boundless Tartarus, grievously
wounding him to the very soul.

Notes

Abbreviations

In the Notes that follow, the following abbreviations have been used:

AHS T. W. Allen, W. R. Halliday, and E. E. Sikes (eds.), *The Homeric Hymns* (2nd edn., Oxford: Clarendon Press, 1936)

Loeb M. L. West, *Homeric Hymns, Homeric Apocrypha, Lives of Homer* (Cambridge Mass.: Harvard University Press, 2003)

Notes to Hymn 1

It was only with Christian Friedrich Matthaei's discovery in 1777 of the manuscript referred to by scholars as M (a book of fifty pages, with the Greek written in two columns throughout and about twenty lines in each column), that the Hymn to Dionysus came back to light. Unfortunately, unlike the other Hymn also freshly present in the manuscript (the Hymn to Demeter), no more than the last twelve lines of the Dionysus Hymn were in place: the missing part of M included some eleven leaves on part (or perhaps all) of which the rest of this long poem must have been written.

We possess, then, the end of the Hymn to Dionysus (fragment D); other bits and pieces exist in scattered form, and some lines look likely to be from close to the poem's beginning (fragment A). Diodorus Siculus, the Sicilian historian of the first century BC, quoted these nine lines as work of 'the poet in the Hymns', and 'Homer in the hymns'.[1] A papyrus of the second or first century BC in Geneva was identified in 1992 as containing these same lines, with fragments of some more.[2] A single line quoted in the work of Athanaeus (c. 200 AD) as being 'in the ancient hymns' seems likely, also, to belong somewhere in the poem (fragment B).[3] Finally, one of the Oxyrhynchus papyri contains fragments of about twenty-six lines which may be given a measure of conjectural restoration as part of the Hymn (fragment C).

In any attempt to say what the Hymn to Dionysus must have

---

1   Diodorus Siculus, *Bibliotecha Historica* 3.66.3 and 4.2.4.
2   Of these, four can be identified with surviving lines in a poem from the fifth century AD, the Orphic *Argonautica*, and thus can be used to complete the gaps at that point in the papyrus.
3   Athenaeus, *Deipnosophistai* 653B.

been like, this would appear to be little to go on. Nevertheless, there is enough here to permit an informed guess; and Martin West, whose guesses are better informed than anyone else's, has argued convincingly for the centrality of one particular myth.[4] The Hymn, West suggests, must have contained an account of the story in which Hera is trapped and bound by her son Hephaestus, who cannot be persuaded to release her by Ares, but is then successfully won over by the offices of Dionysus: Hephaestus and Dionysus (probably in an inebriated state) journey back together to Olympus, where Hera is set free to much rejoicing while, as his part of the bargain, Hephaestus takes (a possibly disgruntled) Aphrodite in marriage. For all of this, Dionysus is rewarded with a place at Olympus amongst the other gods.

The story is one that would fit well with a Homeric hymn, since it provides a potentially elaborate and entertaining narrative framework for the serious business of explaining how a deity first took his place of honour amongst the other gods. It is clear, too, that this particular myth is one that had considerable currency in classical Greece, and the lost Hymn (probably considered as the work of Homer) is very likely to have been its principal literary expression. The story features, for instance, on a black-figure krater of the mid-sixth century BC known as the 'François' vase, signed by the artist Kleitias: here, amongst many other mythological and Homeric episodes, Dionysus and an assorted company bring Hephaestus, who is riding a mule, up to Olympus before both Hera and Zeus, while the goddess Athene seems to be taking some pleasure in the failure of a submissive Ares.[5] Later, a disapproving

---

4   See Martin West, 'The First *Homeric Hymn* to Dionysus', in Andrew Faulkner (ed.), *The Homeric Hymns: Interpretative Essays* (Oxford: Oxford University Press, 2011), 29–43.

5   This piece, discovered in Chiusi in Italy and therefore probably an export from Greece to the Etruscans, is in the Museo Archeologico, Florence. It survived substantially intact until 1900, when a museum attendant hurled a chair at it, and it broke into many fragments: these have since been twice reassembled, not without some losses.

reference in Plato's *Republic* to 'the binding of Hera by her son', as one of the themes in poetry which the ideal society would be better off without, suggests this myth's continuing prevalence.[6] This whole story may have its origin in ritual, as a worked-up 'literary' version of cult practice on Samos, the Ionian island which was especially connected with Hera (the first temple to her on the island is from the early eighth century BC). Here, a practice existed (probably already established at the time of the Hymn) of *Tonaia*, the 'binding', in which the goddess's cult image (originally, it seems, so fully stylized as to be no more than an ancient piece of timber) was brought to the edge of the sea, and there tied up with wood from the *lygos* (willow) before a subsequent ritual unbinding.[7]

What remains of the Hymn, however, is very little. The fragment which would most strongly suggest a connection with the story of the binding of Hera (fragment C) cannot, of course, be proved conclusively to belong to the piece which must have stood first in the collection of the Homeric Hymns; and between its first publication in 1904 and as recently as 1973, the identification had not been proposed. Nevertheless, there is a good chance of its belonging to the original Hymn, and very little plausibility in claims that it might be the remains of something much later. What is certain is that the Hymn must have contained a narrative of some length (working back from the size of the quires in the M manuscript, this can be estimated at around four hundred lines). With this extent, the Hymn was indeed probably one in which the story of Dionysus' reception into Olympus could told in detail, and this narrative of a god's assumption of his place in the pantheon would thus accord well generically with others of the Hymns – with all of the longer

---

6   Plato, *Republic* 378d.
7   The sources for this practice on Samos are relatively late ones (third and second centuries BC), but archaeological evidence from Samos gives them plausibility as relating to earlier centuries. See Joan V. O'Brien, *The Transformation of Hera: A Study of Ritual, Hero, and the Goddess in the* Iliad (Lanham, MD: 1993), 54ff.

ones, in fact, excepting the Hymn to Aphrodite.

At an unknown point, somebody decided to make the hymn to Dionysus the first in a collection of the Homeric Hymns. This will have been a lot further back in time than the creation of the M manuscript (in the later fifteenth century), and may well be as long ago as the Hellenistic period. It is possible that the Hymn was thought to be the oldest, but since all of the Hymns were putatively the works of the same poet (Homer), this is not especially likely. The currency and relative popularity of the story which the Hymn contained might very well have been a significant factor (and here, the binding and unbinding of Hera fits the bill): it is possible, too, that the comic nature of its central narrative would have seemed in itself conclusively Homeric to those who knew the *Odyssey*, and in particular the Hymn-like set-piece in Book 8, in which the poet Demodocus recites another story of divine trapping and setting free.[8] It may be relevant, also, that the Hymn began with reference to the (now unlocated) place called Nysa, etymologically read into the very name of Dionysus, where a significant phase of the action in the following Hymn (to Demeter) is set.

M's preservation of the Hymn to Demeter is ample evidence that it was a compilation of important hymnic poetry which went beyond the standard canon of Homeric hymns preserved in other medieval manuscripts; and it is fair to assume that the Hymn to Dionysus, too, was a work of considerable literary importance. What we possess allows us to say hardly any more than that; but disappointment in this regard need not give rise to flat despair over the loss. The leaves that were separated from M some time between its creation at the end of the fifteenth century and its discovery in Moscow nearly three hundred years later were not necessarily destroyed – many things, besides outright destruction, happen to discarded segments of manuscripts. The whole Hymn to Dionysus might even, one day, turn up again.

---

8 *Odyssey* 8: 266–366 (translated as Appendix 1). This same passage was, on the other hand, evidently rejected as Homer's work by a number of ancient critics (though on moral rather than textual grounds).

page 3: Bull-god] The Greek word here, *Eiraphiōta*, is of uncertain meaning; it is, however, of very great antiquity, and may contain several elements. It is a term which recurs at the end of the poem, and is thus of some importance for the Hymn. In a scholion to *Iliad* 1:39, the commentator glosses the Homeric verb *erephō*, to cover: 'from which root also Dionysus is called *eiraphiōtēs*, for he is crowned with ivy.' In Euripides' Dionysus play *The Bacchae*, the verb *erephō* is used in this way, and the covering/crowning is done with ivy (323). Another aspect of this 'covering' root (as the same commentator says) might connect the word with the myth of Dionysus having been sewn into Zeus's thigh after his mother had been struck by the thunderbolt. The 'bull' element of the word, if this is indeed present, would connect it ultimately with Sanskrit, and Dionysus is, of course, a god imported from outside Greece; another possibility, of connection not with bulls but with goats, arises if the word *eriphos* (kid) is detected in this title: and this was in fact a title of Dionysus at the Greek colony of Metapontum. The Hymn's word turns up in an inscription from the island of Amorgos dating from the fourth century BC, where it is the name of a month in which ditches are to be dug (*Inscriptiones Graecae* XII: 7.62, 1.28). Amorgos in the south-east Cyclades is just to the south of Naxos, and further to the south of Ikaros, both places mentioned in these lines of the Hymn. The island was colonized originally by Naxos, but subsequently (in the later seventh century BC) by Samos. The Hymn's word looks very much like a cult title of Dionysus, and it is one which may connect the god not just specifically to the islands being mentioned at this point of the poem (which, we are told, are incorrectly adduced as his birthplace) but indirectly to the culture of Samos, with its major cult of Hera.

Drakanos] This is the name of a promontory on the island of Ikaros. There was also, however, a Drakanos on the island of Cos (where there was a temple of Dionysus in the Hellenistic period).

Semelē] The mother of Dionysus: she was the daughter of Cadmus, the king of Thebes, and it was here that she was seduced by Zeus. Traditionally, her fatal request to her divine lover for him to reveal himself to her as a god, which resulted in her immediate death, was made at the mischievous suggestion of Hera.

Alpheios] This river is close to Olympia in mainland Greece, and is the name of a river-god in *Iliad* 11: 727.

Ikaros] If Drakonos is in fact on Ikaros, it would seem odd to name the island separately here. It lies close to Samos, and is the legendary site of the failed flight of Deadalus' son.

Naxos] The largest of the Cyclades, this island was indeed often taken as the birthplace of Dionysus. Ancient sources mention a cave in which the god was born, and Naxos was also held to be the place where Dionysus met Ariadne: the priest of Dionysus was a key official in classical times, and from the fourth century BC onwards all coins from Naxos bore a portrait of the god. It seems fair, then, to assume that the Hymn's dismissal as possible birthplaces of Naxos, along with Ikaros and Drakonos (if that is indeed a separate place) means that it has its own origin somewhere else.

Nysa] The place-name itself here is not uncommon – up to fifteen locations are mentioned in various ancient sources. The earliest trace comes in *Iliad* 6: 133, where Lycurgus son of Dryas 'once drove down, over the sacred mount | of Nysa the nurses of crazed Dionysus'. It would seem to be the point of the Hymn, however, that this Nysa is a place where no one has ever visited, far away and almost unknown.

by fresh springs … grazing land] The poem as I translate it here incorporates a speculative reconstruction on the basis of the Geneva papyrus fragment. What can be made out of the words is given literally by West (*Loeb*): 'occupied by a deep … extended … away from the surge … by skill … lovely pastures …'

page 4: Fragment B] This is a single line of Greek, quoted by Crates of Mallos, the librarian of Pergamum in the second century BC, as being 'from the ancient hymns'.

Fragment C] This fragment comes from one of the papyri (*P.Oxy.* 670) discovered at the Egyptian site of Oxyrhynchus in the late nineteenth century. An edited version appeared as early as 1904, but at this stage the subject matter remained unidentified. The argument for these lines belonging to the Hymn to Dionysus was first made by R. Merkelbach, 'Ein Fragment des homerischen Dionysos-Hymnus', *Zeitschrift für Papyrologie und Epigraphik* 12 (1973), 212–215, and this attribution is accepted by West, who includes the fragment in this position in *Loeb*. As translated in my version, the lines are speculatively rendered. The papyrus contains 26 lines or parts of lines, most of which require reconstruction. West's account, incorporating such reconstructions within square brackets, runs as follows:

> ... you wish. What else could happen to [you worse than this? I was stupi]d myself, from [...] left of his own accord [...] as they [sur]mise ever [... he tricked you and pu]t you in hellish fett[ers. Who] could set y[ou] free, my dear? [A painful b]elt encircles y[our body, while he,] heed[ing neither co]mmand [nor entreaty, has formed] an unshakeable r[esolve in his heart. It's a cruel] son you have borne, sis[ter ... craf]ty, even though a cripple [...] in front [of ...] feet good [...] wrathful [...] ... angry [...] Let us find out [if he will soften his hear]t of iron. For there are [two] clever [sons] of mine at hand [to help with] your [suffering. There is Ares, who] has raised his [keen] spear, a th[ick-hide fighter ...] to look and bra[ndish ...; and there is] also Dionysus [... But let him] not stir up a quarrel with me, [otherwise he will be on his way belab]oured by my [thunderbolts in no tidy style ...] of sweet [...] this lad [...

If the lines do belong to the Hymn, and are part of the story of the binding and release of Hera, then it must be Zeus here who is addressing his helplessly trapped wife. It is as well to be reminded, however, how speculative reconstructions such as this must be; and that the attribution of the fragment to the Homeric Hymn, however ingenious, is itself an act of speculation.

page 5: *Fragment D*] These lines are at the very beginning of the M manuscript, and form the end of the Hymn. The first three lines of the Greek are spoken by Zeus, presumably after he has set his seal on new arrangements for giving honour to the god Dionysus. The reference to offerings being made as a festival which occurs every three years actually means that this takes place every other year, since the Greeks counted such things inclusively. In the second line of the Greek here, *AHS* proposed an emendation which would have introduced the idea of a ritual cutting-up into three (presumably of the god himself, in his avatar of Zagreus); but this introduces a theme for which the (admittedly scanty) remainder of the surviving poem gives no hint. I have worked from the reading of M, which suggests the mere business of biennial celebration (*ta men triasoî*) rather than the more dramatic and gory proposed emendation, which indicates somebody being chopped into three parts (*tamen tria*).

page 6: *you who can send the women mad*] This ability of Dionysus is the theme of Euripides' play *The Bacchae*.

So, Bull-god, Dionysus, take | *this tribute*] It has been suggested that from here onwards the text proposes an alternative ending to that which has just been delivered in the previous sentence. The lines may be to an extent repetitive, but it does not necessarily follow that M somehow (as West claims) 'incorporates two alternative endings to the hymn'.

Thyonē] This alternative name for Semelē is also found in Sappho, and in Euripides (where, however, it is an alternative for Dionē). When she was brought back from the dead (by her son) to join the gods on Olympus, Semelē was sometimes thought to have been given this divine name. The apotheosis is mentioned briefly by Hesiod:

> The child of Cadmus, Semelē,
> made love to Zeus, and bore him then
> a splendid boy, uproarious
> Dionysus: a woman, she
> gave an immortal birth, and now
> the two of them are gods.   (*Theogony* 940–942)

In Latin literature, in the work of Ovid, Horace, and Statius, Dionysus (Bacchus) is referred to as Thyoneus.

Notes to Hymn 2

The Hymn to Demeter, 495 hexameter lines in length, was for many centuries lost from view: it was not amongst the Homeric Hymns as they were available to the scholars and readers of the renaissance and after, and only came back into sight with the discovery of the M manuscript by Matthaei in 1777 (see Notes to Hymn 1). It is one of the major works of ancient Greek literature, but is has only been in common currency for the last two and a half centuries.

The poem (we know from M) will have stood second in the arrangement of Hymns in the manuscript tradition of which the bundle of parchment, found by luck one day in Moscow, is the last survivor. Textual specialists have worried over the extent to which this tradition can be said to be more authentic than the other line of descent, witnessed by the other surviving medieval manuscripts of the Homeric Hymns. Was the Hymn to Demeter (like the Hymn to Dionysus that stood before it) editorially removed? When, and (more importantly) why might this have happened? No firm answers are either possible or presently conceivable; but the questions remain important nonetheless. All we can conclude is that there was in late antiquity more than one way of counting and collecting 'Homer''s Hymns, and that this particular work – which most modern students of ancient poetry find exceptionally powerful and compelling – was at some point, whether on grounds of content or attribution – thought not to belong with the other work of 'Homer'.

It is likely that the poem is in fact extremely old. Various modern scholars have come to particular speculative conclusions, but a consensus would place the Hymn between 650 and 550 BC. Small papyrus fragments (from the third century AD, and another more tentatively connected from the first century BC) preserve parts of the Hymn independently of M, showing that at least some of the poem was a text in currency in antiquity. It is unlikely to have been the only substantial narrative connected with Demeter; and later hymnic works seem both to draw upon it, and to relate to other (lost) accounts of the myth. Hymns in the so-called 'Orphic' corpus seem occasionally to be in touch with the poem, while poets in the Hellenistic tradition, such as Callimachus, appear to have known and imitated the Hymn; both Ovid and the later Roman poet Claudian show signs of familiarity with its content.

Demeter is the god of corn, and of the general fertility of the fields. It is important that her name means in part 'mother' (*mētēr*), and in myth she is generally in company with (or, of course, painfully separated from) her daughter Persephone. So close is this association that one common way of referring to the two divinities was not by name at all, but simply as 'the two gods' (*tō Theō*). The connection of the story of the daughter's abduction and return to the nature of the mother as a fertility god would appear to be logical enough: with the return of green shoots in spring, so the child would return to the mother.

If the myth of Persephone's abduction and return was a widespread and important one, the Hymn is its most extensive early literary incarnation. Before this, there are only a few lines of Hesiod to go on:

> And then Demeter, the bounteous god,
> came into [Zeus's] bed: she bore
> pale-armed Persephone, whom Hades
> stole from her mother's side – but Zeus
> in his wisdom granted that to him.

> (*Theogony*, 911–913)

This insistence on Zeus's involvement is maintained in the Hymn, so it is a vital part of the early formation of the myth. The first substantial treatment of the story after the Hymn comes in a chorus of Euripides' *Helen* (412 BC), which may very well be drawing on the Hymn itself (especially if, as some scholars think, the Hymn has an Attic provenance). In Euripides, Demeter is conflated deliberately with her mother Rhea, although she is accorded her cult name of Deo, while Persephone is (as custom generally demanded) not named directly:

> Once, the gods' Mother dashed
> with fast steps on the mountain,
> right through its deep glens,
> their swift-running streams, and then
> the waves that rumble past
> each other down on the sea,
> all taken up with yearning
> for her child who mustn't be
> named, her child who had gone.
> Cymbals went wild, turning
> out their shrill noises, when
> she harnessed up her team
> of beasts to the car
> and went out to search far
> and near for her stolen daughter,
> snatched from the round-and-round
> dances of little girls; and after her
> on foot, fast as the wind,
> Artemis with her bow,
> stern-eyed Athene with her spear.
> From high on the summits now
> Zeus was looking down,
> with another fate in his mind:
> and then the mother put an end
> to the work of running high and low
> in search of a girl who had been
> taken so deviously, her own
> beloved child. She went
> up on Mount Ida where the snow
> lies all year, where only

the nymphs are about to see,
and there she sent
herself headfirst down into the icy
treeline, in her grief.
Then she made the fields of the plain
barren, with no grass for men
who cultivate the land;
choking the ground, she
was going to utterly
wipe out all of humanity:
no fodder for the herds,
no fresh shoots, not a leaf,
nothing for cities to live on,
no fragrances sent up towards
the gods from altar-fires.
She even stopped up springs
where the dew-clear water flows,
all for grief,
grief unassuageable for
her daughter. And as things
got worse, and more and more
food went, then even the water,
men's sufferings foreclosed
all of the gods' dues.

(Eurpides, *Helen*, 1301–1338)

As the Ode continues, Euripides has Zeus send Aphrodite on a musically-enhanced embassy to Demeter, which results in her beginning once again to laugh. This is where the story is left, but there is the broad implication that it is through some kind of amusement that the mother can be persuaded to relent from her destructive grief. In the Hymn, it is human beings in the household of Celeus who attempt to cheer up the grieving goddess, but there in ignorance of her divine identity; the sending of famine comes later, once the goddess has been revealed, and it requires more than light entertainment to bring it to an end.

The Hymn, then, offers a glimpse of the Demeter and Persephone legend before it became fully elaborated for the kinds of literary purposes of which Euripides provides a good example. With the passage of time, these artistic demands became more pronounced, and the subtlety of elaboration more advanced. How far the Hymn itself continued to be a major or even a significant poetic account of a widely-known myth into the fifth and fourth centuries BC cannot be known. The Demeter myth, like all the Greek myths, will have been fluid: that is, the act of telling or retelling in poetic form always enjoyed the liberty to adapt, re-shape, or elaborate the traditional elements of a story. The Hymn might reasonably be supposed to exercise such liberty with whatever materials came before it, and it might very well have itself been subject to subsequent adaptation.[1] Certainly, there were so-called 'Orphic' hymns in use in the fifth and fourth centuries BC (and after), and there are no grounds for considering the Homeric Hymn to be any kind of 'original' poetic account.

For all that, the Hymn is a remarkable achievement, the quality and distinctiveness of which meant that, at some stage, it was thought worth preserving and passing on as the work of 'Homer'. Its rendering of the abduction of Persephone, followed by the frantic search of her mother Demeter (joined by the goddess Hecate) has all the pace and intensity of the best

---

1   It is not always possible to say confidently that the Hymn is being adapted in later instances, or whether these are witnesses to another similar poem. A case in point is the fragmentary Hymn to Demeter attributed to 'Orpheus', preserved in a mixture of quotation and abstract in a Berlin papyrus of the first century BC (*P. Berol.* 3044). Here, there appear to be a number of near-quotations from and allusions to the Homeric Hymn; but on closer inspection, the divergences may suggest the use of another similar (but perhaps earlier) text. The paraphrase of the Orphic poem offered by its ancient commentator is not in line with the content of the Hymn, and this might suggest caution. For an expert discussion of these problems, see Bruno Currie, 'Perspectives on neoanalysis from the archaic hymns to Demeter', in Øivind Andersen and Dag T.T. Haug (eds.), *Relative Chronology in Early Greek Epic Poetry* (Cambridge: Cambridge University Press, 2011), 184–209.

of epic poetry; and the whole poem is plainly enough indebted to the stylistic worlds of both the *Iliad* and the *Odyssey*, not least through its subtle and skilful use of repeated formulae and epithets. After the tragic concentration of its initial narrative, the poem takes a daring swerve, when Demeter assumes human form, and is taken into the family of Celeus, where she becomes a child-carer. It is almost impossible to imagine this turn of events as somehow traditional in the Demeter myth, and much more natural to see it as a piece of literary narrative: in terms of the meaning and effect of the Hymn itself, it makes all the difference.

There must be, of course, a reason for the poet making this particular departure; and the most likely one is connected with the location of Celeus' seat in the Attic town of Eleusis. The Hymn provides abundant detail about Celeus' own family and the other leading families of the place; and as the story progresses, Eleusis itself becomes a principal focus, as the centre of Demeter's worship (in the temple built at her command), and the scene in which the goddess first launches her campaign of starvation against mankind and the other gods, before she is reunited with her lost daughter there, and relents. Eleusis was the site of the mystery rites of Demeter and Persephone (the latter often referred to simply as Korē ('the girl')), which by the sixth century BC was a place of national religious significance. There is evidence for the worship of Demeter going back to the Mycenaean era, and the site was enlarged and enriched regularly into Roman times. A sacred road led from Athens to Eleusis, and processions from the city ended with mass initiation rites in the Mysteries, in a major festival which took place at the beginning of autumn each year.

It is not possible to tell how the Eleusinian Mysteries were conducted, but there are plenty of indications in the Hymn that these rites are of direct relevance to the poem and its audience. The Hymn may, as a number of scholars have believed, incorporate aspects of the Mysteries into its narrative:

the use of torches, for example, and the drinking of a barley and pennyroyal mixture known as the *kykeon*, very likely reflect aspects of the religious practice. The poem also explicitly endorses the benefits of being initiated into Demeter's cult, and provides something like a tourist guide to the locality of Eleusis. This could mean that the Hymn comes from Athens, though not necessarily that it is intended solely for Athenian consumption. The fact of the Hymn's preservation means that it did make the transition, at some point, from local to national circulation; and it is as easy to imagine it as a promotional narrative for Eleusis as it is to see it as a kind of souvenir for the already-initiated.

But it is as an artistic work rather than a piece of promotion that the Hymn has its real meaning. The fundamental subject is that of a mother being parted from, and subsequently reunited with, her stolen child; and the Hymn manages to explore this in two different (though connected) situations. Besides the original act of abduction, in which a god's daughter is stolen by another god, the poem's shift into human-centred narrative makes possible a second narrative statement of maternal care and loss, in the story of Demophoön. Demeter's job, when disguised as an old woman, is to take charge of the raising of the little son of Celeus and his wife Metaneira: this she does expertly, and even determines to make him immortal, but her nightly procedures (which include putting the baby into the fire that burns in the house's hearth) are noticed by the child's mother, with predictable shock and alarm. In terms of the narrative, this is the point at which Demeter must reveal herself as a god, and from which she can begin a more aggressive and potentially catastrophic phase of her grief; but the effect and meaning of this whole central episode in the Hymn are important.

An initial puzzle, which the Hymn does nothing to solve, is why Demeter has chosen to assume this particular role at all. One might think that, if concentration of effect were being aimed for, the poet could have passed straight from Demeter and Hecate's initial search to the decision to wreak vengeful havoc on the earth.[2] This would have meant, of course, bypassing Eleusis; but Eleusis could still very easily have been used simply as a setting for the eventual resolution of events. The Hymn's diversion into human life – and Demeter's own diversion into that life – offers a way to increase the poem's acuteness of anguish on the whole subject of children lost and found.

When Demeter arrives at Eleusis, she is not only in disguise, but operating with a falsified back-story. The long account which she offers to Celeus' daughters of her having been captured and transported by pirates is in line with aspects of epic composition – the obvious point of comparison being the detailed false accounts offered in the *Odyssey* by an undercover Odysseus. Gods can, however, lie just as well as heroes; and like Aphrodite in Hymn 5, who presents herself to Aeneas with a fictitious identity and lineage, Demeter spins this story with a particular end in view. In her case, it is to win access to Eleusis' noblest family, and to become there a nurse of its prince. Under her assumed name of *Dōsō*, Demeter mentions her qualifications as a nurse even before she hears of the baby boy in Celeus' family, Demophoön, 'a son | born later in life, hoped for and prayed for' (page 12). One obvious explanation for all this is, in a manner, a psychological one: Demeter wants to replace her lost daughter with another child, and she intends to give this child immortality, the more exactly to replace Persephone. But in this case, why nurse a boy rather than a girl? And it is to be remembered that Demeter does not get over her grief the moment she crosses Celeus' threshold: instead, she sits for a time in silent (and, to the human hosts, inexplicable) mourning, until she is first entertained by the banter of the servant Iambe and then given the herb and barley drink prepared to her own particular specification. Perhaps

---

2 In his magisterial edition of the poem, N.J. Richardson remarks the 'Demeter's wanderings on earth and visit to Eleusis have no special purpose' (*The Homeric Hymn to Demeter* (Oxford: Clarendon Press, 1974), 81. This view has been shared by a number of critics.

it is here that the traces of Eleusinian rites (or at least, the preparation for those rites) may be discerned: Iambe's words (which the poet of the Hymn is too discreet to quote or dwell upon) could correspond to the mocking and indecent humour used on initiates on their way to the Mysteries in the *aischrologia* ('filthy talk') part of proceedings (Iambe's name then becomes suggestive of the 'iambic' verse in which poets engaged in such scurrilities), while the drink mirrors the mixture given to fasting participants just ahead of the rites themselves. Yet these parallels do not in themselves provide a full explanation for the actions of Demeter; if anything, it is her actions as narrated in the story which give an explanation for the ritual routines.

Demophoön is in no simple sense a replacement for Persephone, but the care he is given by Demeter serves to point up the importance in this of her role as a mother. Like the rest of her disguise, though, the maternal impulse is human only up to a point. Time and again in the Hymn, the poet insists on the completeness of the divide that separates men and gods; this is a standard enough theme in Greek poetry, but here it is something other than a commonplace. When she is discovered by Demophoön's natural mother, Demeter's reaction is forthright and unsparing:

> You stupid creatures, you witless and ignorant
> humans, blind to the good as well as the bad
> things in store for you, and no use to each other:
> I swear to you here, as gods do, by the rippling
> dark waters of Styx, that I would have made
> this child of yours immortal, honoured, a man
> untouched by age for eternity; but nothing now
> can keep the years back, or keep death from him.

(page 15)

How are these lines to be taken? First, they show that Demeter's sympathy for human beings, in which we have been tempted to believe all through the account of her desolate arrival at Eleusis and her encounter with the family of Celeus, is wholly our own error of interpretation: this will become abundantly plain when Demeter imposes a crippling famine on the whole earth, not concerned in the slightest with its human costs. Second, how great a tragedy – and for whom – is Demophoön's missing the chance of immortality? The child is denied the chance of becoming a god, but Demeter's words leave little doubt that this transition would essentially take him away from everything that is human: the precedent of Ganymede (see Notes on Hymn 5 (page 281)), who goes to Olympus leaving behind him a distraught father, is not in human emotional terms a promising one. Demeter gives compensation to Demophoön – just as Zeus compensates the father of Ganymede – of eternal commemoration at Eleusis as a state hero. Third, the audience cannot help but share Meteneira's horror when she witnesses her child being put into the fire: this procedure is not exactly on a par with being fed on ambrosia, for it is both terrifying and alienating, a sharp reminder that the world of divinity and that of human flesh are utterly distinct. Metaneira does what any mother would do when she screams out in distress; for Demeter, this is proof of her contemptible mortality.

As Demeter hardens her heart against the gods who have failed so far to re-unite her with Persephone, she uses human suffering as a weapon. That the gods should be denied their customary sacrifices from men is clearly a serious matter – and the treatment of the story later by Euripides confirms this – which will in the end force Zeus (so far, and somewhat sheepishly, on leave of absence from the unfolding events) to bring about a resolution. The people of Eleusis do everything that is asked of them by the goddess, but this in itself is not enough to help the situation: only Zeus, now, can make a difference. At this stage in the poem, our own ways of sensing and understanding Demeter's grief have been somewhat complicated. For whereas in the Hymn's opening episodes our feelings for Demeter turned her into a large-scale version of a human mother, and made our reactions to her shock and sorrow at the abduction of her daughter profoundly sympathetic ones, we are now obliged to witness grief at work on (literally, not figuratively) a more than human scale – a scale in which, indeed, humanity figures as nothing but an expendable mechanism for bringing force to bear. From this point onwards, we are inevitably, as an audience, on the side of conflict-resolution, and the perfectly-timed delays in the narrative's achievement of this resolution add to the sense of urgency. It would be fanciful – too fanciful, in fact – to say that the audience is from this point onwards in the place of the Eleusinian initiates, waiting in the great hall for the rites to be accomplished and their happiness to be made good; but the Hymn does now take us to a place where our sympathies are with the wretched people on a starved earth, and where the reunion of the divine mother with her divine child matters most of all because of the reprieve it will bring to those who are merely mortal.

In the last episodes of the Hymn (though of course there is no way of being sure of this), the poet may be writing in a less 'original' way than in the phase of the poem where Demeter lives amongst Celeus' family. Here, the fate of Persephone, and the subterfuge of the god Hades in securing her annual return as his winter bride, are much more likely to have been narrative elements inherited by the composer of the Hymn. Nevertheless, the depiction of Hades makes him into a distinctly knowing kind of participant in the drama, and his giving of the pomegranate seed to his unwilling bride feels both surreptitious and momentous. It is here, and with her return to her mother, that we begin to have a close encounter with Persephone herself; and the poet's decision to have her recount events to an anxious parent is both bold and entirely justified. According to Persephone, Hades forced her to eat; in the narrative of only a few lines before, no such compulsion was mentioned (the Greek adverb for his action is *karpalimōs*, 'secretly', which implies only that Hades did not want Hermes to notice). Undoubtedly, there is some dimension of sexual meaning to the story here, and of course the whole myth is partly about the passing of control over a daughter, by means of sex, from mother to husband.[3] Persephone's garrulity on her return, not matched by completely full disclosure, helps to confirm the limits that have now been set to Demeter's union with her daughter. Zeus's designs, although they have required strenuous and unanticipated measures to see them through, have not been ultimately frustrated, for Persephone will indeed be the bride of Hades.

The Hymn's conclusion offers a happy ending to a distinctly uncomfortable story. In terms of explanation of a particular divine function, it works perfectly well: Demeter will be the goddess of crops and their cultivation, and her rites will give comfort and illumination to mankind while, on the divine side of the gulf that separates men and gods, the goddess will have Persephone, along with the helpful and powerful Hecate, as her own for at least a large part of the year. Perhaps, though, the conclusion is not altogether satisfactory – albeit from the unsatisfactory point of vantage which is all that is available to a human audience. What was experienced at the beginning of the Hymn as a shocking crime is not, in the end, treated as a crime at all, but as a difficulty requiring diplomatic resolution; and the emotions which had been given free rein by the poet have been shown as, in some ways, mistaken or misplaced

---

3   For interesting discussion of this, see Helene P. Foley (ed.), *The Homeric Hymn to Demeter: Translation, Commentary, and Interpretive Essays* (Princeton: Princeton University Press, 1993), *passim*. Amongst many parallels between the Hymn and marriage practices, Foley cites the following (p. 108):

> In Attic marriage the bridal couple was showered with dried fruits and nuts (*katachysmata*) and presented with a basket of bread; the bride ate a quince (and probably a wedding cake made from sesame seeds) on arrival at the groom's house; the bride's acceptance of food (*trophē*) was a form of acknowledging the groom's authority (*kyreia*) over her. Another aspect of the standard marriage rite was the carrying of torches by the bride's mother; in the Hymn the bride's mother Demeter carries torches alone and after the event. The abduction comes to resemble marriage more fully only at the point of the final compromise, when Persephone eats and Hades mitigates his original violence with persuasion – a promise of honours to his bride.

sympathies. We are left with the existing order of things – in particular, as represented in the Mysteries; but there are no reasons for supposing that those rites (whether as hinted at in the poem, or in most of their historical existence) are intended to bring men and women any closer to the gods. Rather, they are in the nature of an insurance policy, one against ill fortune after death indeed, but also (and one suspects, more importantly) against ill fortune in the business of life. One of the last divinities mentioned in the Hymn is the god of Wealth, *Ploutos*, who was sometimes depicted as a child of Demeter; and the poet himself closes proceedings by asking for a life of comfort. All through this extraordinary poem, the reality of human sympathy, and the precariousness of fate, have been balanced against the implacable otherness of a divine order: and in this context, no source of potential comfort is to be turned down lightly.

In translating this Hymn, I have been a little more willing than usual, in the cause of narrative momentum, to cut and compress here and there, and to leave untranslated some of the epithets used by the poet: I have tried to signal a number of these omissions in the notes below. The version here is that which first appeared in my volume of poems *Torchlight* (2011), and subsequently in my *Collected Poems* (2012). There, the translation is intended to make contact with themes and expressions in a number of the short poems that surround it; but it is nevertheless a faithful enough account not to require revision for the present volume.

page 7: long-haired goddess] This compresses and alters the Greek, which is 'lovely-haired, holy goddess'.

skinny-legged] The epithet here is *tanisphyron* ('slender-ankled'): it may be that the Greek carries hints of imminent sexual maturity which my translation does not.

Demeter's | protecting sword, made all of gold] The Greek has two epithets here for Demeter: *chrysaorou* ('of the golden sword') and *aglaäkarpou* ('of glorious/shining produce').

the god Ocean] Ocean was the son of Ouranos (the sky) and Gē/Gaia (the earth).

as Zeus demanded, and as a favour to Death] Here, close to the very beginning of the Hymn, Zeus is implicated as a prime mover in the abduction. 'Death' is the god Hades, here referred to in the Greek by the name *Polydegmōn*, 'the host of many'.

the plain of Nysa] This location is primarily a mythical one, rather than a specific place. It is used in relation to Dionysus in Hymn 1.

page 8: not even the laden olive-trees] I have translated the adjective *aglaokarpoi* here as 'laden', but it is the same epithet used to refer to Demeter a few lines above, and here means 'of shining fruit'. This arresting detail will be echoed later in the poem, when Demeter sits in disguise beneath olive-trees at Eleusis. It may be significant that these are food-bearing trees, since Demeter is so intimately associated with agriculture.

Hecatē, Perses' daughter] The goddess Hecatē is not mentioned in Homeric epic, but is known to Hesiod as Perses' daughter, whose mother is Asteria:

> Asteria conceived, and bore Hecatē
> to whom Zeus, son of Cronos, gave
> honour most of anyone:
> he gave her the most splendid things –
> a share in the unploughable sea
> and in the earth; and from the starred
> heaven too she has due honours,
> for she is held in highest esteem
> by deathless gods. Even today,
> whenever some man bound to earth

looks to find favour by his acts
of sacrifice in holy rites,
he calls aloud on Hecatē [...]   (*Theogony* 411–418)

As this passage continues, Hesiod expands on Hecatē's ability
to be a sponsor of hunters and fishermen, of those in charge
of livestock and even of athletes. At the close of the lengthy
account, Hesiod renews an earlier emphasis on the goddess's
being an only child, and mentions a last affinity with infant
children:

And thus, her mother's only child,
she has great privilege and fame
among all the immortals: Zeus
made her the nurse of children who
with her help see the light of Dawn –
Dawn who sees everything. So from
the start she was a nurse, and these
things are her marks of honour.   (*Theogony* 448–452)

All of this may be relevant to the Hymn's introduction of Hecatē
at this point. The Hymn says first that she is *atala phroneousa*
('thinking blameless things'), and this initial insistence on her
essential innocence is evidently important in contributing to
the force and urgency of Demeter's search.

Helios] The god of the sun: see Note to Hymn 31.

prince of the teeming dark] My translation of the epithet used
for Hades here, *polysēmantōr*, is very free: more literal would be
'the commander of many'.

she tore | in two the veil] This is a conventional sign of violent
grief: in *Iliad* 22, Andromache when she hears news of the
death of Hector throws off her veil:

The same veil golden Aphrodite gave

to her that day when, in his flashing helm,
Hector led her from the house of Eëtion,
with the costly marriage fully paid for.   (*Iliad* 22: 470–472)

Demeter here may be formalizing a breach with Zeus – he is
now, as it were, dead to her – and more generally, in this and the
wearing of a dark shawl, she may be declaring herself a figure
outside of divine society.

For nine whole days] Here, the Greek calls Demeter by
the name Deo. The nine-day duration is unlikely to be one
randomly arrived at: in epic, nine days is a way of referring
to a long period of waiting, with the waited-for event coming
on the tenth day. There is a plague of nine days in *Iliad* 1,
while the gods are at odds with one another for nine days in
Iliad 24; it takes Odysseus nine days to sail from Aeolia to
Ithaca. In the religious business at Eleusis, nine days would
probably be too long a period for a practical fast for initiates,
though it could possibly have figured in the preparations of the
priests.

a blazing torch in each hand] In visual representations of Demeter
and Hecatē, these torches are very common. Often, one hand
carries a torch aloft, while the other holds a torch downwards.
An important religious official at Eleusis was the *daidouchos*
('torchbearer'), and it is thought that part of the Eleusinian
initiates' routine involved a night-time, stylized search for the
lost Persephone, carried out by torchlight.

page 9: my daughter's voice was lost] The translation compresses
what Demeter actually says in the Greek: there, she mentions
'The girl I bore, my sweet shoot, beautiful to behold: I heard her
voice …' Persephone is a 'shoot' (*thalos*), and the same word will
be used later in the poem to describe the infant Demophoön.

page 10: when things were split three ways] The three brothers,
Zeus, Poseidon, and Hades, drew their respective domains of

the heavens, the sea, and the underworld by lot. This is spoken about in the *Iliad* by Poseidon:

> All things have been divided into three,
> and each has the power apportioned to him:
> when the lots were cast, I drew as my fate
> dwelling forever down in the grey sea,
> and Hades drew the darkness and the dust,
> while Zeus drew the wide sky, the air and clouds:
> the earth and great Olympus we must hold
> in common, one and all.

> *(Iliad* 15: 189–193)

Celeus] The broad implication here is that Celeus is the most eminent man in Eleusis; he is called *koiranos* ('master'), the word used by Helios only a few lines earlier to describe Hades. He, like the other leaders in the city, is also called a *basileus* ('king'); in the Hymn, he seems to be senior to them, though all form what looks like an aristocratic caste.

the Maiden's Well] This may be the well later called *Kallichōron* which was part of the religious landscape at the sanctuary of Eleusis.

the daughters of Celeus] The poet takes care to name these four girls, and it is possible that a priestly caste at Eleusis claimed descent from some or all of them. One girl is called Dēmō, and this stands out from the rest, partly because it is a form into which the name of Demeter was sometimes changed.

page 11: good day to you girls] Demeter's narrative here is of course wholly fabricated. The goddess claims in this speech to be a native of Crete, and 'Cretan tales' are notoriously false in literature: in the *Odyssey*, Odysseus is a master of the form when he has to maintain a disguise on his return to Ithaca. Demeter puts together here a story in which an abduction is frustrated by the escape of the hostage, perhaps in a telling contrast to what has happened to Persephone. There is no pressing reason to connect the Cretan backgound here with theories of a Cretan origin for the goddess Demeter herself, as some commentators have done.

I am called Grace] In Greek, Demeter gives herself the name Dōsō or Dōs: its meaning is unclear (and the form is disputed), but there is probably some root connection to the idea of giving. I have tried to find an English word that would convey this whilst also being recognizably a name: any Christian overtones of 'Grace' are, of course, wholly unwanted here.

Thoricos] This town in Attica is to the north of Sunium; before the time of Solon, it was independent.

page 12: *calling her Grandma*] The Greek word used by Callidicē here is *maia*, a term of familial endearment for elderly women such as grandmothers.

Triptolemus] This passing mention is in fact a reference to a figure who would carry a great deal of significance in the Eleusinian myths: Triptolemus became the person who would spread the knowledge of cultivation across the world, and he figures in visual art as the rider of a winged chariot, armed with the crops given to him by Demeter. He was an Athenian addition to the Eleusinian cult, and it is possible that his small walk-on part in the Hymn is a sign of its being shaped by a tradition that pre-dates the Athenian control of both Eleusis and the Mysteries.

Diocles] This name is connected with Megara, which seems at one point to have been the rival of Athens for control of Eleusis. According to Plutarch, he ruled Eleusis for the Magarians before being driven out by Theseus (*Life of Theseus*, 10).

Eumolpus] Another significant Eleusinian name. Eumolpus was held to be the founder of a hereditary caste of high-priests of the Mysteries; if the Hymn were no more than a piece of promotional work for Eleusis itself, then much more information about Eumolpus would be expected.

Polyxeinus] Otherwise unknown, but the name is the same as one of the titles of Hades. What (if anything) the poet intends by this is obscure.

Dolichus] The name is mentioned in an ancient commentary on Homer as the son of Triptolemus.

Metaneira] The wife of Celeus and mother of Demophoön, Metaneira has an important part to play in the Hymn. She clearly had a life in myth outside the Hymn: she is depicted for example (with Demeter) in a red-figure hydria (from southern Italy) of the mid-fourth century BC (Museum Antikesammlungen, Berlin), and Pausanias (first century AD), in a passage that also gives evidence of a poem very like the Hymn at this point, which was believed to be the work of a pre-Homeric poet from Attica called Pamphōs, mentions a sanctuary to her near Eleusis:

> The other road from Eleusis goes to Megara. When you take this road, you pass a well by the name of Anthion: Pamphōs wrote of how it was by this well Demeter sat in the likeness of an old woman after the abduction of her daughter: from here, the daughters of Celeus brought her, as a woman from Argos, to their mother, and how Metaneira then employed her to rear her son. just a little further on from the well there is a temple of Metaneira [...]   (*Description of Greece* 1:39.2)

page 13: *Iambe*] This character seems to be connected in particular ways with the religious proceedings in and around the Mysteries at Eleusis. The name has a connection with the kind of poetry known as Iambic, which was scurrilous and often indecent. The deliberate staging of mocking and perhaps obscene humour was part of the Eleusinian procession, and it may be that Iambe in the Hymn is intended to figure this.

By the second century BC, the Hellenistic poet Philicus of Corcyra (a fragment of whose Hymn to Demeter survives) made her a garrulous old woman, who had come to Eleusis from the country, and set out to talk Demeter into forgetting her mourning: 'If you want to untie the bonds of your grief, I will set you free'. Much later accounts of the myth transfer Iambe's role to other named characters, who are openly obscene in their acts and remarks.

page 14: barley-water and pennyroyal | mixed up together] This mixture was the *kykeōn*, a drink consumed by initiates at Eleusis. It would have had no intoxicating qualities, and was instead a formal mark of the breaking of a fast. The Hymn's specificity here must indicate that a relation to the Mysteries is intended to be explicit.

the son | of Celeus and Metaneira] Demophoön is in fact named at this point in the Greek. He does not figure in a major way in later Eleusinian myth, though his name does keep some currency; in general, though, he is a more obscure figure than Triptolemus.

page 15: smuggled him | into the burning fire] A connection between fire and immortality is suggested by the immolation of Heracles on Mount Oeta; but Demeter's action here is all the more strikingly supernatural for its taking place right at the centre of the human household.

set him gently on the floor] This is at once an act of ordinary preservation of the child, and a symbolic returning of him to the mortality of earth.

the sham fight] This is probably the *balletys*, a stylized encounter between teams of young men held at Eleusis. The poet might here be working back, so to speak, from current practices towards the protagonists in his story. This assumption colours the translation, and is widely accepted by scholars of the poem, though the Greek says only that 'the sons of the Eleusinians will forever make war and loud battle amongst themselves.' I have adopted the phrase 'sham fight' from the annual mock-battle (a re-enactment of the Battle of the Boyne (1690)) staged by the Royal Black Preceptory near the village of Scarva, Co. Down.

page 17: Iris] Zeus employs this god of the rainbow as his messenger in the *Iliad*; according to Hesiod, she is the daughter of Thaumas and Electra, and the sister of the winds of the storm. She is often depicted (like Hermes) with winged footwear.

page 18: Hades] Hades has special access to the underworld, symbolized here by his golden staff. In the Greek, he is given his honorific title *Argeiphontēs*, 'the slayer of Argus': this comes from the story of his having killed the monstrous hound which Hera set to guard Io, after Zeus had turned Io into a cow.

just the hint of a smile | on his face] In the Greek, Hades 'smiled … with his eyebrows' (a difficult feat, even for experts in eyebrow control).

page 19: the tiny, sweet seed of a pomegranate] The pomegranate is a symbol both of sex and of death. Hades simply gives this to Persephone to eat: there is no suggestion that she does so unwittingly, or against her will. The act is full of associations of marriage (husbands gave food to brides as they entered their new home) and, like Demeter's breaking of her mourning fast at Eleusis, it is heavy with consequence. This takes place in the underworld at a time when the enforced fast of an imposed famine is ravaging the earth above.

like someone possessed] In the Greek, Demeter rushes 'like a maenad': maenads were the female devotees of Dionysus who ran wild in their orgiastic outdoor rites.

Persephone leapt out … What tricks | did he use to bring you away to the dark?] A tear in the manuscript means that substantial portions of these sixteen Greek lines have been lost. The translation here follows the conjectures of the poem's textual editors.

page 20: *me and all my friends*] Here the translation radically compresses the Greek, in which Persephone lists the friends with whom she was playing: these are the daughters of the god Ocean mentioned at the beginning of the Hymn, but now listed one by one. In addition, Persephone now says that the gods Athene and Artemis were of the party. The seven lines have been omitted from my version in the interests of its momentum. The Hymn, though, does pause at this point; and Persephone's list of names adds a certain gravity to her account:

> We were playing together in the uncut meadow –
> Leucippe and Phainō, and Electra and Ianthe,
> Melitē too, Iachē, Rhodeia and Callirhoē,
> with Melibosis and Tychē, and Ōcyroē whose eyes
> are like flower-buds, Chryseis and Ianeira,
> Acastē, Admētē and Rhodopē, Ploutō
> and the captivating Calypsō, Styx and Ourania,
> the lovely Galaxaurē, warmongering Pallas
> and Artemis with her arrows – gathering for fun
> handfuls of the wild flowers that were growing there […]
>
> (*Hymn 2*, 417–425)

If there is something naturalistic about all this, with Persephone giving her mother every last saved-up detail of what has happened to her, there is also something jarring about the inclusion of the goddesses. Artemis and Athene are both mentioned in later versions of the story, so perhaps the poet of the Hymn is working here to find some place for them in his narrative.

page 21: *Rhea*] The sister of Cronos. It is presumably significant that Rhea is the mother of Demeter, since at this point of the narrative the bonds between mother and daughter are especially apparent in the restoration of Persephone to her mother.

Rarion] This plain in the vicinity of Eleusis had great significance, since it was held to be the spot at which crops were first cultivated.

Rhea delivered her message from Zeus] Again, the translation here compresses the Greek text, in which Rhea repeats Zeus's promises almost verbatim (another tear in the manuscript means that portions of lines are missing, but enough is preserved to make clear the repetition). The effect of this repetition of a message is to bring the narrative closely into line with epic practice.

to give them instruction | in her liturgy and rites] The shift from Demeter's permitting the crops to grow to her instituting the Mysteries is immediate. The religious rites are put into the keeping of the Eleusinian families mentioned earlier in the poem, and the poet adds a few lines of general commendation for the Mysteries' power. The initiate is said here to be *olbios*, a word whose meaning stretches from from 'blessed' to 'fortunate' to 'rich'. According to *AHS*, 'This is the earliest allusion to the happiness of the initiated after death' (180), but such happiness is by no means to be understood as a compensation for any lack of felicity in life. As Jenny Strauss Clay has pointed out (*The Politics of Olympus*, 262), *olbios* is distinct in its meanings from the word *makar* (which can more confidently be rendered as 'blessed', and is used of the gods themselves). It is *olbios* that is in a fragment of Pindar which seems tantalizingly close to what is envisaged here by the Hymn – according to Clement of Alexandria, who quotes the lines, Pindar is 'speaking of the Eleusinian Mysteries':

> He who witnesses those things
> and goes under the ground
> is a rich man [*olbios*]: he has found
> out about life's end
> and its god-sent beginnings.   (Pindar, fr. 137)

The emphasis here still seems to be on knowledge rather than some kind of guaranteed beatitude. This sits well with the worship of Demeter, who is generally celebrated as a disseminator of vital knowledge about the fundamental means of life. The Mysteries, perhaps, found one of their meanings in the myth's emphasis on Demeter's change of heart when re-united with Persephone, returning fertility to the land and so putting back in place the basic conditions in which men could again be *olbioi*.

page 22: the god Wealth] This is Ploutus, the son of Demeter and Iason according to Hesiod (*Theogony* 969).

You who protect [...] now and always] Here, as in many of the Hymns, the poet concludes by asking for blessing on his work, promising in return to keep the god or goddess in reverence at all times. The five lines here are unusually extensive: Hymns 2, 4, and 5 (the other major narratives that have been preserved in the collection) allow this content to occupy no more than a couplet.

Antron, and Paros] Antron was a town in Thessaly, near to a temple of Demeter at Pyrasus; the island of Paros had strong connections with the worship of Demeter and Persephone.

Notes to Hymn 3

The Hymn to Apollo is a poem of 546 lines, which narrates both the god's birth on the island of Delos and his establishment of his temple and oracle at Delphi. Each of these two main stories is given in some detail, and each contains a great deal of topographical detail: in the birth narrative, Apollo's mother Leto travels between a number of possible birthplaces before persuading the (relatively barren) island of Delos to host the event, and in the Delphi foundation story, Apollo himself makes a long journey by sea and land before arriving at the destined spot. The Hymn, then, addresses two distinct aspects of the Greek worship of Apollo, in the veneration of his place of origin in the Aegean, and the history of the beginnings of his most important oracle, on mainland Greece. In its geographical sweep, and its narrative celebration of the capacities and daring of Apollo, the Hymn provides a suitably grand framework for the praise of one of the most important of the Greek gods.

It seems that the Hymn to Apollo was also one of the most current of the Homeric Hymns in antiquity. The historian Thucydides, in the later fourth century BC, adduced the Hymn (with Homer as its author) in the course of his account of arrangements on the island of Delos. In the third book of his History, Thucydides sets modern ritual purifications of the island in the context of events longer ago, and specifically the kinds of purification undertaken by the powerful ruler of adjacent Samos, Peisistratos. In the course of this, Thucydides quotes twice at length from the Hymn:[1]

---

1 Thucydides, *The Peloponnesian War* 3.104.1–5.

[1] And in the same winter the Athenians purified Delos, in keeping with a certain oracle. The ruler Peisistratos purified it in the past – not the entire island, but as much of it as was visible from the temple. Now, though, the whole place was purified in this way: [2] the graves of all those who had died on Delos were dug up, and an order went out that in future nobody was either to die or to give birth on the island, but instead such people were to be ferried to Rheneia. (Rheneia lies so close to Delos that Polycrates, the ruler of the Samians, at the time of his strength at sea when he added Rheneia to the other islands under his control, dedicated it to Delian Apollo by actually connecting it to Delos with a chain.) The first thing the Athenians did after this purification was to inaugurate the quinquennial festival, the Delia. [3] There was, in fact, at one time in the past a huge assembly of the Ionians and people from nearby islands on Delos, when they would come to the festival there along with their wives and their children, just as nowadays the Ionians attend the festival at Ephesus. They held contests there of both athletics and music, and the cities brought over their trained choruses. [4] Homer makes all this absolutely clear in the following verses, which come from his Hymn [*prooimion*] to Apollo:

Yet you keep Delos closest to your heart,
where the Ionians in thousands come
together, in long trailing cloaks, and start
processions to your sacred stadium,
children and wives and all, to watch the art
of boxers, dancers, in your honour; some
singing to you themselves in a great hymn.

[5] Again, it is clear that there was a musical contest which the Ionians went to take part in, from evidence in the same hymn [*prooimion*]; for having sung about the Delian chorus of women, he finishes his praise with these verses, in the course of which he also makes mention of himself:

But now may Apollo, and Artemis too,

> be good to me; and you girls who can boast
> of living here, remember me when you
> are asked by some new pilgrim to this coast
> from far away, tired out with travel, who
> has sung the best of all the singing host
> that visit you, and delighted you the most:
>
> tell him, all of you, it was a blind man
> who lives on Chios ...

These two substantial quotations from the Hymn are being used by Thucydides very much as primary evidence for his historical argument, and there is no sense at all that he regards his source as being especially obscure. Furthermore, he makes an emphatic connection between the Hymn and ritual activity on Delos itself; he accepts the great antiquity of Apollo's worship on the island, and suggests that it goes back further than the times of Peisistratos, to those of Homer himself.

Thucydides seems to assume widespread familiarity with the Hymn. This is plausible, for it may well be that the Delian festivals through the fifth century featured its performance. In a fragment of Pindar amongst the Oxyrhynchus papyri, what appears to be a piece in honour of Apollo commissioned by one delegation to Delos (dating presumably from the mid-fifth century BC) contains a reference to 'going on the worn cart-track of Homer', and contrasts this with the 'winged chariot of the Muses', which Pindar apparently intends to mount.[2] By this, as Martin West has put it, Pindar 'probably means that he is going to give an account of the birth of Apollo that departs from the Homeric Hymn.'[3] It looks as though the Hymn

---

2   Pindar, *Paean* 7b (P.Oxy. 2240), 11 ff. The words which can be certainly made out here are 'Of Homer ... on the cart-track | going': the term 'worn' translates a conjectural completion of the word before 'cart-track'.

3   M.L. West, 'Pindar as Man of Letters', in Dirk Obbink and Richard Rutherford (eds.), *Culture in Pieces: Essays on Ancient Texts in honour of Peter Parsons* (Oxford: Oxford University Press, 2011), 60.

was by this time the kind of classical text which a successful contemporary poet like Pindar had to both acknowledge and transform.

Another ancient text, one that is more fiction than history, puts together Delos, the Hymn, and Homer. This is the so-called *Certamen* – 'Concerning Homer and Hesiod, their origin and their contest' – which is a work of the second century AD, but is probably very heavily dependent on something much older. This likely source is by the sophist Alcidimas, from the first half of the fourth century BC, the *Mouseion*. In the course of this strange fantasy meeting between the two great poets of Greek epic, Hesiod sets Homer a series of challenges in composition, which he successfully meets, only to be deprived of his prize on the grounds that, while he writes the poetry of war, Hesiod is the poet of peaceful human activity – something more to be encouraged in society. The whole narrative has the feel of one of Walter Savage Landor's *Imaginary Conversations*: it is fundamentally implausible, but its points of detail have a certain verisimilitude and, in the process, enable a not unsophisticated critical appreciation of their subjects. One such point of detail concerns the Hymn to Apollo. After Homer has spent some time in Argos, winning public acclaim there, he goes to Delos for the festival:

> Having spent a certain time in the city [Argos], he made the sea voyage to the festival (*panēgyris*) at Delos. With his position taken up in front of the Horn Altar, he read aloud the Hymn to Apollo, whose beginning is 'Let me bring to mind, and let me not forget, Apollo the far-shooting'. Once the Hymn had been read out, the Ionians conferred on him [Homer] associate citizenship, and the Delians engraved his verses on a white tablet, which they set up in the temple of Artemis. (*Certamen*, 18)

The single line which the author quotes is evidently quite enough to identify the poem. (Another reading might suggest that a number of Hymns to Apollo would be known beyond this one in particular; but even in this case, a single line is still sufficient to establish the work in question.) One of the interesting things here is that the Hymn is honoured by being written and displayed: this implies both the extent to which oral poetry could be accommodated in written form, and the possibility of enough public literacy to appreciate the written artifact once it was put on display. There was at the time no suitable temple of Apollo on the island, and archaeological evidence seems to support the assumption that Apollo did not receive a significant separate temple on Delos until the late-sixth century BC, while the temple of Artemis was there from c. 700 BC.

There seems to be no sign of the Hymn in any other surviving literature until the second century AD, though when it is cited then the poem is not presented as something especially obscure.[4] The most fascinating of all the ancient witnesses to the Hymn, however, comes from a commentary on Pindar, which draws on the writings of Hipparchus of Sicily, a chronicler who probably lived in the first century BC. In this brief note, the Hymn is not only noted, but given an author and – exceptionally – a date:

> They used to say that the Homeridai in antiquity were those from the family of Homer who performed his poetry in a line of succession from him. Later on, this name was also taken by rhapsodes, who no longer traced their family line to Homer.

---

4   Pausanias, writing c. AD 150, mentions the Hymn in relation to the place-name Crisa (*Description of Greece* 10.37.4), and Athenaeus (c. 200 AD) quotes some lines from near the close of the Hymn as by 'Homer or one of the Homeridae' (*Deipnosophistae* 22 B). The sophist Aristides (mid-second century AD) in his *On Rhetoric* quotes some of the lines from the Hymn as they were quoted by Thucydides – though probably taking these straight from the historian rather than the poem itself. (It may be for this reason that Athenaeus takes Thucydides' phrase 'finishes his praise' to mean 'bring the poem to a conclusion': there is no ammunition here for the theory that Thucydides was referring to the poem in its 'Delian' incarnation only, without knowledge of the 'Pythian' narrative that follows.) Later, a line is quoted as the work of 'Homer, in the Hymn to Apollo', by the grammarian Stephanus of Byzantium (sixth century AD).

Especially prominent were those around Cynaethus, who they say inserted into the poetry of Homer many verses of their own making. Cynaethus was from Chios, and of those poems attributed to Homer he is himself said to have written the Hymn to Apollo, attributing it to Homer. So, it was this Cynaethus who first performed the verses of Homer at Syracuse during the 69th Olympiad (504/1 BC), as Hippostratus says.

The Homeridai were a professional caste, it would appear, who began with the convenient fiction of being descendants of the epic poet himself, but who evolved over time into a looser network of 'rhapsodes', also performers of epic, who were not averse to adapting and augmenting their original inherited texts. The meaning of 'rhapsode' itself includes the work of assembly (the verb *rhaptō* means to stitch, or join together), and the line of Pindar being commented upon in the passage refers to the 'singers of stitched (*rhaptōn*) verses'. The author of the note, or his source Hipparchus, identifies the rhapsode Cynaethus as a stitcher-together who, when he came to perform the Hymn, already had past form as an interpolator, as well as an interpreter, of Homeric works. Does this note, then, really identify an author for the Hymn?

Unfortunately, there can be no very clear-cut answer to this question. But Cynaethus has some chance of having once existed as an individual (more chance, some would add, than 'Homer'): in 1957, at Gela in Sicily, the base of a statue dating from the sixth century BC was discovered bearing the name 'Cynaethus son of Epochus'; and this location and date both accord with the time and possible movements of the rhapsode.[5] If a rhapsode called Cynaethus was around to perform at Delos in the 504–501 BC period mentioned, he might very easily have found himself in Sicily too, where patrons and festivals also existed. However, the given date poses problems of its

5 See W. Burkert, 'Kynaithos, Polycrates and the Homeric hymn to Apollo', in G.W. Bowerstock, W. Burkert, and M.C.J. Putnam (eds.), *Arktouros: Hellenic Studies presented to B.M.W. Knox* (1979), 53–62

own, for the Hymn is almost universally acknowledged to be considerably older than the end of the sixth century: while the scholiast's date for Cynaethus may very well be correct, it will not do as a way of dating the Hymn. It follows – probably – that Cynathus cannot have been the Hymn's author.

All of this depends, of course, on what precisely we mean when we refer to 'the Hymn'. The theory that the Hymn to Apollo is not one poem but two – the Delian birth-narrative, with its celebration of the festival on the island, and the Pythian oracle story, in which the god travels far and wide before establishing his seat at Delphi – has been around for a long time, and remains very much in currency. Ever since the scholarship of David Ruhnken in 1782, it has been possible to read the Hymn as a composite piece, in which two essentially distinct and self-contained narratives have been welded together in a manner which it is often implied (and sometimes even said) is crude and botched, as though some kind of cut-and-shunt operation has been carried out in order to sell off a fundamentally unreliable poetic vehicle.[6] Postponing a fuller consideration of this theory's merits (for which, see below), it is possible to see how Cynaethus can be fitted in to the scenario proposed: Polycrates of Samos, who organized a festival on Delos around 523 BC and was the same man who Thucydides tells us connected the island to its neighbour by means of a physical chain, was told by no less an authority than the Delphic oracle itself that his event should be 'both Pythian and Delian'. A tradesman like Cynaethus could very well do the job of creating a dual-purpose Apollo hymn, by putting together two previously finished works, or possibly by adding his own to another, and passing the result off as 'Homer'.[7]

---

6   David Ruhnken's *Epistola Critica I. in Homeridarum Hymnos et Hesiodum* was published in Leiden in 1782: he divided the Hymn after line 178, and was followed in this by a number of subsequent editors.

7   There are fairly elaborate reconstructions of possible scenarios for this: see e.g. Richard Janko, *Homer, Hesiod and the Hymns* (Cambridge: Cambridge University Press, 1982), 113–114 and Martin West, 'The Invention of Homer', *Classical Quarterly* 49/2 (1999), 372.

Whatever was going on at the close of the sixth century BC, no scholars believe that the bulk of the Hymn(s) was composed from scratch at that point. There are strong grounds for regarding much of the composition as being a lot older than this. Thucydides, after all, ascribed the lines he quoted simply to 'Homer' – a figure he would have thought of as belonging to the fairly remote past, and not to fifty or so years ago. As with so many of the Homeric Hymns, there are very few strong pieces of evidence to help with giving this poetry a date: elaborate statistical analysis of language has shown up relatively little to aid any firm dating. There are perhaps various kinds of circumstantial evidence which are relevant: here, the 'Pythian' narrative may have something to offer, in the shape of Apollo's warning to his newly pressganged Cretan priests that if they do not behave well, they will find themselves having to answer to new bosses (page 49). It is hard to explain this without reference to the so-called First Sacred War of c. 594–584 BC, when control of Delphi was fought for by an alliance of northern Greek states (the Amphictrionic league).[8] That would suggest the Hymn was composed after 584 (and perhaps quite soon afterwards, since the reference would quickly lose its point); but its position very close to the end of the poem, its abruptness, and its lack of obvious connection with anything that has come before would all point to at least the possibility of interpolation. If a narrative about the founding of Delphi as a religious centre

8   On the other hand, Jenny Strauss Clay is confident both that the passage
     fully belongs in the hymn, and that it has no reference to the First Sacred
     War, which 'never had any bearing on the interpretation of the hymn':
     her argument is made strongly, but there is not enough evidence in this
     whole area to guarantee its strength. She is right, though, to resist the
     incursions of (sometimes very uncertain) history into the field of literary
     interpretation: 'The question a classicist initially asks of a text is not what
     does it mean, but when was it composed and by whom. In dealing with
     anonymous texts of unknown date, these questions become the focus of
     inquiry. Any passage that can be construed to contain a contemporary
     allusion or to betray the author's circumstances or prejudices is wrenched
     from its context' (*The Politics of Olympus: Form and Meaning in the Major
     Homeric Hymns* second ed. London: Bristol Classical Press, 2006), 88.

was already in circulation and performance by the early sixth century, the events of the First Sacred War would be likely to prompt some kind of update of the story. Another potentially indicative element of the 'Pythian' narrative is its account of Apollo's slaying of the serpent, since this looks likely to be connected to the celebration of the same event which was part of the Pythian games: the first winner of this musical contest was recorded in 586 BC. Again, however, interpolation must be a possibility. The building of Apollo's temple (page 37), which goes so far as to give names for the builders, may possibly relate to something archaeologically datable, since the first stone-built temple remains at Delphi go back to the second half of the seventh century BC; the poem shows no signs of this being a building lost to the past and, since the temple itself burned down in 548 BC, it seems likely that the Hymn's account is from before that date, and possibly well before it. Here, where the action is properly at the centre of the Hymn's narrative, interpolation seems unlikely.

The 'Delian' narrative is also hard to date. The ancient references (cited above) tend to support an early date; the activities of Polycrates, on the other hand, point towards at least a performance of the Hymn late in the sixth century. But a Samos-sponsored performance would have been a revival, even if Cynaethus was adding material of his own; and there are strong suggestions that Ionians were gathering at Delos for Apollo's worship as early as the beginning of the eighth century BC. The festival described in the poem could have been one taking place at any time between then and the time of Polycrates. The festival certainly occasioned poetry from an early stage: Pausanias mentions a commissioned piece for the Messenians by the poet Eumelus of Corinth, who was active in the mid-sixth century BC, and names the commissioning king as Phintas, before the First Messenian War against Sparta (743 BC).[9] Material relating to Apollo's birth must have been central

---

9   Pausanias, *Description of Greece* 4.4.1.

to poetry such as this, and there seems no particular reason to think that the Hymn is breaking new ground in this respect. It should perhaps be added that there is no necessary reason why the poem – in its 'Delian' part or indeed as a whole – should have been composed specifically for recitation at Delos: both the Delian festival and the Pythian oracle were sufficiently famous to be readily imagined by audiences in many different Greek locations (the *Iliad*, after all, did not depend on being performed near Troy).

Venerable as it is, the question of the 'unity' of the Hymn is not perhaps all that important when it comes to literary evaluation of the poem itself. The Hymn was – as far as anyone can tell – understood and transmitted a single literary entity until the attentions of Ruhnken in the eighteenth century: it is one piece, just like all the other hymns, in all of the surviving manuscripts and these, though none of them is older than the fourteenth century, almost certainly reflect an editorial tradition that stretches back into the ancient world. Division of the Hymn is, then, an act of modern editorial ingenuity: and it *is* ingenious, in many of its versions. Detailed analysis of diction has generated 'evidence' that the two parts of the Hymn are distinct, for example: but in fact this is very far from conclusive, and not without its internal contradictions. In this respect, the sample-size, and the nature of the sample itself, compromise any clear-cut conclusions: not only do we not possess enough datable text with which to compare the Hymn, but the possibility that different aspects of its narrative might generate differing registers of poetic diction lies beyond the scope of the analysis. The more detailed such examinations become, the more they begin to resemble the kinds of 'scientific' analysis carried out on the texts of Shakespeare over the years, which have in practice either yielded very little in the way of hard information, or suggested a number of implausible (and critically unsustainable) conclusions on matters of authorship and attribution. Of course, no 'scientific' enquiries on matters like these are without their critical impulses: research methods are in general driven by the kinds of questions being asked, and those questions come about only through prior convictions concerning the text. In the case of the Hymn, a readerly doubt about unity looked for stylistic and philological proof, and found enough to feel (to some degree) confirmed.

Yet the feeling that there is something wrong with the Hymn in terms of what we recognize as literary 'unity' is fundamentally a literary judgement like any other; and like all such judgements, it can be argued against. A lot of the sources of critical dissatisfaction have been, in fact, relatively naïve in their levels of sophistication: there is, for a start, the apparent conviction that place-names being used in a poem indicate only that the poem must relate to those places in a very direct way – essentially, by being performed there, so that a single piece containing material relating to places as far apart as Delphi and the island of Delos must be some kind of artificial splicing. Then there is the recurrent belief amongst advanced philologists and textual scholars that a poem such as the Hymn, because it emerges from the culture of oral poetry, must be the *record* of a performance, rather than what we understand generally by a finished text. Thus, the poet is held to make mistakes, unwittingly contradict himself, or forget about things as he goes along. The obvious point here needs to be made: the Hymn was preserved as a poem and not as primitive footage of an event; it was written down, and spent the centuries as a written text. It is not, then, to be regarded as some kind of straight-from-the-horse's-mouth evidence of the incompetence of a muddled post-Homeric bard. If the philological expertise of scholars from the late eighteenth century to the present is impressive – and it undoubtedly is – we should remember that the competence of the ancient authors and audiences in their own language probably exceeded it in all the ways that matter for literary composition and appreciation. Whatever else it is, the Hymn to Apollo is not a botched job that requires low marks from the examiners.[10]

10 See e.g. Janko op. cit., 100: 'It is to be hoped that whoever lopped them [the two parts of the Hymn] into a unity may have no more disciples'.

There is no need, then, to make a case for the Hymn's compositional unity, since the case against this has never been satisfactorily framed. Sometimes, the calls to 'defend' the Hymn's unity, in their tone as well as their techniques, resemble the demands made by partisans of Bacon (or others) that 'Stratfordians' should make good and defend something which is not, in fact, on trial. Debates about the Hymn to Apollo are less extreme than this, of course, as well as being much better informed. Without conceding the point that the Hymn's unity if *prima facie* in need of any defence, it is still worth admiring the skill and subtlety with which the poem balances its two major centres of narrative concentration, Delos and Delphi. These two phases of the Hymn can be seen to mirror each other structurally: Leto's search for an accommodating birthplace for the god is reproduced in a different key when Apollo travels in search of the right place for his major oracle, and then again when the Cretan sailors make their journey around the Peloponnese; the festival at Delos is re-figured in the building of the Pythian temple; and the breaking of deadlock with the fetching of Eilytheia from Olympus is repeated in Apollo's killing of the destructive serpent Pytho (both obstacles to his progress having been provided by the jealous Hera). Motifs repeat at both major and minor levels throughout the poem.[11] As a whole, the Hymn is a celebration of Apollo by way of two narratives, each of which delivers a complex account that is probably intended to go somewhat beyond narrative as such: the coming into being of a divinity who is so new that he has the potential to make the existing order of things fearful, and the bringing into existence of a source of oracular authority so powerful that it can transcend the politics of localized strength and influence. Apollo is capable of great violence, and this is perhaps the point of his dealings with the river-spirit Telephousa;

11 See the concise and powerful account of the Hymn's thematic arrangements given by Nicholas Richardson in his *Three Homeric Hymns: To Apollo, Hermes, and Aphrodite* (Cambridge: Cambridge University Press, 2010), 9–13.

it is demonstrated at length, too, in his killing of Pytho. In the poem's opening scene, when Apollo enters Olympus, it is with the threat of engaging in a new war amongst, and against, the gods; he is made safer by the figure of Leto, his mother, and this leads naturally to the birth narrative itself. The question of the god's birth is linked with that of his role in the world, and the first thing he says on Delos is an announcement of the three symbols of that role: 'The bent bow and lyre ... I here declare | my symbols; and to humans everywhere | I shall pronounce the will of Zeus the King' (page 30). The Hymn, accordingly, addresses Apollo's destructive strength (the bow – which is the focus of that arresting opening entrance to Olympus also), his gift of music (with its apogee in the *panegyris* of the Greeks on Delos, and the wonderfully performing choir there), and his foundation of the key oracle of Zeus's will on earth (at Delphi).

In its narrative style, the poem seems closer to various points in Homeric epic than the other major hymns. In this respect, it is less subtle (or at least less sophisticated) than the Hymn to Demeter, less snappy and pointed than the storytelling of the Hymn to Hermes, and less concentrated and artful than the arrangements of material in the Hymn to Aphrodite. Nevertheless, it is a poem of powerful effects and sustained momentum, keeping throughout its seriousness of commitment to the god being honoured. Apollo was one of the most complex figures in the Greek pantheon, and the poem's religious commitment is accordingly a matter of the resolution, through both narrative and celebration, of a series of fairly involved tensions. The god's potential for destructive energy, so strong that it can be feared even by the other gods on Olympus, is neutralized, or put in abeyance: first by his mother, and subsequently by the accommodation of the Greek lands themselves. The personified Delos overcomes initial fear to become a beneficiary of the new god; and the mainland Pythos (Delphi) offers an oracular home, again greatly to its own eventual benefit. In the process, the Hymn revolves around major geographical inventories. As *bravura* performances on the poet's part, these are immediately impressive (and reminiscent, in their way, of the extraordinary catalogue that dominates the second book of the *Iliad*). But in the larger scheme of the whole Hymn, they are absolutely crucial, creating as they do a depth of field that insists upon Apollo as a god for all of Greece. It is, naturally, because of this universality that delegations from so many Greek states visit Delos for the *panegyris*; and Delphi is also a central point in Greece's sense of divine geography. The journeys of Leto and Apollo in the Hymn, and that of the Cretans who will become the Delphic priesthood, give the poem a centre of gravity in panhellenism. Just as by the time of the Hymn's likely composition the poetry of Homer was being received and valued as belonging to all Greece, so the events in the poem are made parts of a panhellenic imagination that must have seemed profoundly Homeric from the beginning. Hence, perhaps, the incorporation in the Hymn of a first-person voice belonging to the 'Homeric' poet himself, which is pitched so as to accord with the already strong traditions of Homer being a blind bard who comes from the island of Chios, but belongs to the whole of Greece.

In translating this long poem, I have used a seven-line rhymed stanza throughout. I have not, however, kept the rhyming patterns consistent from beginning to end. In the portion of the Hymn dealing with Apollo's birth on Delos and the celebration of the *panegyris* there, I have used a configuration of *abababb*, while the story of Apollo's founding of his oracle is in the rhyme royal stanza of *ababbcc*; for the part of the poem which deals with the Hera's creation of Typhaon and Apollo's slaying of Pytho, I have adopted a rhyme-scheme of *abaabcc*. Whatever suspicions of disunity in the text this may arouse, I can confirm that the translator is the same person throughout.

page 23: he strides through [...] when he draws | his bow is stronger still] This very dramatic opening scene makes a point of Apollo's great power as something potentially threatening to the gods

on Olympus. There are near-eastern parallels for this, as there
are for the aspect of Apollo as an archer-god. The Canaanite
Resheph (Rešef) was identified with Apollo in Idalion on
Cyprus (where Greek presence dates from the mid-sixth
century BC, and where there was a sanctuary of Apollo-Rešef):
like Apollo, this god is also identified with war and pestilence.
Such deities cause alarm at assemblies of fellow gods in Hittite
and Babylonian stories, and there is a suggestive parallel to
the Hymn in the Sumerian hymn to Ninurta, *An-gim* (dating
from no later than 1000 BC, but copied with translation into
neo-Assyrian and neo-Bablyonian in later times). Here, in
Martin West's summary, the god's entrance bears some striking
resemblances to the opening of the Greek hymn:

> As Nimurta drives furiously towards Enlil's city of Nippur, raging
> like a thunderstorm, his chariot draped with defeated monsters,
> Enlil's page comes out and begs him not to strike terror into the
> hearts of his father and the gods assembled in the council chamber,
> but to accept honour and recognition for his mighty deeds. Ninurta
> lays aside his whip and goad, leans his club against them, and
> enters Enlil's mansion with his booty. The gods, deeply impressed,
> bow down before him, his mother Ninlil soothes him with praise,
> and his chariot and fighting equipment are received into Enlil's
> temple. (M.L. West, *The East Face of Helicon: West Asiatic Elements
> in Greek Poetry and Myth* (Oxford: Oxford University Press, 1997),
> 355.)

Apollo's destructive potential is always present when he comes
into contact with mortals. This has its most arresting expression
at the beginning of the *Iliad*, where the god responds to the
pleas of his priest Chryses for vengeance on the Greek army:

> He spoke the prayer; Phoebus Apollo heard him,
> and left Olympus' peaks then with his heart
> all anger, with his bow and the ornate quiver
> slung on his back, where they rattled together
> as the god rushed on in fury, coming down

like night; but still more dreadful was the sound
his bow of silver made once he sat above
the ships, starting to open fire: at first
he hit the camp-mules and the running dogs,
and then it was men he shot at, and struck
with his bitter arrows: soon everywhere
fires jostled for the burning of the dead.　　(*Iliad* 1:43–52)

Apollo was often represented with his bow in art, but it is as well
to remember that this bow was not just there for decoration; and
the Hymn's opening scene shows an appreciation of the god's
capacity for harm. His disarming is important from the point
of view of the other gods, but it is also important for a human
understanding of his propitiation: for it is Apollo's mother,
Leto, who puts the bow away safely, thus proving that Apollo's
violence can be put by; and in honouring his mother, through
venerating his birthplace on Delos, this act of disarming may
be perpetually repeated.

Leto ... pause | to take our worship and our mute applause] The
translation here is an expanded paraphrase of a condensed (and
important) line in the Greek, which hinges on the verb *chairë* (a
word that may mean 'welcome' and 'rejoice' as well as 'farewell',
and can also serve as a more general verb of salutation): '*Chairë*
O blessed Leto, for you bore glorious children'. The verb's
ambiguity is a significant part of the verse's literary effect, as it
will be later in the poem also, since it can introduce a closing as
well as an opening sequence: 'We first interpret it [as farewell],
but as the passage progresses, we realize that it does not signal
the end of the composition and reinterpret it as a greeting'
(Jenny Clay, *The Politics of Olympus*, 32).

page 24: the mother too | of Artemis] The association of Apollo
and Artemis in worship is well-attested. In literary terms,
the most important point of comparison here is Hymn 27
(pp. 99–100), where another act of disarming is central. In
that poem, the setting is Delphi rather than Delos; but this

shows that Leto as the mother of Artemis and Apollo could
be perfectly legitimately praised in a Delphian setting as well
as the Delian one, so that the two sites are complementary in
literary myth, rather than incompatible or mutually exclusive.
The Hymn to Apollo, as a whole, shows this on a much larger
scale.

Ortygia] The name, which means 'quail island', occurs twice
in the *Odyssey* (5:123, 15:406); it is also an honorific title of
Artemis in Sophocles' *Trachiniae* (213). It may be Delos'
neighbouring island, Rheneia.

under a palm tree] Palms were relatively rare in Greece and the
islands. The palm on Delos was a celebrated devotional feature
of the island.

page 25: *Past all the people [...] to all these places*] This is the first of
the Hymn's major geographical catalogues. It gives an itinerary
for Leto's search for a place willing to be the scene of Apollo's
birth; but the poetry is composed in such a way as to keep this
purpose concealed until the catalogue's completion: initially,
the list seems to be an enlargement upon the compliment to
the god of 'now you rule all mankind'. The places listed do in
fact often have associations with Apollo, but all of them (we
deduce at the end) were either unsuitable or unwilling sites for
his coming into the world. Leto's journey around the Aegean
and Greece is also an important sign, early in the poem, that
an extensive and *virtuoso* awareness of a variety of places on
the part of the poet is to be taken as an appropriate artistic
means of registering the Panhellenic nature of the god himself.
For reflections on the importance of this kind of catalogue in
renaissance English poetry, from Marlowe to Milton by way of
George Chapman's translation of the Hymn, see Introduction,
page xxii. In the annotations below, I have identified only the
less well-known points of Leto's journey.

Aegae] The location of this place has always been uncertain, though the name is not uncommon. There is often some connection to Poseidon, as with one likely candidate mentioned by Hesychius of Alexandria (fifth century AD), an island off the north of Euboea.

Iresiae] Pliny in the *Natural History* (4.23) mentions an island called Irrhesia on the Thermaic Gulf in the NW Aegean.

Peparethos] An island to the north east of Euboea. (In the translation, I have shifted this island a little further down in the order of places: the Greek text has it in the same line as Aegae and Iresiae.)

Macar] In the Greek text, Macar the Aeolian: Macar (or Macareus), whose name means 'the blessed', was a legendary first colonizer of Lesbos (itself sometimes referred to as 'Macaria' after him). In the *Iliad*, Achilles mentions Macar to King Priam in connection with Lesbos (*Iliad* 24: 544).

Phoceia, Autocanē] Phoceia was the most northern Ionian city on the coast of Anatolia; Autocanē a mountain range that faces the southern coast of Lesbos. A number of coins survive with the name, including some with the head of Apollo.

steep Aisagea, then Claros] The Greek text has these two places in the opposite order. Claros on the Anatolian coast had a sanctuary of Apollo and Artemis (see notes to Hymn 9); its epithet here, *aiglēessa* (which I have rendered as 'luminous') is used in Homer, but only of Olympus. Aisagea is probably nearby; the name's only other occurrence is in the work of Nicander of Colophon (near Claros) in the second century BC, whose *Theriaca* (Dangerous Animals) includes a line on 'the strong foreland of Aisagea' (212).

Mycale] A mountain on the west coast of Anatolia, facing the island of Samos. The Hymn's phrase here repeats exactly that of *Iliad* 2: 869, 'the steep crests of Mycale'.

Cos and Miletus … the Meropes] Cos was supposed to be the island home of a people called the Meropes, whose name somehow becomes a Homeric epithet for men in general (its meaning unknown, despite strained attempts to make it signify 'voice-dividing'). Miletus was a city much associated with the worship of Apollo: there is evidence for a temple of Apollo Delphinios from the fifth century BC, and it was the starting point for the annual procession to nearby Didyma, an important oracular site.

Cnidos] This city, on the mainland to the south of Miletus, also had significant Apolline religious links.

Carpathos] Island in the southwestern Aegean, where there was a temple of Apollo.

Naxos and Paros] Coming closer now to Delos, these islands were also sites of devotion to Apollo.

Rhenaia] This is the western neighbour of Delos, which Polycrates dedicated to Delian Apollo in the late sixth century BC.

page 27: *this Apollo will turn out wild*] Delos here uses a very strong term, along with an intensifier, *lien … atasthalon*, to describe Apollo's rumoured character. With regard to the adjective *atasthalos*, 'No single English term', as Clay puts it, 'can convey the full range of this Greek word', and "overbearing,' 'violent,' 'reckless,' or 'lawless' offer only partial translations for this highly charged term' (Clay, 36).

Leto … swore] Leto's oath secures Delos as a place of Apolline worship and pilgrimage; what it does not do is bind anyone to making the island an oracular site. In fact, though, Delos has asked for just this. The omission is pointed (and there is little evidence for any oracular shrine to Apollo on Delos in the likely period of the poem's composition); it also quietly lays the groundwork for the importance of Delphi later on in the Hymn.

page 28: *Eileithyia*] This goddess may be more familiar in her Roman form of Lucina (as employed by George Chapman in his translation of the Hymn). This goddess of childbirth is thought to have Minoan origins, and her name probably comes from somewhere other than Greece, but in both Homer and Hesiod she is daughter of Hera. On Delos, she seems to have had both a temple and an annual festival.

page 29: *paired* | *like rock doves*] The line in Greek repeats almost word for word one in Homer, where the goddesses Hera and Athene 'both moved with steps like timorous doves' (*Iliad* 5: 778).

Apollo's birth] Throughout this account, the Greek verbs shift between the third- and second-person. This makes for slightly confusing English; but the translation retains it, partly because it is impossible to know that this was not intended to be tonally significant in the Greek. It is certainly the case that frequent switches between 'he' and 'you' establish a special register in which narrative relation and religious address merge into, or perhaps continually shadow, one another.

page 30: *Where the Ionians in thousands come* | *together*] This account of the festivals in honour of Apollo on Delos must have a good deal of historical foundation. There was a religious link with Delos from at least the time of Homer. In the *Odyssey*, Odysseus himself mentions a visit he made to the island, including the plam tree which became significant in Apollo's birth-cult, and which plays a role in the Hymn:

> On Delos once I did see one such thing,
> when by Apollo's altar I saw spring
> up the delicate young shoot of a palm

(for that was another place to which I came,
with many a good man following behind,
on the long road where I was doomed to find
so many woes): and then, in just that way,
the sight made my senses all swim and sway
at once, for never before did I see
growing up from the earth any like tree.   (*Odyssey* 6:162–167)

The Ionian delegations' 'long trailing cloaks' were often
mentioned in accounts of these peoples. Boxers, dancers, and
ritual singing are a unique combination of festival activities in
the surviving literature; but they are not far, in spirit at least,
from Homeric events such as Odysseus' visit to the Phaeacians
(*Odyssey* 8), where there are athletic contests, dancing, and
singing. The extravagance of the Hymn's praise of the Ionians
may perhaps indicate that an original audience would have had
many of them in its number.

page 31: *the great choir | of girls from Delos*] The Delian choir is
evidently well-known, and by the fifth century BC was widely
active: the poet Cratinus (mid-late fifth century BC) staged
a comic play with the title *Deliades*, possibly with reference
to these singers. The choir probably performs some kind of
choral lyric (which, though it is not said so here, would have
also involved dancing). The account here conforms to a pattern
which may cast some light on the kinds of contexts in which
the Hymn itself (and the other Homeric Hymns) could belong.
First, there is specific praise of a deity (here, the standard Delian
trio), then there are stories of 'women and men long gone, and
ancient lore': this sounds rather closer to epic narrative than
choral lyric, but such subjects were also covered in lyric modes.

how to imitate | exactly voices] This aspect of the performance
raises some puzzling issues. The concept which lies behind the
Greek verb used here is *mimēsis* (roughly, imitation): but why
would a girls' choir busy itself with imitating the voices of its
audience? For *AHS*, this is a problem easily solved, since 'the

accomplishment ascribed to [the choir] is that of singing in dialect' (225). But the Hymn actually seems to go further than this: the verb *phtheggesthe*, when the poem says that anyone might recognize their own sound being imitated, is to do with speaking, and not singing. Another word, translated here as 'the babble they create', is the evocative *bambaliastun*: but it is worth bearing in mind that this is in fact a marginal correction in only three of the medieval manuscripts, and the majority of the manuscripts transmit at this point the word *krembaliastun*, which would probably be a kind of percussive instrument, rather like metallic castanets. The word is very rare, but this is no reason why it should not be correct (and the copiers of manuscripts would be less likely to have changed the word for 'babble' to this one than the other way around). This still leaves, however, the problem of imitation. It may be the case that an ability to speak in different (though of course neighbouring) Greek dialects was an admired and remarkable skill.

a blind man | who lives on Chios] At this point, the author of the Hymn seems to step forward and identify himself; the identification, moreover, is with the figure of Homer as traditionally conceived – a blind bard from the island of Chios. Of course, this traditional image of Homer derives in fact from these lines in the Hymn (as may be seen from the passage in Thucydides discussed above, page 209).

and I will spread your fame] The Greek here goes into the first person plural, speaking of how 'we will carry your reputation as we journey': this might be considered a tell-tale sign of a guild of Homeridae rather than the single poet who has only just announced himself. When the first person instantly returns, it is to say that 'I will not cease from my singing of hymns'. This has been taken to show that the supposedly separate 'Delian' segment of the Hymn is here drawing to a close; but it is not really part of a closing formula (the poet is not addressing the god here, for one thing), and the words could indeed be taken more naturally as a sign that the narrator is about to resume the larger theme from which he has briefly departed – 'he makes a virtual apology for intercalating a personal episode into his proper theme', as *AHS* put it (227).

page 32: the god Ares ... gods when they dance and sing] This celebration of Apollo as a maker of music and leader of dance voices a fundamental aspect of the god's significance. The inclusion of Ares dancing alongside Artemis and the younger Hermes may seem unusual, given that he is the god of war; but this deity is also shown as being appreciative of music in Pindar's first Pythian Ode, where the 'Lyre of gold, belonging as of right | to Apollo and the Muses with jet-black hair' produces such an effect that 'Even strong Ares sets aside | his spears with sharpened points, and makes his heart | happy with sleep' (*Pythian* 1: 1–2, 11–13).

page 33: *Azan's daughter ... Leucippus*] Apollo woos Coronis (who became the mother of Asclepius) in rivalry with Ischys: a rather different account from that given here is included in Pindar's third Pythian Ode, where Coronis has already conceived a child by Apollo before her marriage to Ischys. On the discovery of what has happened, her angry family burn her alive, but her child is saved by the timely intervention of Apollo: 'He came, and with his first step the baby from the corpse | snatched up' (*Pythian* 3: 44–45). The Hymn's name for the father of Coronis, Azan, is something of a puzzle: in both the Hymn to Aphrodite and Hymn 16 (as well as Pindar) this is Phlegyas. Azan is associated with Arcadia (as is Ischys in Pindar) while Phlegyas was from Thessaly, but the Greek word meaning 'the daughter of Azan', *Adzantida*, is given in the M manuscript as *Atlantida*, 'the daughter of Atlas'. According to one fragment of Hesiod, Asclepius' mother was Arsinoe, a descendant of Atlas (Hesiod fr. 53b. (Most)), so it is possible that the Hymn alludes to this rival genealogy. Phorbas the son of Triopas is mentioned in later literature as a lover of Apollo, though here he seems to be a rival suitor; the poet suggests a race between him and the god, which Apollo wins: the translation attempts to maintain some element of ambiguity about whether the god won the competition or the boy. Erytheus is otherwise unknown. The chariot-race against Triopas and Leucippus has no parallel outside this poem, but may again be associated with Apollo's career as a divine suitor: in Pausanias (*Description of Greece* 8.20.3) Leucippus is a suitor of Daphne.

how you travelled] This second geographical itinerary in the poem maps out Apollo's journey from Olympus across the north of Greece to reach Delphi. The places mentioned here tend to have associations with Apollo, though they do not correspond with any precision to e.g. the Amphictrionic League members, or the route taken every eight years by the representatives of Delphi coming from Tempe and its Apolline festival of the Septarion. The journey is clearly intended to parallel that of Leto in search of the god's birthplace; here, though, Apollo makes two significant stops on his progress, while Leto moves quickly through places until she reaches a deal with Delos. Leto's itinerary of repeated rejection is thus matched by one in which it is the god who does the rejecting.

Messapion] The proper name is not given in the Greek, but this mountain on the Boeotian coast is clearly intended.

page 34: the site of Thebes] This pause is important in registering the extreme antiquity of the mythic time in which the Hymn sets itself. Jenny Clay's account is persuasive:

> Traditionally, Thebes was considered one of the oldest cities in Greece, founded, according to legend, by Cadmus on orders from the Delphic oracle. The apparent digression in Thebes thus has a twofold function: it coordinates the divine narrative of the founding of Delphi with human history. The events recounted in the hymn take place in the remote past, not only early in the reign of Zeus, but also long ago in the earliest phases of human history. (Clay, 58)

Thebes did have a cult of Apollo Ismenius in historical times, but the Hymn (while still calling Thebes 'holy') discreetly insists on the priority of Delphi.

Onchestus] The detailed account of the cult of Poseidon at this site in Boeotia seems, at first sight, to be both a digression and indirect evidence for some first-hand knowledge of the place on the poet's part. Artistically, the *suggestion* of this kind of knowledge is important to the effect of a lengthy itinerary such as this – as important, perhaps, in the context of a performance on the relatively far away island of Delos as it would be in the much closer Delphi. The Hymn is the sole evidence for what goes on in this particular cult activity, and as such it has been variously interpreted. One significant aspect may be the mention of newly-broken horses here: Poseidon's strong divine connection with horses (one of his titles was Poseidon Hippios) is relevant, and may support an interpretation of the rite as one which symbolically makes apology to the god for the taming of his creatures. What seems to happen at Onchestus is that travellers must dismount from their vehicles, presumably to make sure that the horses are rested. Whether by accident or as a part of the rite, some driverless carriages carry on into the sacred grove itself, where they may crash: in this case, the vehicles themselves become the property of the god.

page 35: *Telphousa*] The location of this site is unknown, but it is referred to also in a fragment of Pindar quoted by Athenaeus (*Deipnosphistae* 2.15.41):

> Water as sweet as honey is,
> ambrosial water coming from
> Tilphōssa's lovely spring.

The spirit of the place, who engages in a negotiation with Apollo, is in a somewhat similar position to Delos when she is approached by Leto; here, however, she decides to send the god in another direction, by stressing the disadvantages of the place to which he has come. These disadvantages are principally those of threats to his sanctuary's peace and quiet – and they are not easy to reconcile with the bustling activity associated (in the Hymn itself, and elsewhere) with the business of Delphi. Talk of passing traffic does, however, pick up on the account just given of Onchestus. Telphousa manages to dissuade Apollo quite easily at this point, by suggesting the loneliness and peace and quiet offered by Crisa, a place which would have been understood as being in the general vicinity of Delphi.

page 37: the Phlegyae] These are the descendants of Phlegyas, son of Ares and the father of Ixion; they are mentioned briefly in the *Iliad* 13:302 as 'huge-hearted', and associated there with warmongering. Their bad reputation stems from a particular hostility to Apollo, who personally drove them from his shrine at Pytho; thereafter, they attacked those on the way to and from Delphi, before being finally wiped out by the god.

page 38: Trophonius and Agamenes] These are legendary first architects, to whom various famous ancient buildings were commonly attributed. One received version of the history of Apollo's sanctuary at Delphi had the pair as the fourth, and not the first, of its builders: according to Pindar and Pausanias, they built the first stone temple of Apollo, which had been preceded by a temple of bronze made by Hephaestus, one of beeswax and feathers, and an original building made simply of branches of bay. The pair are 'dear to the gods', having been granted (in a tradition recorded by Plutarch) by Apollo the privilege of dying in their sleep after a solid week of feasting.

A stream runs clear nearby] This is often identified with the spring Castalia.

the serpent Pytho] The monstrous serpent which guards Delphi here was the offspring of Gaia, the Earth. In being destroyed by the new god, Python may offer a symbolic expression of the passing of the Delphic site from the older, chthonic cult

to the Olympian dispensation. In a late account from the
second century AD, the Roman writer Hyginus gives a digest
of received version of stories about Python, and this locates the
monster as a protagonist in the persecution of Leto (Latona)
by Hera (Juno):

> Python, offspring of Terra, was a huge dragon who, before the time
> of Apollo, used to give oracular responses on Mount Parnassus.
> Death was fated to come to him from the offspring of Latona.
> At that time Jove lay with Latona, daughter of Polus. When Juno
> found this out, she decreed (?) that Latona should give birth at
> a place where the sun did not shine. When Python knew that
> Latona was pregnant by Jove, he followed her to kill her. But
> by order of Jove the wind Aquilo carried Latona away, and bore
> her to Neptune. He protected her, but in order not to make void
> Juno's decree, he took her to the island Ortygia, and covered the
> island with waves. When Python did not find her, he returned
> to Parnassus. But Neptune brought the island of Ortygia up to
> a higher position; it was later called the island of Delos. There
> Latona, clinging to an olive tree, bore Apollo and Diana, to whom
> Vulcan gave arrows as gifts. Four days after they were born, Apollo
> exacted vengeance for his mother. For he went to Parnassus and
> slew Python with his arrows. (Because of this deed he is called
> Pythian.) He put Python's bones in a cauldron, deposited them in
> his temple, and instituted funeral games for him which are called
> Pythian. (Hyginus, *Fabulae* 140, trans. Mary Grant)

This account demonstrates that Python played a role in the
larger story which links Delphi with Delos: the anger of Hera,
which connects the two parts of the story, is also the motif which
joins the Delian and Pythian phases of the Hymn, and just as
Hera attempts to keep Apollo from being born on Delos, she is
also behind the fostering of Typhaon by Pytho. Apollo's slaying
of this monstrous snake was a central element in his religious
celebration at Delphi. It was commemorated every eight years
at the festival of the Septarion, and was also the occasion of
the Pythian Games, thought to have been begun by Apollo

himself to mark the killing of the serpent. A flute-playing
contest also took place, in which there was a representation in
musical form of the god's battle and victory: this was first held
in 586 BC.

Typhaon] While it is natural that the Hymn should make
Apollo's encounter with Pytho a major part of its narrative,
what is more unusual is the apparent interpolation of another
lengthy serpent narrative, that of Typhaon, into the story. It is
tempting to see the poem as incorporating another work here,
and some scholars have been very suspicious of the Typhaon
episode on these grounds. But Hera's major role is perhaps the
key to the episode's prominence, since the Hymn (both here
and in the birth narrative earlier on) makes so much of the
hostility towards Apollo of Zeus's jealous consort. The Hymn
registers throughout a sense of threat from Hera towards
Apollo and what he comes to represent, and with her giving of
Typhaon to Pytho, she embarks indirectly on a campaign both
to harass humanity and to cut off any chance of an Apolline
oracle working for the good of mankind. Typhaon will have
existed as a character prior to the Hymn. The most important
account of this monster comes in Hesiod's *Theogony*, and differs
substantially from the Hymn's version: it was, nevertheless,
closer to being a standard account, and its version of events is
repeated in visual evidence such as a black-figure *hydriai* from
Calchis of c. 550 BC, on which Zeus attacks with thunderbolts
a winged Typhaon with snakes for limbs (Munich, Staatliche
Antikensaamlungen, inv. 596). In Hesiod, Typhaon (or
Typhaeos, as he is named there) is the last of the Titans, and
Zeus's battle with him marks the conclusion of the cosmic war
that sets in place the Olympian order. In the Hymn, the monster
is an instrument of Hera's purposes: these, too, may be read as
essentially anti-Olympian, though they come later in mythic
sequence. The difference between Hesiod and the Hymn does
not necessarily suggest that the Hymn's author was ignorant of
the *Theogony*; it could show that the poem is here attempting
to remind its audience of the cataclysmic interference with the

established order of things which Zeus first, and Apollo after him, fought to bring to an end. For the whole passage from the *Theogony*, see Appendix 2.

page 40: *Earth and broad heaven*] Hera's address here begins with *Gaia*, the Earth: the chthonic deity's priority at Delphi is being alluded to, and there is little doubt now that Hera intends to keep Delphi firmly apart from any Olympian control. Her invocation of the Titans has the same effect, but it is worth noting that she seems to credit them with giving birth both to the Olympians and to mankind. To give the Titans this role appears anomalous, and there are no close parallels for this in literature, where it is the Olympian gods who give being to mortals.

page 42: *Chimera*] According to Hesiod (*Theogony* 319–325), Chimera is the daughter of Typhaeos. The names means 'she-goat', and this monster is described by Homer, who tells how she was killed by Bellerophon:

> Of supernatural, not mortal, stock
> she was: the front of her a lion, then
> a serpent at the rear, and in between
> a she-goat: out she breathed with awful
> force of raging flames. And Bellerophon
> killed her, obedient to the gods' commands.   (*Iliad* 6: 180–183)

Pytho, a rotten pun] The Greek verb *puthesthai* means 'to rot', and Apollo here makes the most of this coincidence of name and fate for the monster.

the sly piece of deception] Having dealt with Pytho, Apollo turns his attention back to the nymph Telphousa, by whose arguments earlier on he had been swayed. He takes revenge by means of covering her stream with rocks, then setting up his own cult over what remains. That this takes place before Apollo sets up Delphi as a going concern may be an indication that the new God's first task is to punish deception: Telphousa's ability to talk Apollo out of founding his oracle by her stream can be seen to be a version in bad faith of the island of Delos's negotiations in good faith, and just as Delos is rewarded, so Telphousa must be punished.

a title alongside yours … the name | Telphousios] *Telphousios* is a very rare title, attested only twice: in Strabo (first century BC) there is a reference to 'the temple of Apollo Telphousios' (*Geography* 9.2.27), and in the *Alexandra* of pseudo-Lycophron (early second century BC) Apollo is given the name 'Telphousios' (562).

page 43: Cnossos, King Midas' city on Crete] The author of the Hymn might have known of Minos and Crete simply from Homer, where Cnossos is 'the great city, where at nine | years old Minos became king and the close | confidant of Zeus himself' (*Odyssey* 19: 178–9). But there do seem to have been links between Delphi and Crete, and it was on Crete that the cult of Apollo Delphinios had many of its sites (there was even a month of the year which was on Crete known as Delphinios), and Cretans plainly had early connections with Delphi itself: in Pindar, there is a detailed reference to 'the statue carved from a single block | of wood which in a shrine | on Parnassus they put up, | the Cretans with their bows' (*Pythian* 5, 40–42). The valley below the site of Apollo's temple at Delphi, Crisa, was also thought to be linked etymologically to Crete. There is, however, no particular historical evidence for there having been a line of Cretans forming the Delphic priesthood.

when he shakes the sweet laurel] This would appear to be an allusion to some form of divination by tree (for which parallels exist in other Greek oracular cults, such as that of Zeus at Dodona). Evidence for this is scanty, but an ancient annotator of Aristophanes' *Ploutos* reports how 'they say that close by the tripod [of Apollo] there stood a laurel tree which the Pythia would shake to provide oracular divination'. There are later accounts of the Pythia (the serving priestess of Apollo) chewing laurel leaves, and of laurel leaves being burnt in oracular ceremony.

page 44: with Cape Malea ... to Crisa] This is the third major topographical list in the poem, coming (like the other two) at the beginning of a distinct – and now the final – phase of the narrative. Just as the first list began with Crete ('Past all the people that there are in Crete' (page 25)), so here the sailors set off from the same island, this time ending up by sailing around the Peloponnese. Between them, the Hymn's three voyages add up to a fairly comprehensive journey through the waters of the Greek world.

Taenarum] This place, with its flocks of sheep sacred to Helios, recalls the Island of the Sun in the *Odyssey*, and the adjective used for Helios, *terpsimbrotou* (delighting man's heart), is exactly repeated from *Odyssey* 12:269 and 12:274 (I have not translated the word here). Flocks sacred to gods include the cattle and sheep of Helios at Thrinicia in *Odyssey* 11:104–9, but there were also flocks dedicated to Apollo in Epirus (Herodotus, *Histories* 9.93). There is evidence of an early settlement at Cape Tynaerum on the southern Peloponnesian coast.

Arenē ... Crisa] Arene is mentioned twice in the *Iliad*, and is thought to be Samicon on the eastern coast of the Peloponnese. Thryon and Aipy occur here in a line repeated exactly from *Iliad* 2:592: Thryon is probably Thryoessa from *Iliad* 11: 711–712 ('There is a city on a rugged hill, | Thryoessa, far off by the Alpheios, | down towards Pylos in its sands'), and Strabo identified this as Epitalion in Elis; Aipy is unidentified. Chalcis and Crounoi (a river and a spring, respectively) appear together (though in reverse order) at *Odyssey* 15:295; Dyme is first heard of here in the Hymn: it is a town well up the coast to the north, in Achaea. The Epians is the term given to inhabitants of Elis in Homer. Pheia is a town in Elis, though in fact it lies to the south of the places just named in the poem: this should not rule it out, though, since strict geographical accuracy here is probably neither possible nor called for. With Ithaca, the islands begin to come into view (they are visible from points on the coast): Doulichion's identity is uncertain, but it may well be Leucas (Lefkada); Samē is Cephallenia, lying to the south; and further south again is Zacynthus. The Cretans are propelled towards their landfall at Crisa through the Gulf of Corinth.

page 45: *Apollo shot away | in a sprinkle of sparks*] This is the point at which the god makes his divinity apparent, and it may be compared to moments of divine self-revelation in e.g. the Hymn to Demeter or the Hymn to Aphrodite. As in those narratives, it is a prelude to the god's establishing his or her purpose on earth in explicit terms. There is a similarity, also, to Homer's description of Athene coming down from Olympus. Homer's word *spintheres* (flashing sparks), which occurs here only, is picked up by the Hymn's *spintharides*:

> In just the way that Cronos' wily son
> sends a star down for sailors or the great
> host of an army as a certain sign,
> bright with the sprinkling of many sparks,
> just like that Pallas Athene shot to earth
> and rushed into the midst of things.   (*Iliad* 4: 75–79)

a young man, whose long hair fell] This human form which Apollo adopts is reminiscent of the many *kouros* sculptures of the god from the archaic period.

page 47: *the name Delpheios*] In these lines, Apollo assumes the third of his titles in the Hymn: after Pythios and Telphousios, he is now established as Apollo Delphinios. Just as the other two titles have been explained by narratives (the slaying of the serpent and the stopping of the stream), so this one is given an explanation (the Greek genre of the *aition*) by story of the god's manifestation as a dolphin. Delphic coinage from the sixth century BC and later plays on the place's name-association by featuring dolphin images; but there were cults to Apollo Delphinios across the Greek world (including, notably, at sites on Crete).

page 48: *the Paean hymn*] this famous religious hymn to Apollo, with its refrain *Io Paian*, was closely associated with Delphi. In ancient tradition, it had its origins in Crete: even the metrical term of paeon (for a foot of one long and three short syllables) was a 'resolved' form of the foot called the cretic: this suggests that the paean had musical links back to Crete. This may be very ancient indeed: one of the tablets from Cnossos in the Linear B script has been shown to carry the title 'Paiwon'.

page 49: *but sir, how | are we to live*] The Hymn lays considerable emphasis on the new priests' (not unreasonable) question. Delphi was, indeed, a notoriously barren spot. Apollo's confident response relies on the audience's awareness that Delphi, as a result of its divine patronage, was to be anything but impoverished, and that its controlling priestly caste would be far from deprived. There is a dramatic contrast implicit here, between the stunned and bewildered sailors who are led up to the great temple and the affluence (and, perhaps, over-confidence) of their successors.

you must hold to my straight way] Apollo ends his address with words of warning to the priests. There has been speculation that these lines presume on an audience's awareness of the so-called First Sacred War, when control of Delphi passed from Crisa into the hands of a loose league of city states (the Amphitrionic League); but this cannot be proven (see above, page 215).

Notes to Hymn 4

The Hymn to Hermes, which at 580 lines of hexameter is the longest of the major narrative hymns, is also likely to be the youngest of them, dating probably from somewhere near the end of the sixth century BC.[1] The poem is often seen as more comic in nature than its companions, and it certainly contains strong elements of comedy in its story of the infant god's exploits; but it is far from being a simply comic addendum to the other more solemnly related Olympian narratives. The poem can be understood as an account of how Hermes came to take his place amongst the other gods, and also as an entertaining explanation, in its own narrative content and procedure, of this particular god's nature and powers.

Hermes was already a god in Mycenaean Greek culture, and so he ranks among the longer-established pantheon, but in the Hymn his status as a junior deity is at the heart of things. In particular, Hermes is junior to the god Apollo, and the Hymn tells the story of how a newborn Hermes makes an aggressive incursion on his older half-brother's territory. This is literal as well as figurative territory, for Hermes steals the cows which

---

1   Several scholars have treated at length the question of a date for the Hymn's composition. While earlier opinion put this in the seventh century BC, summarized in the judgement of *AHS*, more recent studies favour a later date: for Nicholas Richardson, 'There does not seem to be any compelling reason to date the hymn later than c. 500 BC' (*Three Homeric Hymns* (2010), p. 24), while M.L. West concludes that the poem 'must be the latest of the major Hymns', and that it 'contains too many words and expressions that are not paralleled before the fifth century' to make any earlier dating plausible (*Loeb*, p. 14). The recent specialist studies by Oliver Thomas and Athanassios Verglassos find the Hymn to be a late-sixth-century piece.

Apollo has been pasturing at Pieria, and this incident sparks off the action of all the rest of the poem, as Apollo attempts to retrieve his property, and Hermes uses the theft as an opening move in a campaign to secure his own special place amongst the other Olympians.

In fact, the Hymn is as much concerned with Apollo as with Hermes. There are several indications in the text that the author of the Hymn knows and alludes to the Hymn to Apollo, but the subject-matter itself in any case makes Apollo a central figure. The Olympian gods were seen generally as having each their own particular areas of concern, places and items of exclusive association, and marks of distinction. The word used for such things in poetry is the hard to translate *timai* (the standard English translation of 'honours' catches little of the concept's importance, and calls up unhelpful images of the holders chatting over tea at crowded Buckingham Palace receptions). As soon as the god is born in the Hymn to Apollo, he announces his *timai*:

> 'The bent bow and lyre',
> Phoebus Apollo said then as he breasted
> the last tight linen band, 'I here declare
> my symbols; and to humans everywhere
>
> I shall pronounce the will of Zeus the King.'
> (Hymn to Apollo 131–132, page 30)

Apollo's bow, and his function as the sole vehicle of divine prophecy for mortals, are central to both his artistic representation in art and his meaning in Greek religious practice. The extra item here is the lyre – again, an essential symbolic object in the representation of a god who was also the god of poetry and music – for which the Hymn's word is *kitharis*. When Hermes is born, his first noteworthy act is the killing of a passing tortoise to provide the means of creating a lyre of his own – in this case the *phōrmynx*, a different word for what is a very similar instrument.[2] As the poem's narrative continues, it is this lyre which proves to be pivotal in the infant god's strategy, and which he uses as a bargaining chip in his negotiations with Apollo. When Apollo accepts the gift of the lyre from Hermes, he allows him in return control of herds, including the herd of cattle which has been stolen, and a number of other *timai*. This transaction is given as a pointed contradiction of the version in the Hymn to Apollo, and is a good example of something more generally apparent in the Hymn to Hermes: the transgression of established boundaries by the new god in the process of achieving his own religious and cultic identity.

The narrative centre around which the whole of the Hymn's action is made to turn is Hermes' theft of Apollo's cattle. The motif of cattle theft is itself a very ancient one, and is common in mythology. There are numerous cattle raids in the material of the Indian Rig Veda, and the motif continues into important episodes in Homer (Nestor's account of a cattle raid in *Iliad* 9: 670–761, and the capture by Odysseus' men of the oxen of the god Helios in *Odyssey* 12: 340–366) as well as later myth and literature. The Irish *Táin Bó Cuailnge* (The Cattle-Raid of Cooley), dating from the seventh or eighth centuries AD, shows how long-lasting the tradition of the cattle-raid proved in mythic composition. The conception of Hermes as a cattle thief, then, has a clear place in the standard set of possibilities for stories of the exploits of gods and heroes. While Hermes is of course a full Olympian presence in Homer, his rise to that status from birth is not alluded to. In Hesiod, where Hermes' parentage is mentioned ('When she climbed into the holy bed | of Zeus, Atlas' daughter Maia | bore glorious Hermes, messenger | to the gods' (*Theogony* 938–939)), there may well have been an account of the young god's cattle theft. This

---

2 The differences between these forms of lyre do not seem to be germane to the poem: it uses the word *phórmynx* twice, but twice also *kitharis*; the verb for playing the lyre, *kitharizein*, is regularly employed as well. A third term for the instrument, *lyrē*, is also used twice in the Hymn.

would have been in the poem known as the *Great Ehoiai*, or the Catalogue of Women, which has been lost: the work is cited as a source for the cattle-theft by a commentator on Antoninus Liberalis (second century AD). The version in Antoninus may derive substantially, or only very partially, from anything that was in Hesiod's *Ehoiai*: there is no way of telling. Certainly, it differs a good deal from anything in the Hymn, although there are points of broad similarity.[3]

The lyric poet Alcaeus, whose poems were ordered so that his first book began (just as all but one of our manuscripts of the collection of the Homeric Hymns does) with a Hymn to Apollo, and was followed by a Hymn to Hermes, used the story of the infant cattle-theft. It is likely that this is before, rather than after, the Homeric Hymn, though there is no firm proof of the datings. All that survives of this poem is its opening stanza:[4]

Welcome, since my spirit desires to praise you,
ruler over Cyllenē, born on shining mountains
to Maia, who mingled in love with the son of Cronos,
master of all men.

Both Maia and the locale of Cyllenē are already in place here. If we possessed the rest of this poem, we would know how

---

3 In this version (Antoninus Liberalis, *Metamorphoses* 23), Hermes steals a herd of over a hundred (including one bull) from Apollo; Battus is a witness to the theft, and is paid by Hermes not to reveal what has happened. When he does so, having been put to the test by the god himself in disguise, Hermes punishes him by transforming him into a stone, and 'to this day that place is called the Peaks of Battus'. The version of the story in Ovid's *Metamorphoses* (2: 683–707), largely similar to this, also contains details which may link it back to the Hymn – Battus, for example, is referred to as a *senex* (an old man), possibly recalling the old farmer of Onchestus.

4 Alcaeus, S 264 in D.L. Page, *Supplementum Lyricis Graecis. Poetarum lyricorum Graecorum fragmenta quae recens innotuerunt* (Oxford: Clarendon Press, 1974). That this poem was fairly well known in the ancient world is suggested by its influence on Horaces's Ode 1.10.

developed was the story of the cattle-theft as inherited by whoever composed the Hymn: one witness, Pausanias, writes, 'that Apollo takes great pleasure in oxen is shown by Alcaeus in his hymn to Hermes, who writes how Hermes stole the cows of Apollo'.[5] One other fragment of information about this poem is that Alcaeus had Hermes make off also with the quiver of Apollo, the archer-god; this may explain the Hymn's inclusion (otherwise somewhat abrupt and puzzling) of Apollo's anxiety that his bow may yet be stolen by the young god (page 80).

After the likely date of the Hymn, the story of Hermes' cattle theft is the subject of a large fragment of a satyr-play by Sophocles, the *Ichneutai* (The Searchers). It is not possible to date the play with any certainty in Sophocles' career, so it may be as early as 468 BC or as late as 420 BC. Just as he had done when using the *Odyssey* in his play *Cyclops*, Sophocles uses the satyr-play format to improvise freely on a received Homeric narrative – in this case, the story contained in the Hymn (which in his time would probably have been considered simply as the work of Homer). The surviving part of this play does not include the ending, but it begins at the point where Hermes' theft has already taken place, and he has stashed the cattle away in a cave beneath Mount Cyllenē. Apollo appears, offering a reward for information, and is joined by Silenus and his satyrs, who make up a search party. The satyrs (who form the play's Chorus) spot the mysterious backward-facing prints, but noises from inside the cave startle both them and their leader. They themselves disturb the nymph of the mountain, Cyllenē, who comes to tell them that she is nursing the infant son of Zeus and Maia. She explains that the strange noises they have been hearing come from the lyre which this baby, Hermes, has made from the shell of a tortoise; but she denies outright that the god, being so young, could possibly have been the cattle-thief. Fragments suggest that Apollo entered next, presumably to reach an eventual arrangement with Hermes. The freedom

---

5 Pausanias, *Description of Greece* 7.20.4.

exercised by Sophocles in altering his source material is largely in keeping with what would be needed for dramatic purposes, not least the need for unity of time and place, and it seems extremely likely that the *Ichneutae* offers proof of the currency of the Hymn to Hermes for a fifth-century BC audience in Athens.

The Hymn itself, then, does not explore a particularly obscure corner of the mythology associated with the god Hermes. Where it does seem to be original, however, is in its dealings with Apollo – and perhaps even with the Hymn to Apollo. The broadly comic narrative is part of an engagement with the whole question of how Hermes and Apollo come to be reconciled as parts of the Olympian family. The tonal contrast which the poem presents to the more epic notes struck in the Hymn to Apollo is not just to do with its being composed a generation or more later, and may be a direct consequence of its establishment of a distinct religious space for Hermes to occupy. Such a space is characterized by the transgressive, the tricksy, and even the downright mendacious; instead of miracles, it features deceptions, sleights of hand, and confidence tricks; and its god is not one who either keeps faith or guarantees good order. Hermes is all of the things Apollo is not, and the Hymn's ambition is to relate the story of the reconciliation of these two gods into a lasting accord in such a way as to retain the full force of Hermes' disruptive energy, while making clear the terms of his ultimate accommodation. If the herd of cattle is at the centre of events, the other element of the story which is vital to the poet's design is the lyre – itself, of course, inescapably a symbol of poetry. One of the questions at issue between Apollo and Hermes is, essentially, that of who is to control the power of poetic utterance: a powerful truth-teller, or a subtle trickster?

In the end, the lyre passes to Apollo. The lyre's invention, all the same, is credited to Hermes, and the Hymn makes its construction the god's first prodigious deed. The fact that Hermes' fatal encounter with a passing tortoise is given this priority may be significant: the previous versions, insofar as we know about them, seem not to have mentioned the lyre at all, while subsequent versions (such as that of Sophocles) make the invention of the lyre follow, and not precede, the cattle-theft. In the Hymn to Hermes, considerable space is given to performances with the lyre (the god effectively begins to sing a Hymn to himself soon after creating the lyre (page 55), and again performs in front of Apollo a hymn enumerating the Olympian gods (page 76)). Apollo's delight at the music, and his desire to become the master of it, is the key to the whole bargain that Hermes wants to strike with him: in return for the lyre and all it can achieve, Hermes will receive something from Apollo in return. Not only does he get to keep the rustled cattle, but he becomes the god of herds of all kinds; he obtains Apollo's blessing, too, for the exercise of his unique skills in passing through solid boundaries, whether as thief in the night or as the conductor of dead souls to the next world. His status as divine messenger and go-between is confirmed, and he is left as an uncontested member of the Olympian pantheon – very much the desired outcome as outlined early in the poem to his cave-dwelling mother, Maia. The lyre does not achieve, perhaps, quite everything that Hermes desires, for despite his hints to Apollo when the terms of the bargain are being drawn up, he does not get a share in the elder god's monopoly on oracular prophetic power. Instead – maybe as something of a sop – Apollo tips Hermes off about the 'bee-maidens' who dwell somewhere at the foot of Parnassus, offering a measure of *niche* prophetic services. All in all, the deal is good enough for Hermes to accept.

The Hymn, then, describes a state of divine balance, or harmony, which is celebrated as part and parcel of the harmony offered to men by poetry and music. But this accord is also something newly arrived at, in some sense; and the poem is 'modern', at least insofar as it relates to the kind of poem represented by the Hymn to Apollo. There seems little doubt that the audience is allowed to see not only Hermes and

Apollo as contrasting figures (albeit figures whose differences are ultimately to be reconciled), but also as gods whose stories belong in, and enable, different modes of poetic celebration. In this respect, the Hymn's prevailing tone of comedy is one that contrasts with the epic narrative procedures of the Hymn to Apollo, just as its Hermes inhabits registers that are much more subtle than those belonging to Apollo, either in his own Hymn or in this. Unquestionably, Hermes is a god; but the Hymn to Hermes incorporates the uncertainty about just how central a god he will turn out to be. The capture of Apollo's cattle leads to the slaughter of two of them, and the attempt at a divine sacrifice; but this is slightly undercut by the infant god's appetite for the offered meat itself (something which, in the event, he manages to overcome). Hermes is a god who doesn't behave entirely like a god – for one thing, he is much too entertaining. On the other hand, Hermes is not to be taken as a representation of a more 'human' face of Greek divinity: on the contrary, the Hymn is emphatic on the degree to which he is not necessarily to be presumed upon as a friend to humanity – 'seldom bringing profit, he | goes through the night randomly, | tricking folk when they can't see' (page 83).

It is unwise, naturally, to venture far on the road of allegorical interpretation, for this or any other piece of Greek literature. Nevertheless, the Hymn to Hermes tempts a modern reader to see in it the celebration of a particular kind of poetry – the self-referring and self-sufficient, the slippery and transgressive, the ironic and verbally light-footed – which sets itself most against the expectations and demands of the world of solid sense. 'Hermetic' poetry is poetry that is always up to something not quite proper: outlandish, doubtless, but also beyond the grasp of sensible society and well-ordered imagination. As such, it is the kind of poetry whose meanings are always elusive, that are not just something else in relation to what is expected, but also something else again. However worthy of celebration all this may be, it is never an unmixed blessing, for Hermes gives us back far less than we bring to him – if, that is, he is not already engaged in the business of relieving us of what we think rightfully ours.

In this translation, I have turned the Hymn into a series of eighteen episodes, with each intended as (more or less) a poem in its own right. Obviously, no such division exists in the Greek text; nor is there variation in metre and form in the original. In the belief, though, that the Hymn is itself something of a 'Hermetic' performance, intensely aware of its own status as a work of poetic art, I have built in (I hope) a degree of significance to the changes and recapitulations of metrical forms throughout, rather as an ambitious poet in the contemporary world might carefully arrange and vary the forms and angles in her or his new poetry collection. Fanciful as such an approach may be, it strikes me as in keeping with the lightness of touch and complexity of intent that are so important to the Greek poem.

page 51: *Maia*] The name means 'mother' (as well as 'nurse'): Maia was a daughter of Atlas, and is thus one of the Pleiades. In a fragment of Simonides (sixth century BC):

> [...] and rightly Hermes gives the prize,
> master of contests, and son
> of Maia from the mountain
> with her long-lashed eyes:
> for Atlas was
> her father, and she was far
> and away the most beautiful
> of his seven daughters with violet hair
> that people call the Pleiades in heaven.   (Simonides, fr. 555)

page 52: *herder of dreams*] Hermes was both *oneiropompos* (conductor of dreams) and *psychopompos* (conductor of souls). In the *Odyssey*, he receives the final libation before a night's sleep:

> Odysseus found leaders and councellors
> of the Phaecians there, all emptying

their drinking cups to Hermes, the far-seeing
killer of Argos; for it was their way
to pour him out the last wine of the day
when they were turning to their beds. (*Odyssey* 7: 136–8)

Homer's word for the Phaecian leaders, *hēgētoras*, is the same as
the Hymn's term for Hermes here (*hēgētor*).

the fourth day | in the month] According to Hesiod, both the
fourth and the seventh of the month were especially propitious
days: he explains the special nature of the seventh by reference
to the birth of Apollo, but does not say why the fourth is equally
important – perhaps a reference to Hermes' birth is silently
understood, or has been lost in the text's evolution (*Works and
Days* 769–771). Plutarch, in the *Moralia* (738F), confirms that
the fourth was generally a day on which to honour Hermes; in
Aristophanes' play *Ploutos* (*Wealth*), cakes are offered to the god
on that day (1126); and according to Hesychius (fifth century
AD), young men used to enjoy riotous parties on the fourth day
of the month.

page 53: his cradle] The Greek word here, *liknon*, is not found
earlier than here, but is related to a word in Homer meaning to
winnow (*Iliad* 5: 500 – 'of men at work winnowing'): a *liknon* is
a winnowing-fan, that is, a large basket, used to hold corn after
it had been threshed and winnowed (by being thrown against
the air). The use of this item as a cradle seems natural enough,
and the word is taken up in Sophocles' *Ichneutai*, very possibly
in allusion to the Hymn (269). The cradle/basket was also
evidently associated with Dionysus (who was then worshipped
as *Liknōtēs*), whose image wore the *liknon* on its head on these
occasions. In two surviving pieces of pottery (a black-figure
water-pot from c. 530 B.C., and a red-figure kylix from c.
490–480 BC), the infant Hermes is depicted in his *liknon*, with
his stolen cattle nearby. Later poets such as Callimachus and
Aratus (in probable allusion to the Hymn) mention Hermes
lying in his *liknon*, and ancient commentators on these writers

inform us that babies were sometimes put in a *liknon* in order to bring them good luck.

page 54: '*Better at home*'] This line occurs exactly in Hesiod's *Works and Days* (365); it may of course be a saying known both to Hesiod and the author of the Hymn. The context in Hesiod is one of safeguarding one's household goods:

> What's safely laid down in his house
> can cause a fellow little grief:
> it's better kept at home – for once
> out of doors, then the danger starts.
> To take what you need from the things
> you have already is the best;
> but to need what you haven't got
> is a great burden to the soul.   (*Works and Days* 361–364)

the seven strings] Essentially, Hermes is here inventing the kind of lyre which would have been more 'modern' than the four-stringed instruments that seem to have existed commonly before the seventh century, but which was still a venerable instrument by the time of the Hymn's likely composition.

page 55: *lads on a night out*] The reference here seems to be to improvised compositions sung in the setting of an all-male drinking party. There are hints in the Greek that these drunken songs might find themselves venturing into risky territory, possibly involving insult or personal abuse. There is a partial precedent in the *Odyssey*, when a still-undercover Odysseus addresses Eumaeus the swineherd:

> Listen, Eumaeus and Eumaeus' men,
> all of you, while I tell for you again
> a story that comes over boastfully;
> it is the drink, of course, that fuels me,
> befuddling drink, that makes a sensible
> man sing and giggle, unable to stand still,

and sometimes as he dances, he comes out
with things much better not spoken about.

(Odyssey 14: 462–466)

he sang of Zeus and Maia] In this, his first performance on the
lyre, Hermes sings what is basically a Hymn to Hermes, its
principal elements corresponding quite well with the standard
elements of at least the opening of a Homeric hymn.

page 56: *immortal prize | cattle*] The cattle are called 'immortal'
at this point because they are the property of a god: they can,
as events will show, in fact be killed. The Greek word here is
not the adjective used to describe the gods' own immortality
(*athanatoi*), but one which in Homer is generally used for
things belonging to the gods (*ambrotoi*).

he turned their footprints round] This stratagem doesn't, perhaps,
bear too much thinking about, even though the Hymn now
goes to some trouble to spell it out in detail. It is faithfully
enough preserved by Sophocles:

> Just look at that!
> The footprints are turned right around, by Jove,
> and they go backwards. Now the prints in front
> are facing to the rear, while some are tangled
> up, going two ways at once: what an odd
> muddle that was for whoever drove them!

(Ichneutai 117–123)

But Sophocles' play (in which irony and comedy are important)
is the last we hear of this rather pointless device: later versions
of the story, such as those of Apollodorus and Antoninus
Liberalis, attempt more plausible methods of misleading any
pursuit. Nevertheless, the technique in the Hymn has had its
adherents: *AHS* point out confidently that 'In the case of horses,
reversal of their shoes to avoid pursuit is found as far afield as
Serbia and Wales, and is frequent in Border literature' (292).

Perhaps, though, this ruse is literary rather than real: pursuers incompetent enough to be taken in by backward-facing (but still forward-progressing) prints must be unusual, even as far afield as Wales.

page 57: a pair of sandals] The English word happens to mirror the Greek one (*sandala*), but this is clearly an altogether exceptional kind of footwear. The term is not attested prior to the Hymn (and is therefore not in Homer), though the word *sambala* is in Sappho. Just as Hermes improvises a wholly new kind of shoe in this passage, so the Hymn comes up with an unusual word to describe the invention.

grassy Onchestus] Onchestus is in Boeotia, and has some (limited) geographical plausibility in the context of Hermes' present journey. However, the Hymn's choice of this as a place to set the encounter between Hermes and the old farmer (and later on between that same farmer and Apollo) is interesting. On the face of it, there is no particular need to name the location in the first place; but there may well be an allusion here to the Hymn to Apollo, where Onchestus plays a significant role (see page 232). Just six lines before the mention of Onchestus in that poem, there is a reference to Teumessos as 'grassy': the word used is the same as that used here, *lechepoiēn*. If this is an allusion, what is its purpose? One possible answer might be that the author of the Hymn wants his audience to be reminded (glancingly, and maybe just remotely) of the Hymn to Apollo in the context of a larger re-approaching of the older poem's themes and, in particular, its depiction of Apollo himself. Where in the Hymn to Apollo the god passes through Onchestus with clear purpose, in harmony with and without hindrance from the place's presiding deity (Poseidon), the poet of the Hymn to Hermes will bring to Onchestus a duped Apollo, angrily in pursuit of a thief who has got the better of him. Here, in the first of the Hymn's two Onchestus episodes, Hermes is the god fully in command and sure of himself, who gives direct (if faintly riddling) orders to the mortal who sees

him. His imperiousness and confidence, as well as his freedom
of movement, perhaps recall ironically the character and
abilities of Apollo in the older Hymn.

page 58: *Alpheios' streams*] The river Alpheios helps somewhat
to locate events here: *AHS* pin this down to the ford at
Thryon or Epitalion in Elis (a spot mentioned in *Iliad* 2: 592
as 'Thryon, the ford of the Alpheios'), thus allowing Hermes
to follow the river on to Triphylian Pylos. There may be all
kinds of reasons for the Hymn placing its action here, but it
may be worth remembering that the Alpheios was thought
to be a particularly complicated and resourceful river, which
would vanish from sight in one spot only to reappear again in
another. A strong sense of this can be gained from Pausanias
(8.54.3):

> It is known that the Alpheios differs from other rivers in
> exhibiting this natural peculiarity; it often disappears beneath
> the earth to reappear again. So flowing on from Phylake and
> the place called Symbola it sinks into the Tegean plain; rising at
> Asea, and mingling its stream with the Eurotas, it sinks again into
> the earth. Coming up at the place called by the Arcadians Pegai
> (Springs), and flowing past the land of Pisa and past Olympia,
> it falls into the sea above Kyllene, the port of Elis. Not even the
> Adriatic could check its flowing onwards, but passing through it,
> so large and stormy a sea, it shows in Ortygia, before Syracuse,
> that it is the Alpheios, and unites its water with Arethousa.

A river that disappears and reappears, and even goes under the
sea to emerge again in Sicily, is well-matched to the abilities, as
well as the immediate needs, of a god like Hermes.

page 59: *Hermes made himself the pioneer | of flame conjured from
little more than kindling*] The Hymn here uses the word *purēïa*,
'fire-sticks'. This alludes to creating fire by twirling a stick in
a base made from another piece of wood, and is the earliest
reference in Greek to the practice. The emphasis on Hermes as

a pioneer in this regard (which may include the use of a novel term) aligns him with Prometheus (to whom, much later, the fire-sticks were attributed (*Diodorus Siculus* 5.67.2)).

there they are still] This would appear to be a clear instance of 'aitiological' content – that is, the poetry providing an explanation (*aition*) for a place or physical feature which can still be inspected. It is possible that the reference is to rock-formations, possibly close to the Alpheios, which were shown as the petrified hides of the cows killed by Hermes; not inconceivably, there might have been a spot in which cultic entrepreneurs kept a pair of venerable hides on public display. In terms of the Hymn's narrative, however, this leaving out of the hides is a point at which the otherwise careful Hermes is failing to cover his tracks.

page 60: twelve of them] This division of the sacrifice into twelve equal portions is often taken to be an allusion to the cult of the Twelve Gods, a formalized cult practice to honour the major Olympian figures in one place. According to Thucydides, the Athenian archon Peisistratos the Younger established an altar to the Twelve Gods in the Agora in 522–1 BC, and some scholars who suspect the Hymn of having Athenian connections see this as a telling parallel to what Hermes does here. But there were other such altars in Greece around this time, including those in Olympia, where according to Pindar and Herodotus, Heracles was thought to have established six double-altars (to Zeus and Poseidon, Hera and Athena, Hermes and Apollo, Dionysus and the Charites, Artemis and Alpheios, and Cronos and Rhea). In view of the fact that Hermes is conducting his sacrifice somewhere by the banks of the Alpheios, which ran through Olympia, and the existence of an important Twelve Gods altar dedicated to Apollo and Hermes together there, some scholarly opinion sees the distinct possibility here of an explicit connection between the Hymn and Olympia.

the roasting smell ... | made glorious Hermes covet his own portion] The gods were believed never to partake of the cooked flesh offered to them: Hermes' hunger, and his temptation to eat some of this roasted meat, may be indications that his divinity at this point is not a condition to which he is properly habituated. He does not, in the event, commit an act which is beneath his dignity as a god – but the Hymn hints that this is a close-run thing. He goes on, having stored the sacrificial portions, to burn everything else. While this will in time offer Apollo another clue about his route, it could also be seen as an attempt by Hermes to get rid of the evidence of his potentially less than divine weakness. After committing the remains to his bonfire, and as he throws away his sandals, Hermes is for the first time in the Hymn referred to as a *daimōn* (god).

page 61: the dogs, who can often | sense these things] The Greek says simply, 'nor did the dogs bark'; but I have expanded this slightly, to reflect the belief in epic that dogs were sensitive to supernatural comings and goings. In the *Odyssey*, when Athene appears to Odysseus, Telemachus does not perceive her, but the dogs do:

> That gods appear to everyone alike
> is not true: but Odysseus could see
> her; and the dogs, who bark usually,
> saw her and hid at the far end of the yard,
> whining for fear.

(Odyssey 16: 161–3)

the autumn wind ... | in at the keyhole] The simile for Hermes' clandestine entry aligns him with the dreams which it was, in fact, one of his divine duties to convey. In *Odyssey* 4, a dream enters and leaves Penelope's bedroom 'by the keyhole' (802, 836). At the same time, the simile drives home the message of Hermes' innate abilities in burglary.

page 62: neither offering nor prayer | to our names] The obscurity of the family cave does not preclude Maia and her newborn son from being divine, but it does deprive them of the full benefits of their divinity.

page 63: Onchestus] How does Apollo know to come here? Although in search of his cattle, he has not yet seen their tracks. The Hymn is a poem, and not a documentary; but as a poem it is exploiting the contrast between Apollo in Onchestus in the Hymn to Apollo (see above) and Apollo having to wait politely while an elderly mortal takes his time in giving a comprehensible account of what he has seen. (The old farmer here is disobeying the instructions given to him by Hermes, but no punishment follows.) It is also worth noticing that the farmer may not be quite aware of Apollo's divinity (or else is being exceptionally obtuse), addressing him familiarly as 'my friend'. The god may be in disguise here, but we are given no information to that effect. Where encounters take place between gods and mortals elsewhere in the narrative hymns (as in the Hymn to Demeter), terms are much more formal.

orange eyes] The Greek here applies the adjective *charopoi* to the dogs: its meaning is uncertain, but may be in the region of 'wild- /fierce-eyed'. I have translated this into a colour instead.

page 64: quare ... hilt nor hair ... forenenst] The word 'quare' is common in the spoken English of Northern Ireland: although a form of 'queer', its force is more that of 'considerable', 'impressive', or 'sizeable'. 'Hilt nor hair', meaning 'nothing at all', is recorded in Scottish dictionaries of the early nineteenth century, and is current in Ulster Scots. 'Fornenst' (meaning 'Right opposite to, facing') was last spotted by the *OED* in the *Glasgow Herald* in 1864, but it remains current in rural Ulster.

page 66: ashes' coverage ... lightly buried] The simile here derives from life, of course, but may also be indebted to Homer. It bears comparison with the lines describing Odysseus' bedding material of leaves:

> He covered his body in the fallen leaves,
> the way a man out on some distant farm
> who has no other neighbour but himself
> beds in an ember under the grey turfs
> to keep a seed of fire going, so that
> he won't have to light it again from scratch;
> just in that way Odysseus hid deep
> in his pile of leaves.   (*Odyssey* 5: 487–491)

page 67: *small souls who never made their mark*] The Greek here threatens Hermes with becoming 'leader of people of little significance' (i.e. the souls of the dead). The phrase used (*oligoisi met' andrasin*) could be taken more literally as 'over little men', and some commentators interpret this as a specific reference to the souls of children (over whom a baby-sized Hermes might indeed reasonably preside). Hermes goes on, in fact, to assume the important function of *psychopompos*, the guide of the soul to Hades.

page 69: *a sharp* crip-crup ... *a huge sneeze*] The two signs delivered here by Hermes, first a fart, and then a sneeze, come as surprises to Apollo. Literally, the fart is described in mock-dignified periphrasis as 'an insolent servant of the belly, an unruly messenger'; a fart, like a sneeze, could be interpreted as an omen, though still retaining its comic effect. There is a momentous confirmatory sneeze-omen in the *Odyssey*, when Telemachus sneezes loudly as his mother Penelope mentions the possible return of Odysseus to Ithaca. This is taken both as significant and as comic:

> Telemachus suddenly made the house shake
> with an enormous sneeze just as she spoke.
> Penelope laughed at this: "Now, please, say
> to the stranger that he must make his way
> up here to me," she told Eumaeus, "for
> don't you see how my son this moment tore
> out a sneeze to confirm my very words?   (*Odyssey* 17: 541–545)

page 71: the scales of justice] This image is carried over from the *Iliad*, and is repeated here in an altogether lighter vein than in the epic poem. For Homer, the scales weigh up the weightiest matters of life and death:

> When the sun had reached the middle of the sky
> Zeus the father lifted his scales of gold:
> in them he placed two fates, and each grim death:
> one for those tamers of horses, the Trojans,
> and the other for the Greeks in their coats of brass.
> He took the scales in the middle, and raised them up:
> down for the Achaeans sank their day of doom.
>
> (*Iliad* 7: 68–72)

Apollo gave his speech] The court-like setting of Olympus here is matched by a forensic speech from Apollo. The extent to which his speech for the prosecution (and subsequently Hermes' speech in his own defence) may be felt to mirror legal realities has interested scholars who see here possibilities for dating the Hymn. In fact, although several rhetorical techniques here could be paralleled in developments in the fifth century BC, they can also be traced back to earlier poetry, including Homer. Having said this, it remains interesting that Apollo should behave at this point so like a professional prosecutor, and that Hermes, after him, should offer so confidently accomplished a defence speech.

page 73: I didn't … drive home his cattle] This is strictly speaking true, for Hermes has not actually brought the cows to his house (he uses the word *oikad'* here, meaning 'home'); in vase representations, in contrast to the poem, they can be seen standing nearby in the Cyllenian cave. However, Hermes is lying outright when he claims not to have crossed the threshold into the wide world.

page 74: this great oath] Again, Hermes twists the expected procedure, for the oath is not a swearing of innocence, but one not to pay Apollo compensation. His final shot is an appeal to Zeus to back the new generation against the older one.

page 75: strong handcuffs] Now that Hermes has obeyed the instructions of Zeus, and revealed (or, if the terms of the Olympian court proceedings are kept in mind, enabled Apollo to discover) the stolen herd, the older god is instantly anxious and distrustful. The attempt to bind Hermes, for which Apollo uses withies (flexible branches from the willow), is instantly frustrated when the younger god works a miracle. There are parallels for this instant taking root of the sticks, including one mentioned in Pausanias' account of Troezen:

> Here there is also a Hermes called Polygius. Against this image, they say, Heracles leaned his club. Now this club, which was of wild olive, taking root in the earth (if anyone cares to believe the story) grew up again and is still alive; Heracles, they say, discovering the wild olive by the Saronic Sea, cut a club from it. (*Description of Greece* 2.31.10)

It is possible that the miraculously overgrown field mentioned here in the Hymn was a religious site associated with the god.

page 76: a hymn] This is Hermes' second hymnic performance in the poem. In outline here, it appears to be a kind of theogony, an account of the births of the gods and their powers. The present translation slightly compresses the beginning of this hymn in the Greek, where Hermes 'began his prelude, and the voice he had was a beautiful one: he honoured the immortal gods and the dark earth, as they were first brought to being and as each received his due portion'. Mnemosyne (Memory), as the mother of the Muses, is the subject of his primary invocation. Plainly, this is intended as part of a recognized convention; whether or not specific memories of Hesiod's *Theogony* are to be triggered is impossible to say. It is in the *Theogony*, however, that the Muses themselves are first invoked, with Mnemosyne given praise as their mother:

Mnemosyne gave birth to them
when she made love to Cronos' son
on Pieria – Mnemosyne
who takes care of Eleuther's heights –
as the surest way to forget
troubles, and a blessed relief
from all life's worries.   (*Theogony*, 53–55)

Hermes, of course, hardly has these blessings for mortals in
mind, so he can concentrate on the Muses' mother rather than
on the muses themselves.

page 77: *How did you get the knowledge?*] In the Greek, this is a
concise question, *tis tribos?* The word *tribos* here is sometimes
translated as 'study' or 'practice', but it comes to mean 'track'
(deriving perhaps from ideas of a much-travelled path). The
cognate word *tribe* is used by Plato to mean a practised routine
as contrasted with *technē*, an accomplished skill.

when the turns go | round to the right] It was good form at a
symposium (literally, a drinking party) to pass the lyre from left
to right amongst the guests. On taking the lyre (or, sometimes,
a branch of myrtle), each guest would be called upon to perform
(whether by singing, or by reciting or composing on the spot
some verses).

page 80: *a brightly shining goad*] The *mastix* presented here is
an everyday object (it is generally represented as such, as being
needful for moving about donkeys or horses), given by Apollo
a coat of bling.

Hermes ... invented the pipes] The *syrinx* would more usually
be associated with Pan, Hermes' son. This is more common,
however, in art from the fifth century BC and later, whereas
from as early as c. 580 BC it is Hermes who is depicted with
the pipes.

if you take the step of swearing a great oath] Apollo offers two possibilities for the form of the oath (the Greek line has a clear 'either … or' at this point), the downwards nod of the head to signify assent, and the divinely binding oath on the waters of Styx: it may be that he believes one will imply the other. Hermes, though, delivers only the nod, so that for the Hymn's audience (if not at this stage for Apollo himself) there is the suspicion of a loophole being made.

page 81: this triple-headed staff made of gold] This item, known later as the *kērukeion* or *caduceus*, is significant in the iconography of Hermes. The elaborate wand can wake men or send them to sleep, and is used by Hermes when he takes souls down to Hades. It does seem that the Hymn rather plays up the properties of the staff itself here, as Apollo heaps up a list of lucky and prophetic properties. As *AHS* have it, 'The line ascribes unheard of virtues to the caduceus' (343). In art, the staff has a pointed lower end, and is decorated on the top. On a drinking cup from Corinth, dated 675–650 BC, there is a depiction of the wand with three points as here, while from the mid-sixth century BC onwards, the decoration is usually augmented by snakes (not mentioned in the Hymn). Other ancient sources suggest that the god constructed it for himself.

page 82: there are three girls] What follows here is a much disputed (and genuinely mysterious) part of the Hymn. The starting point for any discussion must be the fact that we have no historical sources for what appears to be some kind of bee-oracle. This very lack, however, was enough to trigger speculative emendation amongst scholars – something made all the more tempting by the fact that the medieval manuscripts of the Hymn differ at line 552, where the first word is generally *moirai* (Fates), but is in the important manuscript M *semnai* (holy women). For the German editor Hermann in 1806, this was disagreement enough to justify the intervention of historical scholarship, and he changed the word to the proper noun *Thriai*: the Thriai were three oracular priestesses, whose processes involved scattering pebbles. None of the fragmentary ancient sources for these women mention either Hermes or bees; the pebbles, which they do mention, and which may correspond to the many knucklebones which have now been discovered in a cave half-way up Parnassus (very possibly the cave of the Corycian nymphs, who exercised a prophetic office near Delphi), do not find any mention here in the Hymn. Hermann's ingenuity was misplaced; and this leaves the text back where it began, in a considerable degree of darkness. Honey, certainly, could be associated with certain prophetic inducements (sometimes in fermented form), and it is mentioned often in connection with the production of poetry too (the oracles delivered at Delphi, and some elsewhere, were in verse). The Corycian Nymphs, too, may not be entirely irrelevant: a stone relief from the cave has Hermes and three nymphs, while on a later relief from Delphi (fourth century BC) three female figures sit on a mountain with both Apollo and Hermes. But really what is needed is some further reference to bee-women, and this is not to be found. (This is not to say, of course, that it never will be, and there is one piece of evidence, though from a different place, which suggests that bee-women did not stretch the Greek imagination overmuch: an electrum plaque from Kamiros in Rhodes, dating from the seventh century BC (in the British Museum), depicts a figure female from the waist up, with the body of a bee below, and sporting a pair of wings, who appears to be hovering between two flowers). Perhaps, though, this whole passage should be taken partly in the spirit of a riddle, something which would be in keeping with Apollo's oracular character, and which Hermes might be expected to be adept at interpreting.

page 83: *Hades*] The god Hades was not generally offered gifts. Aeschylus, in a fragment of his *Niobe*, gives him the title *Thanatos* (Death):

> Alone among the gods, Death asks for no
> presents; and not by offering to him,

not by making libations flow,
not by anything you bring to him
can you profit; for him, there is
no altar, and for him nobody sings
the songs a worshipper brings.   (Aeschylus, fr. 161)

Notes to Hymn 5

The *Hymn to Aphrodite* is a poem of 293 hexameter lines, and has been considered by some to be the earliest of the Homeric Hymns. Aspects of the poem's language and style indicate that its author was familiar with the *Iliad* (perhaps later eighth century BC) as well as Hesiod's *Theogony* (perhaps early seventh century BC); while amongst the other Hymns, the *Hymn to Demeter* (thought to be from the sixth century BC) shows strong signs of indebtedness to the Hymn to Aphrodite. This and other evidence would suggest that the Hymn was composed in the seventh century BC, and quite possibly in north-western Asia Minor rather than mainland Greece.[1]

The ancient Greeks had a number of different origins for Aphrodite, the goddess of love. One epithet used in the Hymn is 'Cythereia', referring to the island of Cythera off the southern Peleponnese, and there are references also to the common association between Aphrodite and Cyprus: tellingly, Cyprus (where there were important cult centres for the goddess, in Paphos and Amathus) lies close to the near east, with whose love-goddess traditions Aphrodite seems to be associated. Herodotus made something of Aphrodite's

---

1   As with the other Hymns, certainty on the subject of date is impossible. Perhaps the most than can be said is that the Hymn postdates both Homer and Hesiod, and that it pre-dates the Hymn to Demeter; but none of these (unfortunately) can themselves be dated with any certainty, and scholarly opinion seldom agrees, for example, on either Homer and Hesiod's dates or indeed on whether Homer predates Hesiod, or Hesiod predates Homer. Detailed statistical analysis of language is often suggestive, but the sample-size available for this, as well as the element of uncertainty about the amount of dating information it can substantiate on its own, renders such analysis necessarily inconclusive.

near-eastern associations, mentioning a temple for her in
Ascalon (Ashkelon) in Syria (*Histories* 1.105), and identifying
her as *ouraniēs Aphroditēs*, 'heaven-born Aphrodite'. The old
god of the heavens, *Ouranos*, features in an origin story which
locates the goddess's birth firmly in Cyprus. This is in Hesiod,
where Cronos has dismembered his father Ouranos:

> The moment he had sheared clean off
> the cock and balls with his sharp blade
> and flung them from dry land into
> the many currents of the sea,
> they were borne off, for weeks on end,
> while over them, and their god's flesh,
> a pure white foam bubbled around,
> and inside this a daughter grew:
> to holy Cythera she came first,
> and from there to the island next
> of Cyprus; here she soon emerged,
> graceful, beautiful, a goddess,
> and under her slim feet the grass
> grew everywhere. Both gods and men
> give her the name Aphrodite,
> goddess born from the sea-foam,
> and Cythereia, the garlanded:
> the first because she came to be
> from out of all that bubbling foam,
> the second for her coming ashore
> at Cythera; they call her too
> Cyprogenea, because the famous
> isle of Cyprus bore her; also
> Philommeides, lover of smiles,
> who sprung straight from the genitals.
> Eros came with her, and beautiful
> Desire followed her, just as soon
> as she was born and went to join
> the family of gods; and this
> honour she from the very start

has had for her own lot and due
among men and immortals too:
smiles, and girlish whispers, little
tricks, and sweet sudden happiness,
and love with all its gentleness.   (Hesiod, *Theogony* 188–206)

Hesiod hears in Aphrodite's name *aphos*, the word for sea-foam, as well as choosing to detect in her cult epithet *philommēdes* (lover of smiles) the word *mēdea* which he uses to describe the lopped-off genitals of Ouranos. While such etymologies are doubtful (as often amongst ancient Greek sources), they were widely accepted in antiquity; in particular, Hesiod's epithet *Cythereia* was generally adopted, and its connection with the island of Cythera taken as certain. (Modern philologists are much less sure: Hesiod's term has as its second syllable a short *e* where the island's name keeps the vowel long, and some scholars have proposed alternative derivations for the epithet, including one from Kuthar (*Kwtr*), a king of Cyprus in mythology, and his avatar in the Ugaritic god Kothar, who was – like Aphrodite's Greek consort, Hephaestus – a god of craftsmen.)

In the *Iliad*, Aphrodite is given a different origin, as the daughter of Zeus and Dione, the goddess associated especially with Zeus's cult at Dodona. In *Iliad* 5, Aphrodite attempts to rescue her son Aeneas from the field of battle, is herself injured by the enraged warrior Diomedes, and retreats to her mother on Olympus, where 'She fell down on her knees before Dione | her own mother, who hugged her daughter tight, | then stroked her with her hand and spoke to her' (*Iliad* 5: 370–372). For the Hymn, the Hesiodic genealogy is more significant than the Homeric one. However, it is in the *Iliad*, and not in Hesiod, that the earliest reference to Aphrodite's liaison with Anchises is to be found: in *Iliad* 2: 820–821 Homer mentions 'Aeneas, whom great Aphrodite bore | to Anchises on Mount Ida's heights, where she | had gone to bed with him, a mortal man', and in *Iliad* 5: 313 Aphrodite is the 'mother who conceived him [Aeneas] by Anchises, | a herdsman then'. In Hesiod's

Theogony 1008–1010 the same encounter is briefly related: 'Garlanded Cythereia bore | Aeneas, having mixed in love | with Anchises on wind-swept heights | and ravines of Mount Ida'. A fragmentary early reference to the story is found in a now obscure mythographer of the sixth century BC, Acusilaus, who says that 'Aphrodite had intercourse with Anchises who was already well past his prime' (a variant on the story not found elsewhere, and certainly not in the Hymn).[2]

In the Hymn, Anchises is finally left in no doubt about the severity of the consequences should he ever reveal the secret of his mountainside affair with the goddess of love: in that case, he will find himself on the wrong side of a thunderbolt-wielding Zeus. Of course, this sworn secret is revealed in the poem, and had therefore already been on open display in prior forms of the myth, so Anchises' promise cannot have been kept. By the time of Virgil's *Aeneid*, Anchises talks about as his having been lamed by a thunderbolt:

2 Acusilaus (Akousilaos) dates from before the Persian wars, and is associated with the city of Argos. He composed genealogies, some based on the tablets of bronze which (not very plausibly) he claimed to have found in his back garden; he also undertook the unlikely task of translating Hesiod into plain prose. All that remains of his work is a scattering of forty-five short fragments quoted by later authors. This particular remark crops up in a scholiast's note (on a papyrus dating from second-third centuries AD) to *Iliad* 20: 307–8 ('And now will mighty Aeneas rule the Trojans, | and his children's children, in all the times to come'): since it adds a slightly unusual spin (one wholly at odds with the Hymn) to the reading of Aphrodite's conduct, it is given here in full:

> When an oracle issued forth that those descended from Anchises would rule as kings over the Trojans after the dissolution of the monarchy of the House of Priam, Aphrodite had intercourse with Anchises who was already well past his prime. She bore Aeneas and, wishing to furnish a cause for the dissolution of the House of Priam, she threw into Alexander a longing for Helen. After Helen's rape, she appeared to be an ally to the Trojans, but in truth she was consoling them in defeat lest they completely despair and deliver over Helen. This story is in Akousilaos.
> (Acusilaus fr. 39, in Ian Worthington (ed.), *Brill's New Jacoby* (online: Brill): see R.L. Fowler, *Early Greek Mythography* (Oxford: Oxford University Press, 2000), 24–5.

A long time now I've waited out the years,
shunned by the gods, and of no use to men,
ever since heaven's father, mankind's king,
blasted me with the tempests of his thunder
and touched me with his fire.   (*Aeneid* 2: 647–9)

The lameness – which also explains the need for Aeneas to
carry his father away from the sack of Troy on his shoulders,
itself a common visual motif in Greek and Roman art – must
have been present in Greek literary sources from an early point.
There is every likelihood that this punishment of Anchises was
to be found in those parts of the lost Epic Cycle relating to the
destruction of Troy; and its eventual imposition is, in the Hymn,
almost certainly to be felt as a resonance from Aphrodite's stern
words of warning. In the fifth century BC, Sophocles makes
graphic allusion to the punitive lightning-strike in a surviving
fragment of his lost play *The Men of Larissa*:[3]

At the gates now Aeneas stands, the child
of a god, and on his shoulders he carries
his father, whose robes of linen are all stained
and scorched where the great bolt of lightning struck:
retainers in a circle crowd around him.

There will have been various explanations for Anchises' having
survived Zeus's thunderbolt, and there is evidence that one
version of the story had Aphrodite intervene to divert the
strike. There is no doubt, however, that the future of Anchises'
line, as kings of Troy, is important both for the Hymn and in
the myth more generally.

Here Aeneas is the key figure, and the Hymn's narrative
of his supernatural conception follows on from Homer in its
emphasis on the royal destiny of the family. *Iliad* 20 is much

3   Sophocles, fragment 373, in Hugh Lloyd-Jones (ed.) *Sophocles: Fragments*
    (Cambridge, Mass.: Harvard University Press, 1996), 200.

taken up with Aeneas, and part of its narrative concerns
his being spirited out of harm's way when he encounters an
infuriated and lethal Achilles on the field of battle. The two
warriors exchange speeches, and Aeneas is moved to give a
lengthy account of his genealogy (*Iliad* 20: 230–241). Here, his
account includes Ganymede and Tithonus, who both feature in
the Hymn. It is Poseidon who rescues Anchises from the battle,
and his declaration of intent to do this reveals that Anchises'
line, rather than Priam's, is fated to rule over future Trojans:

> Come on then: we must lead him out from death,
> in case the son of Cronos should grow angry
> when Achilles slays him – his fate is to escape
> so that the direct line of Dardanus
> should not perish, and never more be seen:
> Dardanus who, above all of the children
> that mortal women bore to him, Zeus loved;
> yet now he has for all of Priam's line
> nothing but hate, and surely after this
> great Aeneas will rule over the Trojans;
> his sons' sons also, born in time to come.
>
> (*Iliad* 20: 300–308)

It may be significant that the last line here, with its reference to
Aeneas' 'sons' sons', looks as if it is being imitated in line 197 of
the Hymn, when Aphrodite promises Anchises a future of rule
for his children's children (Homer: *paidōn paides*; Hymn: *paides
paidessi*). The degree to which the intent of the Hymn seems
to chime with a passage such as this has tempted some readers
to ascribe it a common origin with *Iliad* 20, and to regard
both works as being pitched towards patrons who might have
professed an ancestral connection with the mythic Anchises. It
is entirely possible that such patrons might have existed when
the Hymn was composed: in Lydia (Homer's Maeonia), the
Mermnad kings (c. 700–546 BC) were able to use the myth
of Aeneas to justify their rule over parts of the Troad, and thus
claim to be his successors by asserting their descent from him.

According to the ancient geographer Strabo (c .64 BC–c. AD 21), the town of Scepsis in this area also had rulers who claimed Aeneas as an ancestor.[4] While this can hardly be claimed as hard evidence that the name of Aeneas was invoked by ruling clans in north-west Asia Minor at the time of the Hymn's composition, the possibility is not an implausible one, and would help to make sense (centuries before Roman myths of Aeneas as a founding dynast) of the emphasis here, and in *Iliad* 20, on the Trojan prince as the inheritor and re-founder of the Trojan royal line.[5]

The Hymn's primary purpose, however, is not as simple as ancestor-praise for some regional elite in search of historical validation. It is a complex and subtle poem, which is certainly heavy with literary allusion (to Homer and Hesiod, probably also to now irrecoverable sources), and which concerns itself

---

4 See Strabo, *Geography*, 13.1.52–3:

> Palescepsis is situated above Cebrene towards the most elevated part of Ida near Polichna. It has the name of Scepsis either for some other reason or because it was within view of the places around, if we may be allowed to derive words then in use among barbarians from the Greek language. Afterwards the inhabitants were transferred to the present Scepsis, 60 stadia lower down, by Scamandrius, the son of Hector, and by Ascanius, the son of Aeneas; these two families reigned, it is said, a long time at Scepsis… [53] The Scepsian (Demetrius) supposes that Scepsis was the palace of Aeneas, situated between the dominion of Aeneas and Lyrnessus, where, it is said, he took refuge when pursued by Achilles. … Homer does not agree either with these writers or with what is said respecting the founders of Scepsis. For he represents Aeneas as remaining at Troy, succeeding to the kingdom, and delivering the succession to his children's children after the extinction of the race of Priam: "'the son of Saturn hated the family of Priam: henceforward Aeneas shall reign over the Trojans, and his children's children to late generations.'"In this manner not even the succession of Scamandrius could be maintained. He disagrees still more with those writers who speak of his wanderings as far as Italy, and make him end his days in that country. (H.C. Hamilton and W. Falconer (trans.), *The Geography of Strabo* (London: George Bell & Sons, 1903).

5 One scholar in modern times has gone so far as to claim that, for this reason, the Hymn and *Iliad* 20 are works of the same poet (K. Reinhardt, 'Zum homerischen *Aphroditehymnus*', *Festschrift für Bruno Schnell zum 60. Geburtstag* (Munich, 1956), 1–14): but no classicist since has endorsed this conjecture.

with both the contacts and differences between the human and the divine. Aphrodite, as the goddess of love, is the centre of attention and, in some senses, the poem is a narrative meditation on what it might be for a human being to be literally loved by the divine. The mythic time in which the Hymn is set is one at which such conjunctions between mortal and immortal are coming to an end – some readers have even seen this process of ending to be the poem's basic subject. 'By explaining and justifying our loss of intimacy with the divine,' Jenny Strauss Clay has written, 'the *Hymn to Aphrodite* bids us to come to terms with our mortal lot.'[6] This allegorical meaning may be a little more serious than the poem's lightnesses of tone and of touch would suggest, but that there is a certain air of momentousness to the Hymn's comedy is certainly true.

Unlike the three other long Hymns, the *Hymn to Aphrodite* does not concern itself primarily with a god's power or special privileges, his or her origins or religious cult, but with an episode of divine misadventure and humiliation. Aphrodite is portrayed in the poem as a source of some discomfort on Olympus, having in the past arranged so many erotic entanglements between the immortal gods and mere human beings. In retaliation for this, her father Zeus has decided to play the same trick on her, and make the goddess fall in love with the Trojan prince Anchises; in the wake of this, the Hymn says, Aphrodite will no longer be so ready to set up such embarrassing liaisons between mortal and immortal lovers.

The story told by the Hymn, then, is in certain important respects a comic one, for Aphrodite is given a taste of her own medicine when she woos and wins Anchises. In expressing her anxiety, after the event, that from now on the gods will laugh at her, Aphrodite (one of whose conventional poetic epithets is *philommeides*, 'lover of smiles' – with its Hesiodic overtones (discussed above) of an appreciator of male genitalia) is already

6   Jenny Strauss Clay, *The Politics of Olympus: Form and Meaning in the Major Homeric Hymns* (Princeton NJ: Princeton University Press, 1989; 2nd edn. revised London: Bristol Classical Press, 2006), 201.

subject to the audience's amusement. It is clear that in Greek poetry of this period the depiction of gods in a comic light did not imply what we might understand as religious irreverence: the episode in the *Odyssey*, told by the poet Demodocus, in which Aphrodite is trapped *in flagrante* with her lover Ares by her vengeful, lame husband Hephaestus, is ample proof of this.[7] The mortal Anchises in the Hymn, too, is shown in something of a comic light, as a handsome but not overly intelligent piece of arm-candy. In so far as the Hymn is intended to demonstrate the workings of the will of Zeus, it shows that the father of the gods has a wicked sense of humour.

Structurally, the Hymn is a little odd. No sooner has the poem got under way with an address to the goddess than it takes a series of diversions, into three mini-hymns to those female deities who have remained immune to Aphrodite's influence. These lines about Artemis, Athene, and Hestia are beautifully written, but it would take more ingenuity than scholars have yet been able to muster to argue convincingly for their full structural integration with the Hymn as a whole. Nevertheless, here they are; and their relation to the main narrative, in being so oblique, suggests that an audience is expected to be alert to unorthodox and sidelong patterns of narrative juxtaposition and implication. Another oddity is one of seeming imbalance: lines 185–290 of the poem are given entirely to a speech by the (now confessedly divine) Aphrodite to a post-coital and terrified Anchises. In the course of this, still other stories are told: that of Ganymede, a mortal boy who became immortal after Zeus chose him as his cup-bearer in heaven; that of Tithonus, the lover of Eōs, goddess of Dawn, whose gift of immortality failed to include any anti-ageing guarantee; and finally that of the tree-nymphs on Mount Ida, whose inhumanly long lives will come to an end with those of the tress they inhabit. After all this, along with a series of fairly aggressive threats about what Anchises can expect if he so much as breathes a word of anything that

7 *Odyssey* 8: 266–366 (translated here in Appendix 1).

has been going on between them, Aphrodite simply disappears (in a single line) back to her own domain. And there, with jarring abruptness, the Hymn ends: Anchises, whom we have seen closely earlier on, and whose thoughts have been made a subject of psychological interest, is not even mentioned again. Aphrodite, the speaker of this last third of the whole poem, is a very different goddess from the lovestruck girl Zeus makes her into, who has to pretend to be a Phrygian princess mysteriously ferried to Troy by the god Hermes, expressly for the purpose of becoming Anchises' finacée.

The seemingly strange distribution of weight in the Hymn's narrative is not without its own logic and rationale, and it is certainly possible to argue for an overall unity of effect in the poem. For all that, its procedures are likely to strike us as disconcerting. They may have been less so in ancient Greece; for digression, and narrative changes of gear, are important aspects of originality within a predominantly oral tradition. If this poem was created in order to tell the story of Anchises' supernatural seduction – which it does, with enormous aplomb – then it was also composed in such a way as to bring into and around that story other parts of the epic and mythological apparatus. It is in the order and relative weights of these elements, one suspects, that the literary originality of the piece must lie.

The seduction of Anchises – which he may believe at the time to be his own seduction of a visiting princess – is naturally the most important of the Hymn's stories. Stylistically, it is not without Homeric precedent, in the narrative of Hera's seduction of Zeus in *Iliad* 14 (the verbal echoes of this in the Greek text are almost certainly meant to be picked up: see note to page 87), where a goddess's elaborate bathing and dressing rituals are lovingly detailed. But the Hymn's narrative here is finally a distinctive one, and the goddess's elaborate fabrication of a back-story to explain her presence on Anchises' mountain-fields is paralleled by her complicated and exotic *toilette* and fashion. It is possible that audiences used to accounts of male warriors being readied for battle, in piece by piece of specialized armour, making rhetorical declarations of war or heroism, and then going into victorious combat, might have seen in Aphrodite's preparations, speech, and bedroom action an interesting inversion of the usual heroic routine; but the Hymn's seduction narrative has its own momentum quite apart from any such generic ironies.[8]

Anchises' situation is simultaneously absorbing (in an erotic sense) and frightening. On the one hand, he is being given sexual opportunities beyond an audience's (or his own) wildest dreams; on the other, he is crossing a line between the divine and the human, the consequences of which are likely to be grave ones. When he discovers for certain what has been happening (though it is possible he had guessed something in advance, and gone on regardless), Anchises is right to be in a state of high anxiety. Aphrodite puts his mind at ease, or tries to, but she also takes her time with that process: her three *exempla* in the long speech offer mixed messages about what lies in store for humans who find themselves sexually entangled with the gods. All three, additionally, are tinged with concerns about mortality; and each of the stories stands at a suggestive angle to the other two. As with the three mini-hymns at the beginning, so these three divinely-narrated stories in the poem's (protracted) closing movement are not so much illustrations of the Hymn proper as indirect and subtle comments upon its theme. Ganymede's father, for example, seems to suffer terribly when his son is snatched away from him; but not all that terribly, in the event, since Zeus makes him a gift of some exceptionally fast racehorses. Tithonus is loved by Eōs, but once the consequences of her administrative error in failing to ask for his eternal youth become obvious, the goddess locks him away, and leaves him where he can cause

---

8 For Aphrodite as an inverted heroic warrior, see the essay by Pascale Brillet-Dubois, 'An Erotic *Aristeia*: The Homeric Hymn to Aphrodite and its Relation to the Iliadic Tradition', in Andrew Faulkner (ed.), *The Homeric Hymns: Interpretative Essays* (Oxford: Oxford University Press, 2011), 105–132.

her no further embarrassment. The wood-nymphs who are to bring up Aphrodite and Anchises' child Aeneas are the regular sexual partners of the gods, and live so long that (like the trees with which they are identified) they seem to human beings to be practically eternal; but this is an illusion, and these nymphs must themselves die in the end. Facing each other like mirrors, the three stories complicate the relations between love, sex, loss, and mortality – themes which crowd in upon the episode of high sexual intensity and comedy, between a goddess and a human being, to which the audience has just been witness.

In translating the Hymn, I have assembled the continuous narrative of the Greek text into a number of episodes, each metrically distinct. The original, of course, is entirely in hexameters, and is not broken into separate parts.

page 85: war-buggies] this translates the word *harmata* (chariots) in line 13, but the line also contains another object of manufacture, *satinas*, which is not translated here. A *satinē* was also probably a carriage of some kind, though perhaps one more associated with female than male use. The word is very rare, and has been thought to be of eastern origin: it occurs (in close proximity to *harmata*) in Sappho fr. 44, in Anacreon, and in Eurpides' *Helen*, describing the chariot of Cybele (1311); in each case some allusion to eastern luxury seems to be implied. For *AHS*, *satinas* is 'a Grecized Asian, perhaps Phrygian, word' (353), and it may be worth remembering that the Hymn does contain later on an explicit reference to the speaking of the Phrygian language.

Hestia] This goddess was rarely represented in human form in figurative art, and remained associated primarily with the household hearth. The Hymn's reference to her as both first- and last-born of the children of Cronos is explained by the story in Hesiod's *Theogony* that she was Cronos' eldest child in order of birth, but that once he had swallowed his children, and was forced by Zeus to regurgitate them, she was the last to be disgorged. This 'first and last' motif is echoed in the giving of the first and the last libations to Hestia (see note to Hymn 29). Hestia's request to Zeus for perpetual virginity does not fit all that well with a divinity more usually figured as the physical hearth rather than in anthropomorphic ways, and it may well originate with the Hymn; but it is mentioned in a scholion on Aristophanes' *Wasps* (846), where 'After the wresting of power from the Titans, and control coming into Zeus' hands, it was entrusted to Hestia to take whatsoever she wished: the first thing she asked for was perpetual virginity, and after that to assume the prime place for herself in the household offerings of mankind' (quoted *AHS*, 355). Apart from here in the Hymn, Poseidon and Apollo are not mentioned in literature or depicted in art as suitors of Hestia. The oath which Hestia swears has points of verbal contact with early lyric poetry, in a fragment of Sappho (fr. 44a) where Artemis also swears a great oath to Zeus to remain perpetually a virgin. This does not necessarily clinch a case for direct relationship between Sappho's poetry and the Hymn: as Faulkner summarises matters, '[the Hymn] is either drawing directly on this fragment, or there was a common exemplar (or examplars) for the two poets … Nonetheless, borrowing from Sappho by the poet of [the Hymn] does seem less likely, and there is nothing to substantiate direct borrowing here in any case. A common exemplar sufficiently explains the similarities between the two passages' (Faulkner, 111).

page 87: *back to Cyprus*] This scene of Aphrodite's elaborate *toilette* in preparation for her seduction of Anchises has close parallels in Homer, which extend to substantial verbal repetition and echo. In *Iliad* 14, Hera determines to distract Zeus from his unwelcome interference in the battle at Troy by seducing him at the post he is keeping on Mount Ida. The passage is heavy with ambrosia, the fragrant substance (sometimes a drink, more often a food) consumed by the gods:

> She went straight to the chamber which her son
> Hephaestus made for her, with doors cut snug

into the jambs, held fast with a secret latch
that not another god knew how to open.
Walking inside, she closed those shining doors,
and the first thing she did was wash each speck
of dirt from her flesh with ambrosia,
and then she poured gently over herself
ambrosial oil, viscous, deeply-perfumed:
a single drop of that in the bronze-fronted
palace of Zeus would fill all earth and heaven.
So she anointed all her gorgeous skin;
she combed her hair out, and with her own hands
plaited the glossy locks, now beautiful
themselves with more ambrosia: they fell
streaming downwards from her immortal head.
She slipped into a dress – ambrosial too –
Athene had made for her, worked all over
with intricate, embroidered ornaments;
she fastened it above with golden pins,
put on brooches of gold, then round her waist
wore a smart belt set with a hundred tassels;
she fixed three-beaded earrings into place
for their glamorous shine; and over herself
next the great goddess began to arrange
a newly-made and half-transparent veil,
white as the blazing sun is white; then on
her flashing feet she put delicate shoes.

(*Iliad* 14: 166–186)

There are further close verbal parallels in three lines (8: 362–365) towards the close of the *Odyssey*'s mini-narrative performed by the poet Demodocus (translated as Appendix 1), again involving the application of ambrosia. Since ambrosia is redolent of Olympus, Hera's liberal use of the substance in the *Iliad* may be a way of reminding Zeus of his primary erotic attachment to another immortal; in the Hymn, on the other hand, Aphrodite is using ambrosia in order to project an allure which would be utterly alien to anything the mortal

Anchises could have previously experienced. It may be, also, that a subliminal taste, or rather fragrance, of immortality is coming Anchises' way: this is in the nature of a tease, rather than a promise (as the narrative of the Hymn will go on to make clear).

page 89: *twisted gold earrings … the gemstone*] Aphrodite's jewellery is designedly exotic. Some of the words used here are rare, and their precise meanings are matters of informed guesswork. Eastern goddesses of love are associated with elaborate jewellery, while statuettes from Cyprus are also so adorned. In Sumerian myth, the goddess Inana [Ishtar], who seduces a mortal shepherd called Dumazid, first clothes herself in jewels from top to toe. In the fragmentary 'Song of Inana and Dumuzid', *The Electronic Text Corpus of Sumerian Literature* 4.08) there are some interesting parallels with the language and imagery of the Hymn here:

> At her mother's bidding, Inana bathed in water and anointed herself with sweet oil. She covered her body with a grand robe; she also took her pin. She straightened the lapis lazuli stones on her neck, and grasped her cylinder seal in her hand. The young lady stepped forward as Dumuzid pushed open the door, and like a moonbeam she came forth to him from the house. He looked at her and rejoiced in her; he embraced her and kissed her. (4.08.29)

O goddess for certain] I have expanded the simple and formal Greek here ('Welcome, lady') to accommodate something which in Virgil Aeneas will say to his mother Venus (Aphrodite) who has appeared in mortal disguise: 'O dea certe' (*Aeneid* 1: 328).

page 90: *I'm no divinity…*] Aphrodite's elaborate back-story, which bears comparison with the tale spun by Demeter in Hymn 2, needs to be detailed enough to explain her sudden appearance on the slopes of Ida, and tempting enough to persuade Anchises that he has just met suitable marriage-material. On the other hand, neither of these requirements may be absolutely necessary, since Anchises is already erotically excited by the new arrival, and ready to believe anything (for the moment, at least) in his hurry. Aphrodite's false mortal lineage is plausible enough: there is a Phrygian chieftan called Otreus in the *Iliad*, where Priam recalls fighting alongside him against the Amazons (*Iliad* 3: 185–189) (in later tradition, he is made a relative of Priam's); and there was a town between Phrygia and Bithynia called Ortoia. The detail of how this princess has come to learn the language of Trojans when she herself was raised in Phrygia is in fact a remarkable one: in Homer, there are a few allusions to the differing languages of the Trojans and their allies, but the matter is never much dwelt upon. Language difference is a realistic touch, and when in the *Odyssey* a returned and disguised Odysseus is giving a false account of himself to Penelope, he gives more plausibility to his story about being from Crete by adding details of language differences on the island: 'For one group there does not possess the same | language as another: their tongues are mixed' (*Odyssey* 19: 175). The Hymn, though, has the first explicit allusion in Greek literature to bilingualism. Here, Aphrodite is clearly trying for the credibility of realism, and her account is enough to satisfy Anchises. However, this may tell us a little more about the Hymn itself, and its possible place of composition: as *AHS* put it, 'this is the first passage where a difference between Trojan and Phrygian is asserted, and where a native of Phrygia being on Mt. Ida thinks it necessary to account for having a knowledge of Trojan … The realization of the difference between adjacent Asiatic tongues points to an Asiatic, perhaps Aeolic, origin for the hymn' (360).

page 92: her head touching the ceiling] Now that Aphrodite can resume the form of a goddess, her stature appears terrifying. Hymn 2: 188–189 and 275–280, in which Demeter also bursts the limits of an earthly room on reassuming divine form (pages 9 and 11), may well by indebted to this passage.

page 93: not to leave me living as half a man] Anchises' fears are well-founded. Some of the previous victims of the desires of goddesses are cited, for example, by the nymph Calypso:

> Gods, you are cruel, and more than anyone
> quick to begrudge, envying what's done
> when goddesses feel love for mortal men,
> should one of them decide to bring again
> a human to her bed: for when Dawn took
> up with Orion, Dawn with her rose-blush look,
> you gods resented her, there at your ease,
> until in Ortygia it would please
> Artemis, goddess of the golden throne,
> to target him and slay him, with her own
> divine arrows. And it was just the same
> when Demeter, with her flowing hair, came
> to give in to desire, and she lay down
> in a ploughed-up fallow field with Iason:
> it wasn't long before Zeus was aware
> of what was going on, and then and there
> murdered him with one glancing thunderbolt.
>
> (*Odyssey* 5: 118–129)

Aeneas, and that very name] In the Greek, *Aineias* has this name because of the *ainon … achos* (shameful/dreadful grief) his birth brings upon Aphrodite. This Greek phrase, which is split across two lines, occurs in Homer, e.g. *Iliad* 4: 169 (where the words are kept directly together, and within the line). The pun-etymology (which is in evidence elsewhere in Homer in relation to heroes such as Achilles and Odysseus) can take the form of wordplay, as at *Iliad* 13: 481–2, where Idomeneus says 'I fear dreadfully | Aeneas' (*deidia d'ainōs | Ainean*).

page 94: Ganymede] A son of the founder of the Trojan dynasty, Trōs. The story of his abduction by the immortal gods (and his eternal job as resident barman on Olympus) is alluded in Homer:

Trōs was the father of three matchless sons,
Ilus and Assarcus, and Ganymēdēs
so like a god, and born the handsomest
of men; the immortals snatched him up on high
because of his beauty, to become the wine-
server for Zeus, and so he could live with gods.

(*Iliad* 20: 231–235)

This does not quite confirm the gift of immortality, which the Hymn seems to take for granted. Zeus's direct involvement (whether in a whirlwind, or – as commonly in later art – in the shape of an eagle), and his pederastic motives, are accruals to the original myth. These aspects were in place by the time Ganymede's name went into Etruscan as *catmite*, and into the Latin word *catamitus*, resulting in the English 'catamite'. The story of Trōs' compensation in the shape of a team of special horses is also in the *Iliad*, where Diomedes mentions their descendants being driven by Aeneas:

For they are of the breed that commanding Zeus
once gave to Trōs as the compensation
for Ganymēdēs: those were the very best
of horses in the dawn or the full sun.   (*Iliad* 5: 265–267)

page 95: *Tithonus*] Tithonus is indeed, as Aphrodite says, in Anchises' ancestral family line: at *Iliad* 20: 237 he is mentioned as the son of Laomedon and brother of Priam, though the Hymn's account here would put him some generations back. The goddess of Dawn, Eōs, had past form in taking mortal lovers (amongst her conquests was Orion), but Tithonus as her consort is present in both Homer and Hesiod. It is not until the Hymn that the question of Eōs' botched request arises, and the issue of Tithonus's eternally protracted old age: here, the closest account in point of time comes with Sappho (writing probably in the later seventh century BC). In the enlarged version of Sappho fr. 58 first edited by Martin West (2005), the lyric concludes by alluding to Titonus in ways that seem to recall the Hymn (though this could equally well be taken to show that both the Hymn and Sappho draw upon some other source, now lost):

> Nothing to be done: for there's nobody
> who goes on living without getting older –
> just as, they say, Tithonus found out
>
> when, crazy about him, the goddess
> of dawn, with her rose-pale arms,
> took him off to the edge of the earth
>
> still fresh-faced and good-looking, only
> for age to claim him in due course, while
> his lover neither grew old nor died.
>
> (Sappho fr. 58 West, 7–12)

In the Hymn, once Eōs has closed the doors on Tithonus forever, his voice continues to sound. The metaphor is probably that of a river's or a sea's flow, as at *Iliad* 18: 402–3, where 'all around the stream of Ocean flowed | seething with bubbles, and unabated' (*rhëen aspetos*: 'flowed unabated'). If *aspetos* suggests force, it seems odd to connect the Hymn at this point to the later tradition of Tithonus' transformation into a cicada; but it is possible to suspect the presence of that development already in the lines. In the *Iliad*, the senior Trojans of Priam's generation sit on the walls by the city's Scaean gates:

> Their age had made them all give up on war
> but they remained the best of talkers still,
> like the cicadas that sit up on a tree
> in the forest, and pour their lily-voices out:
> just so, those Trojan elders on the wall.   (*Iliad* 3: 150–152)

Whether or not these lines inform the portrait of Tithonus in the Hymn, they are very likely an influence on the eventual transformation of the immortal geriatric into a cicada. To return to *aspetos*, it may be worth remembering that its original meaning seems to be 'unspeakable', so that, at some level, the Hymn's use of the word may imply that Tithonus' voice, though still real enough, is perhaps (like the sound rushing water makes) no longer exactly an articulation. By the fifth century BC, Heraclitus could use *aspetos* as an adjective describing time; and it is time, of course, that this myth contemplates through Tithonus' imagined fate. There is one aspect of Aphrodite's telling of the Tithonus story which has continued to puzzle readers: how, if she knows where Eōs went wrong in framing the request for immortality, does she not find herself in a good position now to make the request, in a watertight form, on behalf of Anchises? Jenny Clay's answer to the question, as far as it concerns Aphrodite herself, is convincing: 'Aphrodite knows that her request for Anchises' immortality would meet with scornful rejection on the part of Zeus, who intended from the first to teach her a lesson' (Clay, 190). But the same question would surely occur to Anchises too, though he is hardly in a position to give voice to it; and its answer for him must be as simple as it is true – Aphrodite, although she has been his lover, does not love him enough to want him around forever.

page 97: the nymphs] This is the earliest discursive account in Greek of nymphs as spirits associated with nature. A line in Hesiod's *Theogony* mentions 'The nymphs people call Melians | over the boundless earth' (187): these Melian nymphs are identified with ash trees, and it is highly suggestive that Hesiod moves at this point directly to the castration of Ouranos at the hands of Cronos, and the consequent conception and birth of Aphrodite – a passage which may well be an influence on the opening of the Hymn (see above, page 266) and is now perhaps exerting some kind of pressure as the poem nears its close. The idea that nymphs' long (but not eternal) lives are linked to particular trees may have its remote consequence in Celtic fairy lore, in which trees can be homes to beings whose lives are co-terminous with their natural settings. In the ancient world, the idea was sufficiently curious (and poetically attractive) to occasion a moment in the fourth Hymn (to Delos) of Callimachus (third century BC), in which he may well be thinking of this part of the Hymn:

> and say, Muses, do
> the oak trees and the nymphs both come to birth
> at the same time? For nymphs rejoice when rain
> makes those trees grow, but they cry when leaves
> are gone from the oaks again.
>
> (Callimachus, Hy. 4, 82–85)

Notes to Hymn 6

This short Hymn, twenty-one lines of hexameter verse, is ordered in the collection presumably because of its shared subject with the long Aphrodite poem of Hymn 5. Other than this, there are no direct connections. This poem is of the kind that belongs probably to a prelude to a competition, invoking the deity as an aid to success. Its date is unknown, though it does contain a good number of post-Homeric elements in lexis and diction. Given the emphasis throughout on Cyprus (natural enough, of course, in addressing Aphrodite), there is a possibility that the piece may originate there. The poem from the Epic cycle, the *Cypria* (composed probably in the second half of the sixth century BC) has points of contact with this Hymn. It seems likely that the *Cypria*, which was sometimes attributed to the poets Stasinus or Hegesias, has an origin in Cyprus. Two *Cypria* fragments, preserved in Athenaeus' *Deipnosophistae*, are worth comparing to the Hymn:

> Her dresses, which the Seasons and the Graces
> made for her, clothed her body; they had steeped
> them in every species of spring flower
> the year can bring: crocus and hyacinth,
> the violet just as it comes up, the rose
> with a lovely flush of bloom like nectar, then
> the narcissus with its little cups of buds
> full of ambrosia: so Aphrodite
> was dressed up in clothes that had been perfumed
> by flowers of every single kind.
>
> (*Cypria* fr. 5, 1–7)

They wove themselves sweet-smelling garlands, flowers
of the earth, these gods in their sheer, bright veils,
Nymphs and Graces, Aphrodite in gold
along with them, as they sang finely on
Ida's mountain, with its many springs.

(*Cypria* fr. 6, 2–6)

page 100: *the Seasons*] These are the *Hōrai* (the Hours),
goddesses associated specifically with the seasons of the year.
They are named in Hesiod as Zeus's offspring:

The second thing he did was marry
brilliant Themis, and she gave birth
to the Hōrai: Eunomia
and Dikē, and blossoming
Eirēnē, who all watch over
the workings of men on the earth.   (*Theogony*, 901–913)

(*Eunomia* means lawfulness, *Dikē* means justice, and *Eirēnē*
means peace.) In the Hymn, the exact number of Seasons
is unclear: while it may be three, as in Hesiod, a verb in line
12 of the Greek text is in the dual, and some representations
of the *Hōrai* seem to have featured two rather than three
goddesses.

worked findrinny] The Greek here says that Aphrodite's
earrings are made from *oreichalcos*. The word means some kind
of metal; but, as *AHS* put it, 'The metal, whether copper or
compound, cannot be identified' (374). In Liddell and Scott, it
is glossed as 'mountain-copper, i.e. yellow copper ore'; the word
is unheard of outside the Hymn, though it may have turned
into ōrichalcos in the first-century-AD *Voyage Around the Red
[Erythraean] Sea*. I have translated this with a word introduced
to the 1895 version of his poem 'The Wanderings of Oisin'
by W.B. Yeats. There, annotating 'a bridle of findrinny', Yeats
called the metal 'a kind of red bronze'; in fact, the term should

be taken as referring to white bronze (from the Irish *findruine*, where *fin-* means white). I have used 'findrinny' with Yeats's (mistaken) flash of redness in mind.

Notes to Hymn 7

This poem of fifty-nine lines is clearly a different kind of narrative from that which must have been contained in the long Hymn to Dionysus which is now (in fragmentary remains) the first of the Homeric Hymns. The piece is complete in itself, and gives an account of a kidnapping at sea story, for which there are a number of parallels, the chief one being the well-known story of Arion the poet. Here, as told by Herodotus, the same elements – pirates, a hostage, dolphins, and the favour of a god – are present:

> They say that this Arion, who spent most of his time with Periander, wished to sail to Italy and Sicily, and that after he had made a lot of money there he wanted to come back to Corinth. Trusting none more than the Corinthians, he hired a Corinthian vessel to carry him from Tarentum. But when they were out at sea, the crew plotted to take Arion's money and cast him overboard. Discovering this, he earnestly entreated them, asking for his life and offering them his money. But the crew would not listen to him, and told him either to kill himself and so receive burial on land or else to jump into the sea at once. Abandoned to this extremity, Arion asked that, since they had made up their minds, they would let him stand on the half-deck in all his regalia and sing; and he promised that after he had sung he would do himself in. The men, pleased at the thought of hearing the best singer in the world, drew away toward the waist of the vessel from the stern. Arion, putting on all his regalia and taking his lyre, stood up on the half-deck and sang the 'Stirring Song', and when the song was finished he threw himself into the sea, as he was with all his regalia. So the crew sailed away to Corinth; but a dolphin (so

the story goes) took Arion on his back and bore him to Taenarus. Landing there, he went to Corinth in his regalia, and when he arrived, he related all that had happened. Periander, sceptical, kept him in confinement, letting him go nowhere, and waited for the sailors. When they arrived, they were summoned and asked what news they brought of Arion. While they were saying that he was safe in Italy and that they had left him flourishing at Tarentum, Arion appeared before them, just as he was when he jumped from the ship; astonished, they could no longer deny what was proved against them. This is what the Corinthians and Lesbians say, and there is a little bronze memorial of Arion on Taenarus, the figure of a man riding upon a dolphin.

(Herodotus, *Histories* 1.24 (trans. A.D. Godley))

The Hymn stands in some kind of relation to the story transmitted by Herodotus, but has translated it from the register of history into that of poetry. The Hymn turns a situation in which hostage and god are one and the same into an episode of divine epiphany, when the god reveals himself to the pirates who have captured him, then transforms most of them into dolphins.

Dionysus is already in disguise at the beginning of the poem, where he stands on a promontory in the likeness of a royally-dressed young man, prompting the pirates to select him for capture. The inability of mortals to recognize Dionysus is most memorably put to work in Euripides' great play *Bacchae* (dating from towards the end of the fifth century BC, probably c. 410), in which Pentheus tragically fails to discern the god when in his presence. The Hymn is probably a good deal earlier than this; its bringing together of Egypt and the land of the Hyperboreans as giving the bounds of the navigable world has a parallel in a line of Pindar, 'Beyond even the springs of the Nile, and through [the land of] the Hyperboreans' (*Isthmian* 6: 24), and this, in the middle-earlier fifth century BC, could preserve a poetic turn to which the Hymn also has recourse. A famous piece of pottery, which seems in some ways close to the narrative of the Hymn, may offer some clues as to a possible date: this is the Exekias cup, a black-figure piece which dates from c. 530 BC (Staatliche Antikensammlung und Glyphotek, Munich). Here, the god Dionysus, holding a vine-vessel, steers a ship that is covered in fruit-bearing vines, with seven dolphins in the surrounding sea. (The image is in the inside of the cup, so that in use it would have only become progressively visible as more wine was consumed: the god would be fully visible only once all the contents had been drunk.) This is not, arguably, close enough to the Hymn's content to make the cup an illustration of the Hymn; but it does suggest that stories of Dionysus at sea (and he is not a sea-god) must have been in sixth century BC circulation. It would seem that one version of the story, in the fifth century BC at least, had the pirates acting as agents for an angry Hera. In Euripides' *Cyclops*, Silenus reminds Dionysus of 'When Hera set the Tuscan pirates on | against you, to have you sold as a slave | in some far land' (11–12).

It may be significant that wine flows over the decks of the pirates' ship in the Hymn: while this is naturally a part of the revelation of Dionysus, the god of wine, it is also perhaps a reminder that the Dionysiac condition – drunkenness – is taking control of the nature and order of narrative events. In this context, the transformation of the pirates into dolphins is apposite. Here, some fragments of Pindar are again suggestively parallel: '[The dolphins] who are fond of men, | have not forgotten their past lives' (fr. 236) may hint at the same story told in the Hymn, and the more general 'The dolphin swims fastest at a ship's side' (fr. 234) indicates how standard an item the dolphin is in description of a sea voyage. The link between the mythic and the observed might be provided in a more substantial fragment, quoted by Athenaeus (*Deipnosophistae* 11.782D):

Thrasyboulos, I'm sending you
this carriage full of delectable
songs, which you can have your fill
of once the dinner's through;

may it delight
all the all-night
drinkers with you; may it enhance
the produce of Dionysus
in cups made by Athenians
that you pass round, and spur you on:
for all the cares that weigh on us
go away then,
and the breasts of men
are lightened. And then, on a sea
of sheer well-being, a sea all gold,
everyone is at once enrolled
on a voyage to a further shore
(a shore that isn't really there);
the man with nothing suddenly
is rich, and all with him can be
rich in each other's company.   (Pindar, fr. 124)

(It is this fragment which is recycled at the beginning of Louis MacNeice's poem 'Alcohol' (1942): 'On golden seas of drink, so the Greek poet said, | Rich and poor are alike'.)[1] The sense in which experience of wine can in itself be a kind of sea-going, in the course of which unexpected things occur, makes the dolphins especially apt metaphorical presences in the narrative. It may be, in fact, that such clusters of related ideas and images have their ultimate source in the famously puzzling Homeric epithet for the sea, *oinōpa* ('wine-faced'/ 'wine-dark').

The story contained in the Hymn, then, is quite distinct from the kinds of narrative in the longer Homeric Hymns. At the same time, it has to focus and make meaningful a showing forth – an epiphany – of the god's particular nature and power. As Dominique Jaillard puts this, 'Rather than exploring the position of the god within the divisions of the pantheon and

---

1   Louis MacNeice, *Collected Poems* ed. Peter McDonald (London: Faber and Faber, 2007), 229.

the cosmos, the Hymn instead takes on a strong *iconic* value, which, by means of a dense narrative sequence, renders the god intensely present in the place of performance.'[2]

page 102: *son of Semelē*] The name of Semelē is in fact the third word of the opening line, and it is this matrilineal emphasis (for Zeus, Dionysus' father, is not mentioned here) which is repeated at the end of the Hymn; Dionysus himself also announces that he was born to Cadmus' daughter. There may be some contextual factor, now wholly lost to us, that explains this degree of insistence on the god's mother – and it is women, we might remember, who are at the centre of attention as cult-worshippers in Euripides' *Bacchae*, where the story of Semelē is also important. (For more on Semelē, see Notes to Hymn 1, page 180.)

Etruscan pirates] The Greek calls these pirates *Tyrsēnoi*. There has been disagreement over the place of origin here referred to: as *AHS* put it, 'In the fifth century BC the terms Tyrsenians and Pelasgians were regarded as alternative names for the pre-Hellenic population of the Balkan peninsula' (381). The name went on to apply to settlers in Italy, and was also used to refer to the inhabitants of the island of Lemnos.

but these were not enough] This effortless escape-act is very similar to what happens in Euripides' *Bacchae*, when attempts are made to put the god in bonds; there, to more subtle literary effect, Dionysus deludes Pentheus into tying up a bull in the belief that he is securing his prisoner. Just as in the Hymn the unconstrained Dionysus 'passed his time smiling', so in the *Bacchae* the god says that 'I just sat by, close to all this, | watching it all in peace and quiet' (621–622).

2 Dominique Jaillard, 'The Seventh Homeric Hymn to Dionysus: An Epiphanic Sketch', in Andrew Faulkner (ed.), *The Homeric Hymns: Interpretative Essays* (Oxford: Oxford University Press, 2011), 145.

page 103: *the lands beyond the North Wind's rush and roar*] In the Greek it is the inhabitants of these places who are named, the Hyperboreans: these were a northern race in legend, mentioned by Hesiod and by Pindar, who were thought to be worshippers of Apollo. In one version, preserved in Alcaeus, they hosted Apollo himself each winter, in paradise-like surroundings. The main meaning of the concept in poetry, as here, is that of a place at the very ends of the earth.

page 105: *where they became dolphins*] In the Hymn to Apollo (Hymn 3), Apollo takes the shape of a dolphin as he controls the vessel of the Cretan sailors (see pp. 32–33). Here, it is the humans who become dolphins, as a punishment from the god whom they have attempted to control. In addition to the literary uses of dolphins noted above, a later allusion by Lucian (second century AD) carries memories of early man-to-dolphin transformations involving Dionysus:

> [The dolphins speaking]: Don't be surprised, Poesidon, that we behave considerately to men; it was from being men ourselves that we became sea-creatures. And I do blame Dionysus for that, for he transformed us after defeating us in that fight at sea, when he might just as well have kept us on in submission to him, the way he did with everybody else. (Lucian, *Dialogues of the Sea-Gods* 5.1)

loudest roarer in the pack] Dionysus here announces himself as *eribromos* ('roarer') in an echo of one of the god's cult titles, *Bromios*: his affinities with wild beasts (such as here the lion and the bear) make this appropriate.

Notes to Hymn 8

This is the joker in the pack of the Homeric Hymns. Beyond all possible doubt, it is from a time long after that of the composition of even the youngest of the other poems: West attributes it to the Neoplatonist philosopher Proclus of the fifth century AD – that is, someone writing about eight hundred years after many of the other Hymns. Undoubtedly, the poem is anomalous: in the first place, it is clearly more astrological than anything else, for here Ares is very explicitly the planet Mars; next, it is stylistically quite distinct from anything else in the collection, being essentially a piling-up of elaborate and artful epithets (in this, deriving more from the tradition of the so-called 'Orphic' Hymns of late antiquity); and finally, as a poem it is in the form of a personal meditation, closer to a prayer for peace than an ancient hymn to the god of war. How this ended up in sequence with the other Homeric Hymns is something of a mystery – most probably, a mystery of the most impenetrable kind, since it could well be owing to nothing more complicated than an accident: many of the manuscripts include the 'Orphic' Hymns and the Hymns of Proclus, and it may be that somewhere in the lost history of the manuscript tradition, quite possibly centuries after Alexandrian scholars drew the Homeric Hymns together, a stray hymn by Proclus was inserted in the wrong position, so that subsequent copies (of which the manuscripts we have are the successors) carried on the mistake. In attempting to translate this poem, I have thought it best to try for the idiom of some modern poet intent on simultaneous archaism and anachronism, who has sought out a rare and long-forgotten form in which to encounter and ventriloquise the distant past.

Notes to Hymn 9

This nine-line poem seems to show signs of coming from a particular locality: references here to Claros, Smyrna, and the River Melēs (places not in themselves so strongly associated with Artemis as to be merely conventional) may point towards an origin in Asia Minor, on the Ionian coast. Smyrna, which was a city of some importance, is the starting-point of Artemis' journey in this Hymn, a journey which ends in Claros and a welcoming reception there from her brother Apollo. It may be relevant that the city of Smyrna was destroyed by Alyattes II of Lydia around 600 BC; conceivably, the Hymn imagines a relocation by Artemis in the wake of this. Claros, near the city of Colophon, was the centre of a major temple-complex of Apollo, where oracles were delivered. The Apolline oracle was here from the eighth century BC, and it is mentioned in the Hymn to Apollo (see page 25 and note on page 225). Although there was a temple to Artemis, the temple to Apollo was the most important religious spot, and it is this which is mentioned in Hymn 9. (The temple to Apollo as excavated in Claros is probably from the third century BC, and therefore very probably from a period well after the Hymn's composition, but there is evidence of temples both to Apollo and to Artemis here from the sixth century BC.) Archaeological discoveries have confirmed that water was very important to the oracular process here: a spring of fresh water under the temple of Apollo was drunk by the priest, and the god's words then pronounced. In this Hymn, water is the key image: Artemis waters her horses on her journey from Smyrna to Claros, where she is to be received by her brother. The river is specified as the Melēs (albeit only in the M manuscript; but the location is right, and the other manuscripts carry what look like garbled versions of the name). Here, I have allowed myself the licence of calling this 'Homer's river', on the grounds that the Homeric associations of the Melēs would have been pretty clearly understood by many ancient audiences: Homer was thought often to have been born by the Melēs, and was initially therefore known by the name Melisegenes (as for instance in section 3 of the pseudo-Herodotean 'Life' of the poet, page 142.) It is possible to imagine this short poem being used as the *prooimion* for a recitation from Homer at Claros, perhaps in the sixth or fifth century BC.

Notes to Hymn 10

This six-line poem may well, like the other short poem to Aphrodite (Hymn 6), be intended as the prelude to a recitation in a competition, which asks for the goddess's aid in gaining victory. It makes a feature of using Aphrodite's title of *Cythereia*, and of stressing her origin on Cyprus (all this, in fact, in its two opening words, *Kyprogenē Kythereian*), and in its fourth line hails Aphrodite as *thea Salaminos eüktimenēs*, 'goddess of well-cultivated Salamis': Salamis was a city-state on the eastern coast of Cyprus. In view of all this, a Cypriot origin for the poem seems perfectly plausible. In the M manuscript, this Hymn is in a different position, following Hymn 11 (to Athene); M also omits the reference to Salamis.

Notes to Hymn 11

This poem of five lines reads more as a brief prayer than a prelude to recitation, partly because (like Hymn 12) it is without a closing formula marking the intention to move from invocation to narrative. Athene is addressed in the first line as *erusiptolin*, 'protector of the city', but just because the goddess is powerfully associated with the civic religion of Athens does not mean that the poem originates there: there were numerous other city-states for whom Athene was the guardian. *Erusiptolin* is also used in line 3 of Hymn 28 (to Athene), but the epithet itself may derive from the *Iliad*, in which a Trojan noblewoman makes an offering to the goddess in her temple, beginning with the formal address *potni' Athēnaiē, rhusiptoli, dia theaōn*, 'Lady Athene, protector of the city, fairest of gods' (5: 305). There is much irony in the *Iliad*'s use of the epithet here, since Athene is in fact siding with the Greeks rather than the Trojans. One curiosity of this Hymn is its joining together of the usually incompatible gods Athene and Ares: they are seen here a deities with a common interest in warfare. This is true, though their major literary conjunction in this regard is in Book 5 of the *Iliad*, where they both take to the field on opposite sides (Athene supporting Diomedes and the Greeks, and Ares fighting for the Trojans). Although, according to Pausanias (*Description of Greece* 1.8.4), the Athenian temple of Ares contained a statue of Athene, and there was a joint altar to the two gods at the races in Olympia (5.15.6), it is still highly unusual to find them together as here. Olympus, of course, contains them both; and Pindar has Zeus put them in a single line, rather as a father might quickly mention together two difficult children, passing over their mutual incompatibilities: 'If you want to come yourself, and live with me, | and with

Athene, and with Ares of the black spear, | then that fate can be yours' (*Nemean* 10, 83–85).

Notes to Hymn 12

This five-line poem appears to be without a conventional conclusion (for example, a line of prayer to the deity, or a promise to go on with some narrative). The speculation of *AHS*, that 'Possibly the hymn is the opening of a longer poem' (393) is reasonable, if unproveable. West's proposal that these few lines may originate in Samos (where there were major festivals devoted to Hera) is also plausible (*Loeb*, 17); at the same time, the epithet used in the second line of the poem, *basileian* ('queen') is also attested in cult centres of Heres at Argos, Lebadea, and Pisidia. Both this epithet and *chrysothronon* ('gold-enthroned') turn up in one of Pindar's Nemean Odes (1. 37–39), where the goddess is *chrysosthonon Hēran* ('gold-enthroned Hera') and *theōn basilea* ('queen of the gods'). Brief as it is, the Hymn takes care to give Zeus equal weight to that of his consort: if this is the beginning of a lost narrative, it is unlikely to have followed the commoner storylines in which the pair of gods found themselves at marital odds.

Notes to Hymn 13

This piece, which is three hexameter lines in length, is made up almost entirely from elements of other poems. The first line is that of Hymn 2 (to Demeter), and the second line is line 493 of the same poem. This minute Hymn's third and final line is largely identical to line 134 in Callimachus' Hymn to Demeter (third century BC), save for an alteration of the line end to deliver the request to 'begin my song'. It is something of a puzzle to understand how this Hymn was intended to function in the collection of Homeric Hymns: perhaps it somehow records three lines that might come in useful if a performing poet or reciter had to make an address to Demeter; perhaps it is the patched-together opening of some longer piece addressed to the goddess. Yet the real puzzle is why two lines from the ancient Demeter Hymn should be capped with one written centuries later. Such puzzles may not be worthwhile, of course: it is possible, for example, that both the lines from Hymn 2 here were in fact present in other Demeter poems, whether earlier or later than the Hymn; and the line from Callimachus may not, in any case, be original to him – he might have been quoting it from older tradition, and indeed Hymn 13 might not be quoting him at all, but quoting the lost text from which he drew. Certainty is impossible. As for the quotations from Hymn 2 (if they *are* quotations from there, and not from a place or places to which we have lost access), it is worth remembering that these would be all of that long Hymn we possessed, had not the M manuscript been discovered by Matthiae at the end of the eighteenth century. Bearing all these profound uncertainties in mind, it may still be useful to know the context of the line quoted from Callimachus, which comes towards the end of his Demeter Hymn:

Hail, goddess, keep this city safe,
safe in its wealth and unity of mind;
bring good things to our countryside,
feed the cows, and bring sheep-flocks to us;
bring the ear of corn, bring harvest,
and feed up peace, so that the sower
may reap all that he sows: look well
on me, prayed, prayed, and prayed to,
great governess amongst the gods.

(Callimachus Hy.6, 134–138).

Notes to Hymn 14

Numerous manuscripts give the title of this Hymn as 'To Rhea', and Rhea was often known as the Mother of the Gods. This appellation seems also to have been used for a god from Asia, whose worship shaded into that of Rhea, Cybele. Evidence from inscriptions shows that there were cults of the Mother of the Gods all over Greece, in Epidouros, in Boeotia, Argos, on Cos and Thera, and in Athens; the cult was also practised in non-public contexts. However strong its Eastern associations, the worship of the Mother of the Gods was understood as distinctively Greek by the time of Herodotus, who tells the story of an unwisely enthusiastic convert from Scythia:

> But as regards foreign customs, the Scythians (like others) very much shun practising those of any other country, and particularly of Hellas, as was proved in the case of Anacharsis and also of Scyles. For when Anacharsis was coming back to the Scythian country after having seen much of the world in his travels and given many examples of his wisdom, he sailed through the Hellespont and put in at Cyzicus; where, finding the Cyzicenes celebrating the feast of the Mother of the Gods with great ceremony, he vowed to this same Mother that if he returned to his own country safe and sound he would sacrifice to her as he saw the Cyzicenes doing, and establish a nightly rite of worship. So when he came to Scythia, he hid himself in the country called Woodland (which is beside the Race of Achilles, and is all overgrown with every kind of timber); hidden there, Anacharsis celebrated the goddess' ritual with exactness, carrying a small drum and hanging images about himself. Then some Scythian saw him doing this and told the king, Saulius; who, coming to the place himself and seeing Anacharsis performing these rites, shot an arrow at him and killed him. (*Histories* 4.76.1–5 trans. A.D. Godley)

The importance of music in the worship of the god is shown in this passage by the unfortunate Anacharsis' drum; in the Hymn, the various dedicated instruments are given detailed attention. In the Greek, these instruments are specified as castanets, drums, and flutes, making a tremendous din. I have translated these into instruments of similar volume from an altogether different time and place: fife-bands and lambeg drums are familiar features of Orange Order marches in Northern Ireland each summer and, while worship of a mother-goddess is certainly far removed from any intentions of the marching brethren, the resultant noise is the closest thing in my own experience to whatever musical rites the Hymn records.

Notes to Hymn 15

The title here adds an epithet to the name of Heracles: this word, *leontothumon*, means roughly 'lionheart' and, although it does not appear in any other extant Greek texts, it is not all that odd: *leon-* compounds are not uncommon, and in early literature a fragment of Tyrtaeus (the Spartan poet of the mid-seventh century BC) contains the very similar phrase *megathume leon* ('great-hearted lion'). As a title in English, 'To Heracles the Lionheart' unhelpfully confuses a Greek hero with a Plantagenet King, and perhaps 'To Heracles the Lion-hearted' does little to avoid this; but the epithet might be exerting some pressure on the meaning of the poem itself (one of Heracles' tasks, after all, was the killing of the Nemean lion, and visual depictions of him generally feature him wearing the lion's pelt), so simply getting rid of *leontothumon* in translation would be a loss.

This nine-line Hymn cannot be dated with any certainty. Heracles was being worshipped as a deified mortal, with the goddess Hebe as his consort on Olympus, by the end of the sixth century BC: Herodotus mentions his worship, and Pindar calls him a *herōs theos* 'hero god' (Nemean Ode 3.22). Lines in Book 11 of the *Odyssey* would constitute evidence for an earlier date, but only with the significant caution that they were rejected by ancient commentators as insertions in the text by the Athenian Onomacritus (c. 500 BC). The cult of Heracles was fairly widespread in Greece at this time, but it seems from pottery remains that it had been taken up by the Athenian tyrant Peisistratos in the mid-sixth century BC, and we know of a festival in honour of Heracles held every four years at Marathon, so that an Attic source for a Heracles-related addition to the *Odyssey* in the wake of that is not implausible. If this particular tradition about textual insertion has some foundation in fact, it may be important for the dating of the Hymn, since the lines in the *Odyssey* closely parallel the language of its description of Heracles and his bride Hebe. Odysseus in the underworld has just witnessed the tortures of Sisyphus, and turns his attention to Heracles:

> Just then, I saw the powerful Heracles,
> but only as a ghost – for he had gone
> to enjoy himself at parties with the gods
> and have the daughter of great Zeus and gold-
> shod Hera, their lovely-ankled Hebe.
>
> (*Odyssey* 11: 601–4)

In the Greek, there are a number of close verbal parallels with the Hymn's penultimate line: the verb describing Heracles' enjoyment is the same (Homer: *terpetai*, Hymn: *terpomenos*), as is the verb meaning that he 'has' (*echei*) Hebe – for consort or wife, presumably, though neither Homer nor the Hymn supplies this word of information explicitly. Finally, Hebe herself has in both Homer and the Hymn exactly the same epithet, *kallisphuron* ('with beautiful ankles'): the term is used in early epic, both in Hesiod and the *Iliad*, to refer to beautiful young women or goddesses, but its association with Hebe here makes it almost certain that the Hymn is in a direct relation to the *Odyssey*. If the author of the lines in question was indeed Onomacritus and not Homer, then the Hymn is later than c. 500 BC. As usual, certainty in the matter of dating is not possible; and of course the Hymn could well be later than this. Conversely, there is no way to disprove the assertion that Onomacritus is in fact alluding to the Hymn – if a few lines on Heracles were needed for insertion, then the Hymn might have been the nearest thing to hand.

Heracles was the most prominent example for Greeks of a mortal (albeit a mortal with Zeus for a father) who became a god. The Hymn makes a feature of this dual nature, and it does not attempt to minimize the specifically earth-bound sufferings of its subject. An important line in this respect is line 6 of the Greek text, which is literally 'Many things he did [that were] wicked, and many too he endured'. Amongst the wicked things (*atasthala*, a strong word, often with implications of impiety and outrage) must be the murder of his wife Megara and their children, when Heracles was driven mad by the goddess Hera (Zeus's wife, who was furious about her husband's affair with Alcmene, Hercules' mother). As for what Heracles endured, the story of his labours in the service of the vindictive king Eurystheus was well known in antiquity, and is alluded to in the Hymn. Given the horror of Hercules' mortal end – dying in flames on Mount Oeta, in agony from the poisoned shirt of the centaur Nessus – the happy ending of his deification is notable. The Hymn gives this a lot of emphasis, in line with the general religious hope that the hero-god will want to bring his magic touch to bear on the mortal troubles of those taking part in his cult. The last line of the Hymn, which asks Heracles to send both *aretēn* and *olbon* (roughly, excellence and prosperous fortune), has a cultic resonance. Despite this, it is possible that this short poem is less cultic prayer than epic *prooimion*: it makes much of Heracles' wanderings (in a manner not unlike Homeric references to Odysseus), mentions Eurystheus explicitly, and hints at a mixed bag of adventures and misadventures. Its opening clause, which begins with the hero's name, ends with a verb meaning 'I will sing about'. Perhaps the nine lines are what survives of a much longer poem, in which the stories of Heracles' labours were told, and his eventual deification (which entailed reconciliation with Hera) was detailed and celebrated.

Notes to Hymn 16

In Homer, Asclepius is not a god but a mortal, the king of Tricca, and a physician who learned the healer's art from the centaur Chiron. Fragments of Hesiodic poetry suggest that Asclepius was next made a son of Apollo; he was not yet a god himself, but *orchamon andrōn* ('leader of men'), and was destroyed by Zeus, angered by his over-exercising of healing powers. In Pindar's *Pythian* 3, this account seems to have been accepted, and Asclepius' mother (as in the Hymn) is Corōnis, the daughter of Phlygeas:

> I wish that Philyra's son,
> Chiron, who is gone,
> were living still (if it's right
> to give voice to a wish so common),
> and that he still had oversight,
> offspring of Cronos, the child of Heaven,
> as lord of the green-wooded land of Pelion,
> a wild creature, and yet
> with his good heart set
> on humanity; just as he was
> when once he raised Asclepius,
> that gentle author of relief
> for the body's pain and grief,
> a hero, and sure guardian
> against all manner of ailments in man.
>
> Before the horseman Phlygeas'
> daughter could finish giving him birth,
> the golden arrow-shafts of Artemis
> felled her, sent her down under the earth

to Hades' house, even as she made
use of Eleithyia's aid
on the childbed; for the fury of Zeus's
family is no little thing.   (*Pythian* 3, 1–13)

(The sin of Corōnis had been to marry the mortal Ischys after
already having conceived a child by Apollo.) In the course of
the fifth century BC, Asclepius had gone beyond local places
of veneration such as Tricca in Thessaly and Messenia, and was
a tutelary presence for the college of physicians based on Cos,
who referred to themselves as the *Asclepiadae* (on the model,
perhaps, of the poetic *Homeridae*). The cult of Asclepius
became widespread throughout the Greek world, and one
possible reason for his success as a divinity may well lie in his
human origins and (as in Pindar's Ode) his consequent human
sympathies. The Hymn is impossible to date, beyond being
later than Homer and probably than Hesiod, nor are there any
obvious marks of location. If it once served as the prelude to
a longer narrative recitation, it could have been used in any of
the many sites of Asclepius' worship: one possible venue might
be Epidaurus, near Athens, where the god was important from
around 500 BC.

Notes to Hymn 17

This short Hymn, which is just five lines of hexameter verse, may perhaps (like Hymn 13) preserve lines from another, longer poem. The Dioscuri, Castor and Polydeuces (the Roman Pollux) were believed to be the twin sons of Tyndareus of Sparta, the husband of Leda. The boys, like their sister Helen, were supernaturally fathered by Zeus. In the *Iliad*, the two brothers are said to have died before the Trojan war, when Helen wonders whether they might be somewhere among the Greek army:

> 'I can see the bright-eyed Greeks now, all of them
> that I know well and could call by their names,
> but two of the troop-captains I can't see:
> Castor the horse-tamer, Polydeuces the prize
> boxer, the brothers whom my mother bore.
> Either they didn't follow the army here
> from lovely Sparta, or else when they arrived
> in their trim ships they found no appetite
> to go into this fighting on the ground,
> abashed by the taunts of shame that follow me.'
> She said this, but already the earth that gives
> life was holding them secure in death
> at Lacadaemon, their dear native land.   (*Iliad* 3: 235–244)

In the *Odyssey*, however, the twins' mortality has become qualified, and is now a mysteriously part-time divinity:

> And I saw Leda, Tyndareus' wife,
> who by Tyndareus had given life
> to two firm-minded sons, the horse-tamer

Castor, and the excellent fight-gamer
Polydeuces; for both are held alive
by the good earth, and even in the grave
Zeus grants them a particular privilege:
they come to life in turn, for one day each,
one living when the other dies, and then
changing places with him; and so they gain
perpetual honour on a par with gods.

(*Odyssey* 11: 298–305)

There are other literary versions of how the Dioscuri came to be immortal, but these also involve curious doublings-up: for example, one twin with a divine, one with a human father (in Pindar, Zeus tells Polydueces, 'You are my son, | but the other [Castor] was conceived apart | by your mother's husband, when he came | to her, that hero, and he sowed | his mortal seed' (*Nemean* 10, 80–83). In time, the pair were regularly venerated together, and their cult became very widespread. They appear in sculpture in the mid-sixth century BC, on temple metopes from Delphi, and feature in Attic black figure pottery also from around this time onwards. For further information on the functions of the Dioscuri, see Note to Hymn 33 (page 336).

In translating this Hymn, I have exercised considerable liberties of expansion. The voice of the Muse in the first line of the Greek, for example, is simply *ligeia*, 'clear'. The Taygetus is a mountain-range in the southern Peloponnese, an important natural line of defence for Sparta.

Notes to Hymn 18

This twelve-line poem derives very largely from lines in the long Hymn to Hermes (Hymn 4). The reasons for such acts of abbreviation are perhaps less obscure than those for the tradition's having somehow preserved the results; and the speculative explanation offered by *AHS* probably cannot be bettered, even in more modern terms: 'Perhaps', they write, 'even a hymn of moderate compass came to be thought excessive by rhapsodists who were anxious to begin the actual recitation: the prelude had become a mere convention, just as a few bars of *God save the King* are now taken to represent the entire national anthem at the conclusion of a play' (401). It is possible that the longer poem was filleted for these verses of greeting and praise; at any rate, it seems very likely that this poem is younger than Hymn 4 (i.e., it dates from some time after the late sixth century BC). For the sake of variety, I have given the conventional epithet of Hermes, *Argeiphontēn* ('slayer of the hound Argus') a slightly flippant turn into French. The other references are all explained by Hymn 4 (for which, see also the Notes to that poem). 'Good giver | of gifts' translates *charidōta*: this was in fact a cult title of Hermes, and at Samos the god was *Hermes Charidōtēs*, where at his festival there was a general dispensation to commit petty theft. This is in fact a topic for Plutarch's first century AD Greek culture Q&A: '*For what reason do the Samians, when they are sacrificing to Hermes Charidōtēs, let anyone who wants steal from them and pick their pockets?* Because in following an oracle they decamped from Samos to Mycalē, and supported themselves there for ten years by piracy; after that, they sailed back to their island and defeated their enemies' (*Greek Questions*, 303D, 55).

Notes to Hymn 19

The god Pan, who was in form half-man and half-goat, seems to have originated in Arcadia; his worship spread into the rest of Greece, first through Boeotia and then Attica, from early in the fifth century BC, and became widespread by the fourth century BC. The acceptance of Pan's cult by the Athenians is figured by the story in Herodotus, of events around 490 BC and the Battle of Marathon:

> While still in the city, the generals first sent to Sparta the herald Philippides, an Athenian and a long-distance runner who made that his calling. As Philippides himself said when he brought the message to the Athenians, when he was in the Parthenian mountain above Tegea he encountered Pan. Pan called out Philippides' name and bade him ask the Athenians why they paid him no attention, though he was of goodwill to the Athenians, had often been of service to them, and would be in the future. The Athenians believed that these things were true, and when they became prosperous they established a sacred precinct of Pan beneath the Acropolis. Ever since that message they propitiate him with annual sacrifices and a torch-race. (Herodotus, *Histories* 6.105.1–3, trans. A.D. Godley)

It is almost certain that this Hymn is no older than the early fifth century BC, and it could well come from a time when the cult of Pan was spreading through Greece; but the poem's language, though it has a number of otherwise unattested words, is not that of the Alexandrine poets. There is a possible awareness of the Hymn in Callimachus' *Hymn to Artemis*, when the goddess comes across Pan as he cuts up a lynx: this may just be a recollection of or allusion to the Homeric Hymn's detail of how 'A cloak of spotted lynx covers his back'. There are stronger signs of the Hymn's own awareness of the Hymn to Hermes, which is probably from the late sixth or earlier fifth century BC. Although it is not possible to be certain, the Hymn to Pan may well come from the middle of the fifth century BC.

page 118: *Hermes' dear child*] In fact, there were many different genealogies for Pan in general currency (a total of fourteen), although there was a degree of consensus about Hermes being his father. In the Hymn – and very unusually for the genre – Pan himself is not named at the very beginning.

the bird | who sings all day] This is the nightingale. The verb the Hymn uses for the birdsong, *cheëi* ('pours'), is the same as that used in Homer, when Penelope tells the nightingale's story:

> Just as the daughter of Pindareos,
> the forest nightingale, when spring has come
> sings her heart out from where she perches deep
> among the trees, and with a multitude
> of modulating notes pours out her voice
> in lament for her dear child Itylus,
> King Zēthos' son whom, all unwittingly,
> she slew with a sword of bronze; just so, my heart
> in doubt takes my thoughts first this way, then that.
> (*Odyssey* 19: 518–524)

The metaphorical possibilities of 'pour', then, are already explored pretty fully in Homer, and the Hymn could well be making allusion to them here. But in making the song *meligērun* ('honey-voiced'), the Hymn takes the edge off the bird's conventional lament, and turns it towards celebratory offering: honey, like wine, could be poured as a formal libation.

page 119: *replace | each clear note with its ghost*] The translation's periphrasis here slightly obscures a reference which is implicitly in the Greek, for *echo* there can be simply an echo, but can also be taken as alluding to the nymph Echo, who spurned the advances of Pan (only to find her own advances, to the youth Narcissus, spurned in turn).

Hermes] From this point, the poem records Pan's hymn of praise to his divine father. Mount Cyllene, as Hermes' birthplace, is an important locale for the long Homeric Hymn to Hermes (Hymn 4).

Dryops' sweet daughter] Dryopē, whose father is Dryops son of Arcas. The name here associates her with oak-trees, and this, along with the word *nymphē* in the unusual sense of 'daughter', gives further emphasis to Hermes' character as a deity of transformation. The girl is the mortal offspring of a mortal man, but Hermes' attention brings her close to the condition of being a tree-nymph; he, for his part, comes closer to the condition of mortal life, by entering into the service of her father.

page 120: skins of the hares] The hare was a symbol associated with Pan, and is to be found in this connection in some Greek coinage of the fourth century BC.

they called him Pan] Clearly, this is a case of the poet (or the myth which the poet inherits) inventing an etymology: *pan* is the Greek word for 'all' (though this is not likely, in fact, to lie behind the god's name).

Notes to Hymn 20

Hephaestus is the god of fire, as well as of the skills arising from the use of fire. In Homer, he is a blacksmith and artificer, though also something of an Olympian outsider: he is lame, the cuckolded husband of Aphrodite, and in the past has been cast out of heaven, falling to earth on the island of Samos. It is possible that Hephaestus is a divinity whose origins lie outside Greece, and his position in myth as an anomalous god – conceived by Hera on her own, and a cripple who is often mocked by the other gods – may perhaps strengthen this possibility. In early poetry, Hephaestus and Athene are sometimes mentioned together; this happens in one Homeric simile:

> Just as when a skilled craftsman overlays
> gold with silver, instructed in the ways
> of all such work by the god Hephaestus
> and Pallas Athene, making such fine art,
> so did the goddess pour with a full heart
> beauty and grace on his head and his frame.
>
> (*Odyssey* 6: 232–5)

The same conjunction of gods is in Hesiod, when they work together to create and to instruct Pandora:

> Then Zeus ordered the much-renowned
> Hephaestus to waste no more time
> and mix together soil and water,
> to put in this a human voice
> and motive force, and make the shape
> a beautiful young woman's, like

the gods in heaven to behold.
He told Athene then to teach
her crafts, the weaving of bright cloths [...]

(*Works and Days*, 60–64)

Outside Lemnos itself, where he had a cult site, Hephaestus had a place of worship in mid-fifth century BC Athens. Here, he was worshipped alongside Athene (just as he is coupled with the goddess in this Hymn). In the Theseion above the Agora in Athens, from about 450 BC, there was a sacred area, with sculpture, specifically for Hephaestus and Athene; and it was from here that a major five-yearly festival began, where events honoured the two gods jointly. It is quite possible that this eight-line Hymn has some connection with the Athenian rites; its being a prayer rather than (in any very obvious way) a prelude to some narrative would tend to support this theory.

Notes to Hymn 21

This five-line Hymn offers few clues to help with dating. The present translation somewhat underplays its odd (but authentically ancient) ornithology: in the Greek the swan 'sings from its wings' (*hupo pterugōn*), and this reflects the widespread belief that swans were (except at the point of death) voiceless, so that the sounds they were heard making in flight came somehow from their flapping wings. This began as natural history, and not a poetic conceit; but its longevity as a notion that enabled poetic thought is demonstrated most convincingly by a line in W.B. Yeats's 'The Wild Swans at Coole': 'The bell-beat of their wings above my head'. The River Pēnaios is in Thessaly.

Notes to Hymn 22

This seven-line Hymn opens with a standard prelude formula (*Amphi Poseidaōna … archom' aeidein*: 'About Poseidon … I begin by singing'), but the poem concludes more as a prayer for safety on the sea. As such, it can be compared to the poem known as Epigram 6 (see page 150). In the Hymn, however, the element of prayer is present only in the final two lines; the rest of the poem, in its small compass, includes the standard hymnic elements of address to the god, outline of his powers, and location of his places of worship. About these places, in fact, the Hymn seems to enshrine a mistake: it mentions 'broad Aegae and Helicon', but this is likely to be an ancient error, for the god was worshipped in Helicē in Achaea on the Corinthian Gulf, and not Mount Helicon. Poseidon did have as one of his titles *Helicōnios*, and this was used in his worship at a number of cities in Ionia; perhaps the Hymn originates here. The correct form, Helicē (also here twinned with Aegae), is used in Homer, *Iliad* 8: 203.

Notes to Hymn 23

This may appear a very short Hymn (four lines in Greek) to be addressed to the most important of the gods. In fact, the poem is an opportunity to portray Zeus as the consort of Themis, goddess of Justice. Conceivably, it could serve as the prelude to a narrative in which justice was a major theme; perhaps, in a broader context, it could come before a performance for which the poet might wish to emphasise what would fall due to him by right in the way of reward. Themis was Zeus's second wife, who follows Mētis (Resourcefulness, Wisdom) in the mythic chronology of his marriages. As a personification of right order, she gives birth to the *Hōrai* (who watch over correct arrangements) and the fates (who punish wrong behaviour, and enforce mortality on earth). There were commonly altars of Themis close by those to Zeus on approaches to cities, the message being presumably a double one, of fair treatment to travelling foreigners, and of fair dealing in the matter of those foreigners' commercial business. Thus in Pindar the trading city of Aegina is the place 'where Themis, saviour god, | is seated beside Zeus, | respecter of the foreigner, and most | honoured amongst men' (*Olympian* 8: 22–24). In thinking of possible contexts for this Hymn, the performing poet's status as travelling performer, come to town to make an honourable living from his art before being on his way to other such venues, seems likely to be relevant.

Notes to Hymn 24

This five-line poem is in honour of a goddess who is rarely depicted anthropomorphically (see note to Hymn 5, page 276). Commonly, Hestia is associated with the hearth – in private homes, but also in connection with the more public hearths of civic buildings. In the Hymn, the goddess is being invited 'to this house' from Delphi (Pythō): this could conceivably be a private dwelling, but is more likely to be a public place such as a temple. At Delphi, Hestia had her place at the sacred hearth of Apollo, the symbolic *omphalos*, from which fire was distributed to various Greek sacred sites after the repulse of the Persians in the early fifth century BC. The 'pure oil' that is shining from Hestia in this Hymn may reflect a rite in which the head of a god's statue was anointed with oil. The mention of Zeus possibly adds to the strength of the argument that the Hymn is intended for a public dedication: in a temple, Zeus and Hestia would make an understandable conjunction (more so than in a private home): there is evidence for dedications jointly to Zeus and Hestia from places as far apart as Syracuse, Cos, Rhodes, and Athens.

Notes to Hymn 25

Of the seven lines of this Hymn, six are drawn directly or indirectly from Hesiod's *Theogony*. The opening line bears some resemblance to the first line of Hesiod's poem, while lines 2–5 are almost exact quotations of lines 94–97 of the *Theogony*, with the sixth line being a close imitation of Hesiod's line 104. Clearly, then, the Hymn was run together by someone with the *Theogony* to hand (or rather, in the repertoire), to create a serviceable prelude to some kind of performance. Apollo and the Muses are very naturally conjoined in the context of musical or poetic events, and one title which was used for Apollo was *Musagētēs* ('Conductor of the Muses'); according to Pausanias' *Description of Greece*, there was a temple dedicated to Apollo and the Muses at Megalopolis, and they were depicted together on a gable decoration at Delphi itself. That the Hymn is post-Hesiodic is obvious, but it may be very considerably later (there is, as ever, very little evidence to go on). In translating this Hymn I have tried to convey an impression of a poetic style that is not quite first-hand: the blank verse, together with the particular stretch of syntax, are intended to recall something famous (as the *Theogony* would have been famous) – in this case resulting in a compressed imitation of the opening of *Paradise Lost*.

Notes to Hymn 26

This thirteen-line Hymn looks very much like something intended for a particular festival, with the strong implication in its final line that the event may be an annual one. The opening image of the god as *Kissokomēn Dionuson* ('Dionysus crowned with ivy') preserves an epithet which has also been found on an inscription, and is close to other ivy-compounds used for him from Pindar down to much later literature. According to Pausanias' *Description of Greece*, there was a cult of Dionysus Kissos ('Ivy Dionysus') at Acharnae (1.31.6); a pillar dedicated to the god was wreathed in ivy at Thebes, and this is referred to in a fragment of Euripides ('the god's pillar adorned with ivy' (fr. 202)). The epithet *eribromon* ('strong roarer') is considerably expanded in the translation here: one of Dionysus' cult titles was *Bromios* ('roarer'). For Semele and Nysa, see notes to Hymn 1 (page 180). The young Dionysus was raised (like Hermes) initially in the seclusion of a cave, here in the care of wood-nymphs (compare the nursing of Aeneas in Hymn 5). In translating an epithet from the Hymn's seventh line, which could be rendered as 'god of much song', I have chosen to expand the compliment into an admission of how much 'song' about these events has, indeed, been performed in the past: 'It's all been told before'.

Notes to Hymn 27

Artemis, the sister of Apollo, is one of the most important
Olympian gods; in this Hymn, particular emphasis is given to
her role as a hunter. The Hymn itself is a single continuous piece
of twenty-two lines, but I have divided it into two episodes (plus
a final closing formula). In the first part, Artemis the hunter is
seen in action; in the second, she progresses from the field to
Apollo's temple at Delphi, where her brother-god is waiting to
welcome her. When Artemis enters the temple, she puts aside
her spectacular weaponry, in readiness for dances and religious
rites: in this, the Hymn strongly resembles (and very possibly
shows a knowledge of) the entry of Apollo into the palace of
Zeus on Olympus, at the beginning of Hymn 3. The ferocity
of Artemis in her character as hunter is conveyed in this hymn
largely by elaborate epithets, which the translation tries to render
through a degree of expansion: *elaphēbolon* ('deer-shooter'),
for example, is given a whole line in the present version. The
Hymn stresses how complete the slaughter of wild animals by
Artemis really is: in the tenth line, literally translated, 'she kills
the animals' whole brood'. There may be a nod here towards
one of Artemis' more shocking exploits when, after Niobe had
boasted of her large number of children by comparison with
Leto, Artemis and Apollo together slew all of her children
(six of either sex, according to Homer) in pique. The Hymn's
second episode turns Artemis from violence to celebration, the
symbol of this transition being the hanging-up of her hunting
bow (a moment exactly matching that in Hymn 3 (page 23),
when Leto hangs up Apollo's bow at the court of the gods on
Olympus). The religious celebration which occupies the rest of
this Hymn is in honour of Leto, the deity who is dominant at
the opening of Hymn 3.

Notes to Hymn 28

The birth of Athene from the head of Zeus is at the centre of
this short Hymn. In the *Theogony*, Hesiod gives a version of
Athene's birth which includes her mother, Mētis, the goddess
of wisdom whose name is swallowed in one of her devouring
husband Zeus's epithets, *polymētis* (used twice in Hymn 28).
Hesiod's narrative is this:

> The first wife of Zeus, king of the gods,
> was Mētis, who knew more than any
> god, and more than any man:
> when she was pregnant, and about
> to give birth to Athene, Zeus
> somehow deceived her; and once he
> distracted her with his smooth talk,
> suddenly he gulped her down
> and straight into his own belly.
> This followed from the prophecies
> of Earth itself and the starry Sky,
> for they had told him to watch out
> in case some other god who lives
> forever became king instead.
> The thing that was destined was this:
> Mētis would have the cleverest children,
> a girl first, with huge shining eyes,
> Tritogeneia, the full equal
> of her father in strength and knowledge;
> and after that would bear a boy,
> hard of heart, to be a king
> of men, and a king of gods too.
> Before any of that could start,

Zeus put Mētis into his gut,
where the goddess could whisper to him
all about what was right or wrong.
[...]
And from his own head Zeus gave birth
to Athene with her wide, bright eyes:
fearsome goddess, the stirrer-up
of battles, leader from the front,
untirable, royal, who loves
to hear the loud and awful sounds
of warfare, of armed men fighting.

(Theogony, 886–900 and 924–926)

Hesiod's association of Athene with war mirrors the violence of her unusual conception and birth, in Zeus's swallowing of Mētis. The son who is (apparently) never born, and who seems to be such a potent threat to Zeus (himself, of course, the killer of a murderous father) is perhaps absorbed into the figure of Athene, for the goddess is a virgin with masculine, militaristic associations.

One epithet used by Hesiod is *Tritogeneia*: this became a common cult title for Athena, but its actual meaning is very uncertain. Quite possibly the Greeks themselves (by the classical period at least) were unable to agree on its meaning. The term is used again in the Hymn, where I have attempted a paraphrase of some of its possible associations. We know of places called Tritonis (one a lake in Libya, others rivers and springs in Boeotia and Arcadia) which might be in the word, to give the story of Athene's birth some geographical bearing. On the other hand, the mythical figure Triton was father of Pallas – a boy befriended by Athene, whose name she assumed after his death as one of her cult titles. (Although in this myth Triton might loosely act as a foster-parent to Athene, he is not her father, making '*Tritogeneia*' seem somewhat strained.) Another possibility is that some form of tripling is implied (in '*Trito...*'): yet 'three-parented' may be not just nonsensical English, but nonsensical altogether. Athene is, strictly speaking, Zeus's 'third-born' child (after Apollo and Artemis), so this might lie somewhere behind the epithet. A simpler explanation would work from the fact that *Trito* appears to have been a word for 'head' in the Aeolic dialect of Greek, giving 'head-born' as a meaning for '*Tritogoneia*'.

Hesiod does not mention, as the Hymn does, that Athene is born in full armour – though this may be implied, or simply taken for granted. Certainly, the goddess appears fully armed and brandishing a spear in various sixth and fifth century BC depictions on pottery (as e.g. in the black-figure kalyx in the British Museum, sixth century BC). A figure missing both from Hesiod and from the Hymn is the god Hephaestus, who acts as a kind of midwife, both in pottery depictions and in Pindar's seventh Olympian Ode (where Athene's loud battle-cry closely corresponds to the noises in the Hymn):

> It was thanks to the sheer skill
> of Hephaestus, who forged from bronze
> a special axe, that Athene
> jumped straight out from her father's forehead
> and gave on the spot a tremendous battle-cry:
> Heaven itself trembled then, and mother Earth.
>
> (Pindar, *Olympian* 7, 35–38)

Notes to Hymn 29

This is a fourteen-line poem, in which some editors have found good reason to rearrange the order of particular lines. Like Hymn 24, where Hestia was joined with Zeus, here the goddess is honoured in conjunction with another deity, the god Hermes. The two were associated in antiquity, though the reasons for this can be no more than speculative: Phidias' statue of Olympian Zeus, for example, had representations of Hermes and Hestia together on its base (Pausanias 5.11.8). Both deities had important roles to play in the home, and it is possible that this Hymn is angled towards performance in some private venue: Hestia presided over the (real or symbolic) hearth, while Hermes could often stand at the door. In the house itself, celebrations (as here) would both begin and end with a libation to Hestia; Hermes, for his part, would receive the last libation before sleep. This domestic power-sharing arrangement is summed up by *AHS*: 'Hestia represented the religious focus of family life at meals, and Hermes was the protector of the sleep of the family' (428).

Notes to Hymn 30

This Hymn, along with the two poems that follow it, may be younger than most in the collection. The three pieces seem to be in a deliberate grouping – Earth, Sun, and Moon – which suggests a later kind of composition. The three poems are also all of very similar length. This is not to say than any of the three is unsuitable in itself as a prelude, in the customary way; but it is striking that the poems seem to be composed with a degree of artfulness that enables them to be (so to speak) self-standing. The title of this Hymn (as given in most of the manuscripts) is more explanatory than would be the case in poems simply addressed to a deity (where the name alone is enough); its fairly plain Greek (*mētera pantōn*, 'mother of all') is contrasted immediately by the highly poetic diction of the poem's opening line, and its word *pammēteiran*, meaning much the same thing, but here in an extremely rarefied and exotic verbal shape. In the same opening line comes an adjective which occurs nowhere else in extant writing, *ēüthemethlon* ('deeply-grounded'), and this may be another sign that the very artful poetic style of the piece is late. Gaia, the goddess of the Earth, can claim a much more ancient lineage, and she is a protagonist in a major episode of Hesiod's *Theogony*, where she is the first deity to be born out of Chaos, who brings forth Day, the Air, Heaven, and the Sea, before becoming mother to the Titans (*Theogony*, 116–200). The worship of Gaia as a goddess seems mainly to have been in her aspect of *Kourotrophos*, the nurturer of the young; but she is in no sense a 'mainstream' deity in Greek religious practice. Pausanias preserves what he says is part of an ancient ritual hymn from Dodona:

Zeus was, Zeus is, and Zeus will be;

> O great Zeus! It is Earth sends up
> the fruits of Earth, so you must be
> sure to sing praise, and never stop:
> praise of our Mother Earth.
>
> (Pausanias, *Description of Greece*, 10.12.10)

The idea of the Earth as both the giver and the ultimate receiver of all mortal life has a literary parallel in the *Choēphoroi* (Libation-Bearers) of Aeschylus, where Electra prays 'To Earth herself, who brings all things to birth, | nurtures them, then takes back into herself | that swelling seed' (127–128). In this translation, what are in the Greek simply flowers have been made more specific (and less Greek) as 'herb-robert and loosestrife'. The final address to Gaia as 'wife of the starry sky' probably harks back to Hesiod, where the earth marries Heaven.

Notes to Hymn 31

Helios is the Sun, and references to him as a god are found from Homer onwards. He makes an important appearance as a witness to Persephone's abduction in Hymn 2, and there are signs that his name was invoked in the swearing of oaths and the giving of testimony. As a divine character of literary service, however, he is not commonly encountered in Greek; this seems to parallel the evidence for his worship, which is scanty (the major exception to this relating to Rhodes, where the god had a cult and a major festival, the Halieia.) There was more worship of Helios in later times, especially in the Hellenistic period, and the present Hymn is almost certainly (like Hymns 20 and 22) not early. The opening address is to the Muse Calliope, one of the nine Muses listed in Hesiod's *Theogony*, she was regarded as having epic poetry as a special domain, so it is possible that the Hymn either introduces (or, more artfully perhaps, pretends to introduce) a recitation of epic narrative matter. The genealogy with which the Hymn begins is an unusual one, for the name given to Helios' mother, Euryphaëssa ('wide-shining'), appears to have been made up for the occasion: in Hesiod, his mother is called Theia, and this identification holds for Pindar, though he does accept that Theia can have a number of identities: 'Mother of the Sun, Theia with your many names' (Isthmian 5.1). Nevertheless, the deliberate innovation in the Hymn may be a telling feature of its studied poetic style. The epithet which the poet gives to Euryphaëssa here is *boōpis* (literally, 'cow-eyed'), which is generally accorded to the goddess Hera, in Homer and elsewhere. Helios in this poem drives a chariot across the sky, as commonly in myth: during the Halieia at Rhodes, an entire team of horses, along with a chariot, were sent as an offering into the sea. The 'cheek-plates' worn here by Helios are simply 'cheeks' in the Greek: the word is used of a helmet such as the one imagined here, but is also employed in relation to head-armour worn by horses. The poet lavishes a great deal of descriptive energy on this resplendent armour of the sun – 'the sentence is overfull', according to *AHS* (433) – but this seems typical of the kind of self-consciously poetic effects aimed for in poetry that is later than epic, and it (at the least) anticipates Hellenistic poetic effects. As the poem concludes, there is a clear indication (much clearer, indeed, than usual in the Homeric Hymns) that a story is to follow relating to the acts of legendary heroes. In announcing that 'I will sing' of these things, the poet uses a word (*klēisō*) which is not found in Homeric epic, but is more common in fifth-century BC and later writing.

Notes to Hymn 32

Selēnē, goddess of the moon, is first mentioned (in conjunction with Helios) by Hesiod as the daughter of Theia:

> After she had been tamed in love
> by Hyperion, Theia gave birth
> to mighty Helios and bright
> Selēnē, and to Dawn who brings
> daylight to everyone on earth
> as well as to the immortal gods
> where they possess wide heaven.　　(*Theogony* 371–374)

There is very little evidence, if any, that Selēnē was offered worship in earlier periods in Greece. In the play *Peace* (421 BC), Aristophanes has his character Trygaeus align Selēnē with the religious practices of barbarians:

TRYGAEUS:
I'll let you know this strange and crucial news:
a plot is hatching against all you gods.

HERMES:
All right, then: speak up; maybe I'll believe you.

TRYGAEUS:
Well, crafty Helios and Selēnē
have been laying their plans a long time now
to put Greece into the barbarians' hands.

HERMES:
And why would they do that?

TRYGAEUS:

By God, it's simple:
we sacrifice to you; barbarians
make sacrifice to them; so what more likely
than that they'd want to wipe out all of us
so that they could usurp the holy rites?

(*Peace*, 403–413)

While it could be argued that the hymn still gives to Selēnē something of an exotic air, it is also true that the poetry shows no signs of regarding her cult as inherently foreign or un-Greek. It is likely, then, that the poem (along with Hymn 31, and possibly Hymn 30) reflects a later stage of religious assimilation of Moon- and Sun-cults, more Hellenistic than classical. In the first line of the Greek, Selēnē is given the epithet *tanusipteron*, 'slender-winged', but there is no supporting evidence (from visual art or elsewhere) to support the idea of the Moon having wings: these would be more readily given to Dawn (Eōs). The team of horses driven by Selēnē make her work similar to that of Helios, though she drives colts rather than his stallions: this may indicate that her team is more likely to take an erratic course (thus explaining irregularities in the Moon's apparent transit of the skies). The Hymn's reference to a daughter of the goddess, Pandia, may help to locate a place of origin: the name is attested in the genealogy of the Athenian Antiochid clan, and the Byzantine scholar Photius (who draws on earlier sources) mentions an Athenian festival of 'Pandia, daughter of Selēnē'. Other evidence relating to this festival is scant, but it seems to have come at the end of the great Dionysia, and to have been at the time of the full moon. The Hymn might well have some connection to this festival, and therefore be Athenian in origin, possibly in the fourth century BC or later.

Notes to Hymn 33

Another nineteen-line poem, this Hymn adds to the attributes of Castor and Polydeuces in Hymn 17, concentrating on their status as the helpers of mariners in distress at sea, when they appear as the lights of what is now known as St Elmo's Fire (ball-lightning effects on masts or sails during electrical storms). For the Dioscuri and their genealogy, see Notes on Hymn 17. *AHS* incline to an early date for this Hymn: one plank of their evidence for this seems secure enough, namely the conclusion that, since Theocritus imitates it in his *Idyll* 22, the poem is at least pre-Alexandrian. The other major plank, however, seems (to me at least) something less than weight-bearing: in line 9 of the Greek text, there is the phrase *Dios korous megaloio*, 'the sons of great Zeus', while on a bronze disc from Cephallonia dedicated to the Dioscuri, datable to the sixth century BC, there is the inscription *Di[w]os kouroin megaloio*, 'to the two sons of great Zeus'. For *AHS*, this amounts to an allusion, and 'almost certainly indicates that the Hymn was well known before the sixth century BC' (436). This cannot be said so confidently, however: *AHS* notice that the inscription goes on to use a phrase from the *Iliad* (2: 631: *Kephallanas megathumous*, 'the strong-hearted Cephallanians'), then remark that 'Two literary coincidences in a single couplet can hardly be accidental'. But the Homeric epithet might well have been in common use for the Cephallanians; and even if it is an allusion, it does not make a phrase as straightforward as 'the two sons of great Zeus' an allusion also. So, the Hymn need not be pre-sixth century; nevertheless, there are no reasons to think that it is as late as the poems that immediately precede it. As it stands, the Hymn seems complete, and serviceable as a prelude to narrative performance. At its ending, the reference to 'Tyndareus's boys, riders of fast horses' is the same as that in Hymn 17 – naturally enough, perhaps, since this feels like a standard formula for the Dioscuri: it does not offer evidence that this poem was originally longer, and contained other elements that are picked out to make the shorter Hymn at a later date.

Hymn 33 is not the closing piece in all of the manuscripts. In five of these, there is a final poem, *Eis Xenous* ('To Guests/ Hosts'): this is found also as the first poem recorded in the pseudo-Herodotean 'Life' of Homer, and is now generally known as Eprigram 1 (see page 146). The verbal differences between the Homeric Hymns version and that in the 'Life' suggest that the 'Life' (from perhaps the second century AD, but incorporating poetic materials which are much older) transmits the more reliable text. Why *Eis Xenous* even features amongst the Hymns is something of a puzzle: it has no formal features in common with them, and does not concern itself with any god. One possibility is that the poem was felt to be biographically redolent of the 'Homer' who had written the Hymns, and could therefore form a useful tailpiece to the collection.

Select Bibliography

T.W. Allen, W.R. Halliday, and E.E. Sikes (eds.), *The Homeric Hymns* (2nd edn., Oxford: Clarendon Press, 1936).

Apostolos N. Athanassakis, *The Homeric Hymns: Translation, Introduction, and Notes* (2nd edn., Baltimore: Johns Hopkins University Press, 2004).

Jenny Strauss Clay, *The Politics of Olympus: Form and Meaning in the Major Homeric Hymns* (1989; 2nd edn. London: Bristol Classical Press, 2006).

Michael Crudden, *The Homeric Hymns: Translated with an Introduction and Notes* (Oxford: Oxford University Press, 2001).

Andrew Faulkner, *The Homeric Hymn to Aphrodite: Introduction, Text, and Commentary* (Oxford: Oxford University Press, 2008).

——, (ed.), *The Homeric Hymns: Interpretative Essays* (Oxford: Oxford University Press, 2011).

Helene P. Foley (ed.), *The Homeric* Hymn to Demeter*: Translation, Commentary, and Interpretive Essays* (Princeton: Princeton University Press, 1993).

Richard Janko, *Homer, Hesiod and the Hymns: Diachronic development in Epic Diction* (Cambridge: Cambridge University Press, 1982).

Nicholas Richardson, *The Homeric Hymn to Demeter* (Oxford: Clarendon Press, 1974).

——, Introduction and Notes to *The Homeric Hymns*, trans. Jules Cashford (London: Penguin Books, 2003).

——, (ed.), *Three Homeric Hymns: To Apollo, Hermes, and Aphrodite* (Cambridge: Cambridge University Press, 2010).

Oliver Thomas, *A Commentary on the* Homeric Hymn to Hermes *184–396* (D.Phil. thesis, University of Oxford, 2009).

Athanassios Vergados, *The* Homeric Hymn to Hermes*: Introduction, Text and Commentary* (Berlin: De Gruyter, 2013).

M.L. West, *Homeric Hymns, Homeric Apocrypha, Loves of Homer* (Cambridge Mass.: Harvard University Press, 2003).